Relocating Women's Equality

Edited by

PANKAJ KUMAR
SADHNA GUPTA

RAWAT PUBLICATIONS
Jaipur • New Delhi • Bangalore • Guwahati • Kolkata

ISBN 978-81-316-0742-8

Published by
Prem Rawat for **Rawat Publications**
Satyam Apts, Sector 3, Jawahar Nagar, Jaipur 302 004 (India)
Phone: 0141 265 1748 / 7006 Fax: 0141 265 1748
E-mail: info@rawatbooks.com
Website: www.rawatbooks.com

New Delhi Office
4858/24, Ansari Road, Daryaganj, New Delhi 110 002
Phone: 011 2326 3290

Also at *Bangalore, Guwahati* and *Kolkata*

Typeset by Rawat Computers, Jaipur
Printed at Nice Printing Press, New Delhi

Contents

Preface

Women represent the largest group that has been deprived of political power, economic development and social upliftment. The reason for women being underprivileged and subordinate to men in the Indian society are the role performance and the values attached to women's and men's behaviour, which are not identical everywhere. Nevertheless, variation in activities and attitudes are well attested throughout the world. Although some pattern of gender differentiation exists in all cultures, the degree of separation and the rigidity of boundaries vary. A kind of reductionism, which is evident in the social perception towards women, is subsequently followed by two prime functions attached with women; childbearing and childrearing. The motherhood is perceived in the society as an important and essential condition of women that can glorify and alleviate their social status. This kind of social perception enables us to understand inequality in power relations between women and men.

Women are capable of playing significant role in family, society and professional spheres. But the patriarchal system in India has made women to live at the mercy of men, who exercise unlimited power over them. The elimination of gender-based discriminations is one of the fundamentals of the constitution edifice of India. In fact, the Constitution empowers the state to adopt measures of positive discrimination in favour of women for neutralizing the cumulative discrimination and deprivations which women face. It prohibits all types of discrimination against women and lays a carpet for securing equal opportunity to women in all walks of life, including education, employment and participation. However, despite the laws, discrimination and violence continues unabated, the majority of women are still unable to enjoy the rights and opportunities guaranteed to them. Society has yet not succeeded in framing the required norms to enable them to fulfill the multiple roles that they are expected to play in Indian society. This necessitates the task of empowering women in the society. All the wings and layers of government – legislature, executive and judiciary – at centre, state and local levels have the responsibility towards empowerment of women. A sincere attempt has been made in this book to highlight the problems faced by women and remedies are also suggested which can be helpful for academician and policy makers.

This volume is a result of collective efforts of a number of scholars. We are deeply obliged to all the contributors for sharing their valuable time for the preparation of the papers amidst all the multifarious activities in which our senior academicians are engaged. We wish to express our thanks to Dr Ellina Jena whose work inspired and motivated us to start working on our book. We wish to thank in particular, Dr Nesar Ahmad (BARC, Jaipur) and Dr Manish Kumar Verma (BBAU, Lucknow) for their advice in the initial stage of conceptualizing the thematic note for this work.

We are extremely grateful to Prof. (Dr) Biswajit Ghosh (Department of Sociology, University of Burdwan), Prof. (Dr) S.S. Singh (Retd.) and Prof. (Dr) Manik Chakrabarty (Department of Law, University of Burdwan), who gave us time, guidance and support at various stages of preparation of this work.

We are grateful to our colleagues for providing peaceful environment to make this work possible. Through this book we also acknowledge the love and affection rendered to us by our students, their appreciation and admiration is an important source of encouragement and motivation.

Last but not the least, we express our thanks and appreciation to Pranit Rawat and Rawat Publication for publishing this book under extreme care, precision and patience.

Pankaj Kumar
Sadhna Gupta

Contributors

Saroj Kumar Dhal is working as an Assistant Professor of Industrial Sociology at ITS Engineering College, affiliated to MTU Noida.

Sadhna Gupta is working as an Assistant Professor in the Department of Law, Hoogly Mohsin College, University of Burdwan (WB).

Ayan Hazra is working as Assistant Professor (Sociology) in Hidayatullah National Law University, Raipur, Chhattisgarh.

Khangembam Indira is working as Assistant Professor in the Department of Social Systems and Anthropology, Sikkim University.

A. Kalpana is a Research Scholar, pursuing her PhD in Sociology, Department of Sociology, Sri Venketeswara University (SVU), Tirupathi.

Tukaram N. Khandade is currently working as a Research Officer cum-Zonal Officer with Institute of Health Management Research, Jaipur.

Pankaj Kumar is presently serving as a Head, Department of Sociology, Asansol Girl's College, University of Burdwan (WB).

Rajeev Kamal Kumar is presently working as an Assistant Professor, Division of Sociology and Social Anthropology, A.N. Sinha Institute of Social Studies, Patna.

Barnali Maity is presently serving as a Head, Department of Sociology, Ramnagar College under Vidyasagar University (WB).

Preeti Misra is Associate Professor and Head of the Department of Human Rights, School for Legal Studies, Babasaheb Bhimrao Ambedkar University, Lucknow.

Prasamita Mohanty is currently working as a Associate Professor-cum-Deputy Director, CSSEIP, BBAU, Lucknow.

Niranjan Mohapatra is presently serving as an Assistant Professor in the Department of Political Science, Assam University, Diphu Campus, Assam.

Anirban Mukherjee, PhD in Sociology from Kansas State University, USA, has also served as a Lecturer at Vidyasagar University, WB.

Sudarsana Mukhopadhyay is freelance writer and women activist. She obtained LLB degree from the University of Calcutta, LLM and PhD degree in Law from the University of Burdwan.

Subash Ranjan Nayak is working as Assistant Regional Director in Indira Gandhi National Open University, Regional Centre, Bhopal.

Swapna S. Prabhu is currently working as an Assistant Professor in the Department of Political Sciences, Fakin Mohan University Balasore, Odisha.

Sangeeta Roy Maitra is working as Assistant Professor in Department of Law, Hooghly Mohsin College (WB).

Swati Akshay Sachdeva is Associate Professor and Head of the Department of Social Systems and Anthropology, Sikkim University, Gangtok.

Gurupada Saren is working as Assistant Professor in Rural Development, School of Continuing Education, IGNOU, New Delhi.

Ambey Kumar Srivastava is currently working with IIHMR University, Jaipur.

Introduction

> No nation, no society, no community can hold its head high and claim to be part of the civilized world if it condones the practice of discriminating against one half of humanity represented by women.
>
> — Manmohan Singh, Former Prime Minister of India

Indian society, based on patriarchal values, considers women only an 'object', a thing and not a person. Her value is to provide heir to male-dominated society and to provide sustenance to the family by taking care of home, by remaining within the four walls of the house. The patriarchal culture tries to dilute freedom and equality of women in all walks of life. Patriarchal theory maintains that throughout history, violence has been systematically directed towards women. Economic and social processes operate directly and indirectly to support a patriarchal social order and family structure.

The development in the patriarchal societies has been such that women have become a weaker section of our society. Her functions have been relegated to mere procreation and attending to household chores. The queen of the household, the *ardhangani,* the *sahdharmini,* the *bharya* and the equal participator with her husband in all sacrifices and *yajnas* has become worst target of social and economic deprivation. Equal opportunity and equal treatment are alien concepts to a large number of women in Indian society. Gender justice is a myth for most of the Indian women. In this scenario, women often have to endure a climate of condescension bordering on contempt and hostility.

A profound look into the unfavourable attitude of society towards women reveals that gender inequality is deeply entrenched in policies, legislation and societal institution in our country. The challenges faced by women today, therefore, are alarming and cannot be resolved by laws. We need to change our stereotypical mindset, attitude and perception. What we require are reforms in the policies and greater gender sensitization among the force as well as within the judicial system. More importantly, we require a transformation of relation in our society and within our families.

Atrocities against women are rooted in unequal power relations between men and women in our society and can be understood within a gender framework. While sex is a biological category, gender is a social construct and refers to widely shared expectations and norms within society about appropriate male and female behaviour and roles. While gender roles prescribed a strict division of labour, women are expected to perform largely reproductive functions like maintenance of the household, child rearing and so on. Gender roles also prescribe characteristic of docility, unending patience and servility for women.

Violence against women is sign of discriminatory position of women in patriarchal social structure. It is one of the most persistent human rights violations that are often ignored. This arises due to the culture of discrimination that denies equal rights and equal opportunities to women.

Table1

Incidents of Crime Against Women During 2007–2011 and Percentage Variation in 2011 over 2010

S. No.	*Crime Head*	*Year*					*Percentage Variation in 2011 over 2010*
		2007	*2008*	*2009*	*2010*	*2011*	
1.	Rape (Sec. 376 IPC)	20,737	21,467	21,217	22,172	24,206	9.2
2.	Kidnapping and Abduction (Sec. 363 to 373 IPC)	20,416	22,939	25,741	29,795	35,565	19.4
3.	Dowry Death (Sec. 302/304 IPC)	8,093	8,172	8,383	8,391	8,618	2.7

Cont'd...

...Cont'd

4.	Cruelty By Husband and Relatives (Sec. 498-A IPC)	75,930	81,344	89,546	94,041	99,135	5.4
5.	Molestation (Sec. 354 IPC)	38,734	40,413	38,711	40,613	42,968	5. 8
6.	Sexual Harassment (Sec. 509 IPC)	10,950	12,214	11,009	9,961	8,570	–14.0
7.	Importation of Girls (Sec. 366-B IPC)	61	67	48	36	80	122.2
8.	Sati Prevention Act, 1987	0	1	0	0	1	1.0
9.	Immoral Trafficking (Prevention) Act, 1956	3,568	2,659	2,474	2,499	2,435	–2.6
10.	Indecent Representation of Women (Prohibition) Act, 1986	1,200	998	1,025	845	453	–46.4
11.	Dowry Prohibition Act, 1961	5,623	5,582	5,650	5,232	6,619	26.5
	Total	1,85,312	1,95,856	2,03,804	2,13,585	2,28,650	129.2

Source: Crime Record Bureau Report 2011.

The head-wise details of reported crimes during the year 2007 to year 2011, along with percentage variation, are presented in Table 1. The crime against women during the year 2011 has increased by 7.1 per cent over the year 2010 and by 23.4 per cent over the year 2007. The Indian Penal Code (IPC) component of crimes against women has accounted for 95.8 per cent of total crimes and the rest 4.2 per cent were Special and Local Laws (SLL) crimes against women. The proportion of IPC crimes committed against women towards total IPC crimes has increased during last five years from 8.8 per cent in the year 2007 to 9.4 per cent during the year 2011. There are already enough laws prescribing deterrent punishment for offences against women. What we need is an ordinance, if it can be framed, to infuse sensitivity, understanding and more importantly, the mindset among executive, police and judiciary to implement the laws more in spirit than in letter; only then, deterrent punishment will be awarded in crime against women. The law itself cannot change the society; however, it is an effective instrument to curb abuse against women in a struggling environment. The violence against women has its cause in power imbalance between men and women and hierarchical discrimination. Therefore, gender sensitization and participatory work with men to promote gender equality is essential. There is a need to sensitize policemen in dealing with women-related cases. The behaviour of the police officers dealing with sensitive matters like women and girl child rape cases needs to be a crucial part of their training.

The life of women in India is still surrounded by violence, neglect and exploitation. It is a matter of serious introspection whether the rights guaranteed under the law have any meaning for the downtrodden sections of society. Despite the progressive steps in many areas, a lot more needs to be done to give the marginalized masses a sense of security, dignity and honour in the society. The laws that intended to punish people who commit crime against women and the laws and regulations on the protection of women and girl child should be strictly enforced. These efforts are not likely to be fully successful unless basic changes in the way the girls and women are valued by society takes place. The principle of equality between men and women should be more widely promoted through the media to change the attitude and improve the awareness of the general public on this issue.

A number of strategies have been proposed and implemented by Government of India to address the problems of women. With the independence, women were granted equal status with men. The government made an all-out effort to raise the status of women in various fields through legislation. Mere laws and piecemeal approaches to the development of women cannot ensure an equal status for women unless a multipronged and integrated approach is adopted through which large scale education, opportunities for self-employment and facilities for consolidating themselves into women's organizations are provided. They must enjoy freedom. Women can make a mark in society only when they emerge as a powerful community with distinct ideology, philosophy and strategies to face the challenges of the life.

Against all odds and obstacles, women all over the world have launched powerful movement to reverse centuries of discrimination and injustice. They are mobilizing against violence and oppression and are demanding equal rights, opportunities for development, equitable laws and control over their earning. With the growth of education, women no longer feel that they are confined to four walls of house but are venturing out into every conceivable area of activity. They are increasingly becoming conscious of their inherent rights and have joined hands to assert them, waking up to the idea of 'feminism'. Feminism as a concept has developed from the sense of inequality. Women's oppression and subordination help to develop 'feminism'.

Women's international year 1975 and the international decade 1975–85 played crucial role in creating awareness throughout the world in a new dimension. It symbolizes an awareness of oppression on domestic, social and economic levels accompanied by a willingness to struggle against subjugation and subordination. They have focused their attention on equalizing strategies, which represents attempts to improve women's access to existing education, employment, health care and other opportunities to make resources more responsible to women's need. If women have to be emancipated or empowerment has to take place, it should be all embracing attempt and a constructive effort. Emancipation does not mean the liberty to do what one pleases. It is a movement to acquire self-respect and dignity. A woman gets respect by being upright and traditional bound to some extent. Without changing the mindset of the male dominated society, there can be no gender equality. The fight for women's right is a long and arduous journey and requires patience, courage and sacrifice. It warrants a movement to ensure equality for women. The state must practice equality. The dream and prayer of Tagore for the future state of India can apply very aptly to the changed status of women in India:

> Where the mind is without fear and the head is Held high;
> Where knowledge is free;
> Where the world has not been broken up into fragments
> by narrow domestic walls;
> Where words come out from the depth of truth;
> Where tireless striving stretches its arms towards perfection;
> Where the clear stream of reason has not lost its way into
> the dreary desert sand of dead habit;
> Where the mind is led forwards by thee
> into ever-widening thought and action;
> Into that heaven of freedom, my father,
> Let my country awake.

Part one of this volume examines the rural and tribal women. Chapter one by *Pankaj* precisely attempts to highlight the problems of displaced women who are dislocated by Uranium Corporation of India Limited (UCIL) mining project in Jharkhand. The major impact of displacement and the takeoyer of tribal homelands is the denigration of their culture, custom, language and dress by the mainstream community. Discussion in the paper is based on field data collected by him in the district of East Singhbhum, Jharkhand. Chapter two by *Rajeev and Tukaram* examines Women's health which is one of the important factors for development and emancipation. The economic well-being of the family and society also depends on the health of the people. The present study is carried out in two block PHCs namely – Rajapakar and Patepur of Vaishali district of Bihar state. The main objective of this paper is to understand the women's role in the health decisions. The ability to take health decisions also show women emancipation and level of autonomy enjoyed by the women in the family and society. Since the women's ability to make health decisions depend upon several associated factors such as age, place of residence, education, occupation, family income, etc. these were also studied and their correlation was also analysed. It has been found in the study that most of the women of the studied PHCs are able to take health decisions on their own, but the ability to take health decisions is more among the women who are mature, having better education, better exposure and are engaged in some economic activities. Chapter three by *Ayan* highlights the role of watershed programmes on the poorest among the poor. A study was undertaken in Raipur district of Chhattisgarh during 2008, the primitive tribes from the area are selected like *kamars* and *gonds*, who are mostly inhabited in Mainpur and Gariyaband blocks of Raipur. The tribal women normally follow sustainable rural livelihood approaches, which comprises five kinds of capital assets, viz. natural, social, human, physical and financial. National Watershed Development Programme for Rainfed Areas (NWDPRA) provide a unique opportunity to improve their livelihood and living conditions as a whole. The implementation of NWDPRA was found to be successful in protecting the eco-system and resulted in the tangible and intangible benefits to the tribal community particularly to the tribal women. They have now better understanding of utilizing natural, physical or other resources, judiciously to improve upon their living conditions. However, it was further observed that there was a significant communication gap between project officials and beneficiaries because of illiteracy and the language of programme. Lack of social mobilization was found to be the next constraint. Chapter four by *Anirban* attempts to portray the status of tribal women in the present Indian society. It highlights the worsening condition of tribal women under the lop-sided developmental policies of the Indian government. Further, the paper discusses the educational hurdles faced by tribal women, the impact of environmental degradation on their deteriorating health conditions and the gender bias entailed in the contradictory developmental policies of the government. Finally, the paper narrates the struggles of tribal women towards maintaining ecological sustainability, with special reference to the Chipko movement.

Part two of the volume analyses the crimes of violence against women in India. Chapter five by *Sadhna* deals with rape and Indian society. She examines rape as a crime not only against the person but against the entire society. It has a psychological affect on a woman and pushes her into deep trauma. When a woman is ravished what is inflicted is not merely a physical injury but a deep sense of endless shame. It is crime against basic human right to live with human dignity. Chapter six by *Sadhna* makes a critical analysis of dowry-related cruelty. She examines how dowry has degenerated into a sordid commercial transaction and a vehicle of harassment and torture for married women and extortion from their parents. This system of dowry has ruined many families and created many unhappy homes today. Incidents of dowry death are a blot on civilized society but they occur frequently despite of various legal measures that exist with Indian legal system. Chapter seven by *Sudarsana* highlights the condition of married women as victims of domestic violence in their matrimonial homes. In India, for many married women, family which is considered to be a sacred institution and a place of peace and happiness has became a place of intimidation, fear and violence. Domestic violence towards women is, perhaps, the most pervasive and commonest manifestation of violence in Indian marital life. Majority of perpetrators are men (mainly husbands and other male members of their families) and victims are women, specially the married women. This type of violence cuts across all cultural, socio-economic, educational, religious and ethnic boundaries in India. Chapter eight by *Swati* examines the role of women as a provider of care and love in their families. In every society there are indicators which are used to define equality; some of these are education, occupation, etc. Sikkim, situated in the Eastern Himalayas, represents a meeting ground of several cultures that are manifested in the distinctive lifestyle of its several tribal communities. The status of women in Sikkim, their economic contribution, socio-cultural dimension, autonomy or authority, involvement in the decision-making process in all socioeconomic, cultural and most important of all political sphere gives them a high social status. In Sikkim, there has also been no reported case of gender discrimination, inequality, sexual harassment at work place, infanticide, feticide or dowry-related death. However, there are reported cases of extreme atrocities against women in Sikkim, establishing the fact that the state, although relatively peaceful and prosperous is not immune to the social trend of crime against women. This paper highlights some of the crimes committed against the women in Sikkim and aims to fill some of the existing gaps in this context. Chapter nine by *Preeti* discusses the sexual harassment at the workplace. Sexual harassment in the form of eve-teasing, molestation, sexual assault and rape is crime against the honour, dignity and self-respect of a woman. It damages her personality, hurts her immensely and throws her in the background. She loses confidence in life and her career is also affected adversely. In a country like India, where women are worshipped at par with the Gods, where rivers and various Goddesses are named as women, this kind of behaviour against women is unethical, unjust, unfair and hypocritical. The occurrence of sexual harassment at the workplace is recognized as an infringement of the fundamental rights of a woman under the Constitution of India 'to practice any profession or to carry out any occupation, trade or business'. The object of present paper is to explain the meaning of sexual harassment, understand the situations and types of sexual harassment, to evaluate the legal system dealing with the sexual harassers and to analyse case laws dealing with the problem of sexual harassment. The paper also analyses lacunas of legal system to deal with the problem of sexual harassment, suggests reforms to improve the law dealing with sexual harassment, so as to spread awareness and sensitize the society on the issue of sexual harassment of women at workplace. Chapter ten by *Subhash* delves deep into the vital issue of trafficking in Odisha. An important component of globalization is the transnational linkages created by migration. Increased migration also serves as a cover for traffickers in transporting women to different destinations in the sex industry. Odisha is one of the under-developed states in India; the extent of poverty in Odisha is the highest in the country. His paper discusses how inequality practiced in the society relegates women to a marginalized position in Odisha, how various factors are responsible for pushing the poor and marginalized women of Odisha into the clutches of the traffickers and how trafficking is a serious social problem in Odisha after super cyclone in 1999. Chapter eleven by *Barnali* focuses on the life of single women. In Indian cultural heritage, where women are worshipped as *'Shakti'*, women especially single women are subjected to inhuman treatment by the society. Being single is seen as stigma, they are doubly victimized and exploited by society – first for being a woman and then for not having procurred a marriage certificate, thus a 'single'. In a postmodern democratic society, they now think of their own liberation. But, in playing the dual role of both men and women, they face a lot of problems. Their identities are looked upon with suspicion. The taboo and stigma attached to the singlehood and the negative attitude of the society towards these single women now should be a matter of great concern and therefore, their plight and problems need greater attention. Chapter twelve by

Prasamita picks up a lively debate on the issue of deprivation matters for girls and women from pre-natal to geriatric stage.

Part three of the volume discusses the liberalization and women entrepreneurship. Chapter thirteen by *Swapna and Niranjan* examines the role of liberalization in transforming the nature of women's work in India with a special reference to women in rural India employed especially in the unorganized sector. The paper also places a woman worker, in particular the poor woman worker, at the centre of analysis since it is her hard work and enterprise which creates half of the wealth of the nation, and whose labour leads to national growth. Chapter fourteen by *Gurupada* highlights the condition of Santal in West Bengal. They are deprived of health, education and necessary infrastructure for existence at the place of origin. They are unable to earn enough to sustain their livelihood; therefore, they migrate elsewhere in search of jobs. Initially, they have migrated to nearby places – Bardhaman and Hooghly as agricultural labourers. After certain amount of exposure and economic well-being, the Santal women involved themselves to initiate social entrepreneurship. These energetic Santal women have formed Self-Help Groups (SHG) and undertake entrepreneurship programmes to address the issues like poverty and bring forth the social transformation in the society. The paper examines how the tribal women have been involved in social entrepreneurship to fight poverty. The study attempts to look into the entrepreneurship process which leads them towards social transformation. Chapter fifteen by *Sangeeta* argues quite convincingly that though there has been much progress toward legal parity between women and men throughout the world, important distinctions still exist that may prevent women from improving their own and their families' well-being by working or by running a business. This paper explores women's economic roles and opportunities and their aspirations for advancement. It reviews the sorts of constraints they face in fulfilling them and considers the relationship between women's rights and capabilities on the one hand and development policy and practice on the other. Chapter sixteen by *Kalpana* discusses the impact of Indira Kranti Pathakam (IKP) on empowerment of women in Prakasam District of Andhra Pradesh.

Part four of the volume discusses women empowerment. Chapter seventeen by *Sadhna* seeks to focus on the empowerment which is the effective answer to oppression, exploitation, injustice and other maladies which women have to face. It is about skill formation. The focus on empowerment has given a new emphasis to the building of economic and social capability among women. Chapter eighteen by *Ambey* mentions that the women constitute half of India's population but their participation in Indian economic development has not received the focus equal to that of males because of deep-seated gender discrimination in the Indian society. Gender disparities are manifested in economic participation and decision-making issues because women are primarily perceived as a housewife. The female work participation rate is lower in urban areas than rural areas. The current paper has analysed the participation of women in household economy and decision-making in slums of Jaipur city. Slum women are engaged in spectrum of skilled and unskilled job activities, which exhibit her entrepreneur nature, competitive behaviour, ability to accept challenge and job preferences. She is earning against all the social and cultural inhibitions and male dominant society. But the participation of women in decision-making has not extensively improved. Women are also not able to enjoy the freedom of using their own earnings like their husbands. Making participation of women in household economy measurable is a challenge but also significant for making life of slum women better. Chapter nineteen by *Saroj* examines the era of retreating government, privatization, free market structural adjustment, decentralization, deregulation, empowerment, formulation and implementation of public policy gradually taken over by NGOs. This paper focuses how the NGO *Agragamee* (means forward movement) has successfully made the effort to change the tribal women's condition through education and has empowered them. Chapter twenty by *Khangembam* examines the evolution of *Meira Paibi*, a women's movement in Manipur and traces the nature and extent of changes that have taken place in this movement over the years. The study asserts that *Meira Paibi* is always in the forefront protesting against the injustice done to the people by the state, state agencies or insurgent groups. The paper also questions the movement's excessive preoccupation with the repeal of Armed Forces Special Power Act (AFSPA) vis-à-vis other gender issues occurring in the society. Sceptics have often pointed out that the movement acts as a mouthpiece for insurgent groups in the state even though the leaders of the movement deny the charges. The paper also throws some light on the role it played to bring peace in the conflict-ridden Manipuri society and discusses the limitations of such movements from the societal perspective.

Part I

Rural and Tribal Women

1

Displacement and Gender Justice

PANKAJ KUMAR

After the Independence, with an objective to achieve rapid economic growth, a good number of major developmental projects were initiated and implemented by both central and state governments. These projects included construction of mega irrigation dams, power plants, industries, mining operations and so on. Though these developmental projects have provided irrigation to thirsty lands, energy for growing industries and brought about economic prosperity for the country, nonetheless these mega projects have caused forced displacement of millions of people to make way for these projects. Among the people displaced by various developmental projects, a large number of people belong to scheduled tribe, scheduled caste and other backward communities who are always regarded as the poor and disadvantaged section of the society. India's Planning Commission, almost exclusively manned by economists, did not consider displacement as an issue. Adding to the lopsided character of the commission was the over enthusiasm of the first charismatic prime minister (who occupied the office for 17 years) for technology-driven rapid development, who labelled huge projects as 'temple of modern India' (Oommen, 2008: 76). The 'temple of modern India' has become 'temples of doom' for the uprooted people. In a socialist welfare state like ours, it is an irony that the benefits of development have not been shared by all sections of society. In the developmental process, it is the displaced people, who share only pains of development, while some other people enjoy the gains. It is, in fact, profoundly contrary to the very goals of development.

There have been much greater displacements and many more struggles after independence, because investment strategies for economic progress envisaged by India's five-year plans entail changes in the use of land, water, forest and other resources. These have also led to irreversible changes in the lives of millions who are displaced or otherwise deprived of access to the resources that are their livelihood. There has been an enormous increase in the number of Displaced People (DP) and Project Affected Person (PAP). Despite this, no official database exists on the total number and type of DPs. This chapter presents its arguments within this context.

There are intra household inequalities between males and females in terms of nutrition, ownership of land, access over resources, literacy and so on. These inequalities tend to get aggravated at time of displacement. There have been many cases where women's interests were ignored when rehabilitation policies were being implemented. Most of the time, relief work lacks gender sensitization. The need of the women and the girl child are not taken into consideration, which creates much hardship for women, leading to traumatic experiences. The freedom and independence of women related to their land-based livelihoods was diminished by their displacement. Their economic relationship to the land was neither recognized nor compensated for. Women are the worst victims. But they are rarely taken into consideration while planning for the project and later resettlement and rehabilitation.

The mining projects, of course, have placed the indigenous people in a precarious condition. Moreover, the rights of women are subjugated and were taken away. In the context of gender positioning, mining has only multiplied the exploitation and degradation of women's rights with regard to land and livelihoods. Historically and also in the existing legal framework, women have no legal rights over lands or natural resources. Large-scale mines, which are increasingly dependent on technology, offer no scope for participation to *adivasi* women, as they lack literacy and technical skills because of cultural and social prejudice. While women once formed 32–40 per cent of the workforce in mining, they have now been reduced to less than 10 per cent and in the coal sector alone, to 4 per cent. Schemes, like the Voluntary Retirement Scheme (VRS), have been thrust upon women so as to retrench them first. The mining sector has generated a prejudice that sees women as unfit to work in the mines (Rebbapragada and Kalluri, 2009: 257). There is a strong need for gender perspective in issues related to displacement and rehabilitation. Uranium

Corporation of India Limited (UCIL) mining project in Jharkhand has brought several economic and social problems to the displaced women. Some of the impact that uranium mining project incur for women are discussed here.

Methodology

The focus of the study is land acquisition, displacement and rehabilitation of tribal women and other poor women by the Uranium Corporation of India Limited (UCIL) mining and processing unit, a government of India undertaking under the Department of Atomic Energy (DAE), in Jharkhand. The persons interviewed by the researcher are the people who are displaced due to construction of the UCIL mining and the third tailing pond, I have selected my samples for the study in the following manner: 119 households from Banduhurang uranium mining, 41 households from Bagjata uranium mining, 25 households from Dungridih and 75 households from Chatikocha. In other words, without opting for any particular sampling frame, I have included all the people who are displaced due to construction of the UCIL mining and tailing ponds at Banduhurang, Bagjata, Dungridih and Chatikocha village.

Mining and Gender

The discourse on mining without the gender dimension is incomplete. It is very important to analyse how the mining has affected the male and female members, and how far it is correct to argue that female casualties are more than male in the process of displacement and rehabilitation. The mining projects, of course, have placed the indigenous people in a precarious condition. But women are further marginalized with their rights being taken away and they being forced into male subjugation. In the context of gender positioning, mining has only multiplied the exploitation and degradation of women's rights with regard to land and livelihoods. Historically and also in the existing legal framework, women have no legal rights over lands or natural resources. There is an invisible distinction between rural and tribal women with regard to control over lands in traditional land-based situations in mainstream India. Tribal women enjoy a greater social status with regard to control over resources. This ensures their active participation and decision-making with regard to land utilization, agriculture and powers over cash flow in a tribal economy. Even in the agrarian society, women have a distinct role with regard to participation in agricultural work, livestock management and access to common properties.

On the other hand, in case of mines, the law does not permit the women to work in the underground mines nor to take up mine engineering professional courses.

This prejudice serves to ensure that women do not get space in the formal sector but at the same time it allows for their absorption into informal sector as contract or casual labour under highly exploitative condition. Women wages are always less than those of men, and there are no provisions for paid holidays, not even during pregnancy or childbirth. No equipment is provided to women and worksites lack toilet and other facilities. Women workers are exposed to physical and sexual exploitation by mine owners, contractors and other men. They have to walk miles to return to their villages and are vulnerable to assault on the way. Women in the mining industry suffer from several occupational illnesses, including respiratory problems like tuberculosis, leukaemia, arthritis and reproductive problems. They work with toxic and hazardous substances without any access to safety measures.

When industries shut down and retrench their workers, the men become idle and the entire burden of work falls upon *adivasi* women, who then must find a way to support their families. Women living in the mining communities scavenge on the tailings and waste dumps of big mining companies as a way of earning their livelihood, often illegally and are constantly harassed by company guards, local mafias or the police. They are also at the mercy of local traders for selling their ores.

In most mining situations, communities become aware of projects only at the time of eviction when the bull-dozers are brought in, many a times in police presence. The public hearings are organized in a biased and almost discrete manner where the local administration, the statutory bodies for clearing the projects and the mining companies are in close collusion to ensure that there are no effective objections raised by the public. In case of coal mining, which requires a large area, the coal industry has little choice in the location of its activities as mines can be developed on a commercial basis only where sufficient reserves exist (World Bank, 1996). In India, many areas suitable for coal mining are relatively underdeveloped and are generally inhabited by people from traditional culture, with little contact with the outside world. They mostly live at subsistence level and lack education. Coal mining in such areas produces a profound impact on the lifestyles of the local people (Mathur, 2008: 261). Most mining companies also operate on a deemed consent basis so that even without the mandatory clearances, mining operations are expanded beyond lease areas and periods. The 'public purpose' of a mining activity from a gender perspective and especially with regard to what the women in the communities stand to 'publicly' gain, is highly questionable. Rehabilitation programmes, which are taken up so far, have been entirely insensitive to gender concerns whether in providing land, housing, jobs or cash. Rehabilitated colonies provide no space for women's need for privacy, toilets, washing, domestic, health, recreation or educational facilities. Neither have these provided for taking up economic activities on their own as forests are too far away from the colonies, have no space for livestock rearing or for storage of forest produce. The approach of both industries and governments, towards communities with regard to rehabilitation, has always been one of performing magnanimous favours than with a sense of duty or responsibility. Hence, gender needs have never been a priority in rehabilitation programme.

The anticipated economic development from mining does not accrue to local communities and, on the contrary, reduces the women into worse forms of survival than pre-mining conditions. Hence, when companies and governments give projections of project costs and estimated profits, it is very important that these are analysed from the perspective of social and environment costs in order to assess their actual costs and benefits. This is especially crucial when valuing the extractive industry in terms of the production, processing, consumption and export needs of the country for mineral and weighing these needs and values against the social and environment costs. This should define the basis on which mining projects are sanctioned and cleared where the country has a long-term economic perspective of mining rather than on individual lobbying capacities of mining industries for 'sustenance' of their businesses. It is also very important when weighed from the viability of the projects that social costs are included as part of project costs and if so, then relief and rehabilitation are to be taken up in a socially just manner. Yet, no projects have ever been valued by the state taking into detailed consideration the direct and indirect impacts on communities and the extent of human abuse, deforestation, pollution and ecological destruction and, where industries are bound by rules and guidelines, to pay up for these costs.

Hence, how do we value our minerals? If minerals were to be valued at the cost of exposing women and their bodies to abuse and exploitation and if protecting women's human rights is not a priority for defining our indices of human development, the sanctity of gender justice is completely endangered. Therefore, displacement, acquisition of lands, water bodies and forests, loss of livelihoods of women, atrocities and health hazards that they face, transformation of villages into culturally degraded shanty towns, risks of disasters and mine accidents have to be evaluated and factored in the entire project cost in order to determine whether a mining project is necessary against the other existing economic activities or possibilities of creating other forms of economic activities in each area proposed for mining. Unless the state takes up this exercise seriously, its commitment to communities and ecology and the very economic sustainability of the country stands under scrutiny.

The state has to ensure that the industries first implement complete relief and rehabilitation in the existing and abandoned projects before fresh leases are granted for mining more lands and displacing more people in the green field areas. This is the first step towards building the commitment of the industry and the state to being responsible for mining induced impacts.

Deterioration of Women Economic Autonomy

Access to land, forest, river and grazing land supports subsistence livelihood and provides greater securities against poverty to women. When these resources are not replaced during resettlement, they have to bear the disproportionate share of the resulting cost. It is also noted that if women do not lose complete access to these resources, increase in distance from resettlement to these common property resources will have a long term impact on women and their family income.

Prior to the displacement, indigenous people did not face problems like landlessness, hunger or food insecurity in their subsistence. A self-sufficient economy existed because of their access to forest products and customary right to their household economy through the sale of livestock, baskets, bamboo mats, ropes and pottery. Women had greater economic independence and land rights in the egalitarian tribal set-up. However, displacement has torn the people away from their sources of sustenance of life. Once deprived of their usual livelihood options, women have to depend on the income of their husbands. Only a few women have been able to manage informal jobs of daily wage labourers outside the project. Obviously, many women are reduced to the status of housewives, which is far cry from their earlier role of being contributors to the family economy. Since their role as caretaker of the household remains unchanged, they have to now purchase their basic needs such as food, which they used to get from their land and forest. Under such circumstances, displaced women have to encounter an additional problem. Now they also have to manage their household with little money as their husbands are often seen spending the cash for entertainment and purchase of non-essential consumer goods, having been influenced by outsiders and the new culture.

Declining Job Opportunities

As a result of reduced family income, which is a consequence of displacement, women are over burdened on two counts: searching livelihood to add to the household income and the responsibility of household chores. This is because migration of men in search of employment has increased the responsibility of women.

Table 1

Persons Getting Compensatory Jobs at the UCIL

Compensatory Jobs Given to	*No. of Cases*	*Post Given by UCIL*	*Nature of Jobs*
None	0		
Husband	90	Unskilled	Permanent
Son	50	Unskilled	Permanent
Wife	3	Unskilled	Permanent
Widow	7	Unskilled	Permanent
Others	0		
Total	150		

The compensatory jobs given by the UCIL mainly have gone to men. Data in Table 1 shows that husband and son have been the beneficiaries of the jobs given by the company. Although the UCIL did not restrict women from getting the compensatory jobs, yet because of prevailing patriarchal notions, men (husbands and sons) have been the beneficiaries. Even those women who did receive manual jobs initially, were thrown out of such temporary jobs after technological up-gradations and mechanization of the uranium mines. Caste and tribal structure play important roles in determining distribution of job benefits. Whatever little skilled or semi-skilled employments were given to the selected persons by the UCIL, these went to men as mining labour, fitter, etc. Women were also given jobs that were unskilled and low paid and often on daily wages. Jobs being scarce with the project, the first casualty are the women because they lack skill. Again, in the face of competition between family members for scarce jobs, the women tend to lose out, often almost voluntarily. The point is, while women are being displaced from their traditional occupation, they have not been allowed access to the new sources of employment that may come up in the area (Basu, 2006: 220). The attitude of the rest of the displaced people towards their own women is not always positive concerning job. They consider that women cannot compete in the formal sector, as there is high illiteracy among them. They lack training and professional skill. Some have the opinion that women's place is at home and not outside (Ekka and Asif, 2000).

However, during interviews with Jharkhand's Organization against Radiation (JOAR) people, it was found that in most cases displaced people have not been given satisfactory compensation. In fact, it has been found that several women especially those with a single status are leading miserable lives after losing their life-supporting land. The UCIL uranium mines, which are increasingly dependent on technology, offered no scope for participation of tribal women, as they lack technical skills and face cultural and social prejudices. Management has declared that they do not have job vacancies during the field survey in June 2011.

Change in Occupational Pattern

Tribal women have always played an important role in agriculture sector. They have actively participated at all levels, including that of maintenance, subsistence and sustenance. Any change in land-use patterns, particularly due to displacement and loss of livelihood, thus affects women more than men.

Field survey reveals that the displaced women have been forced out of their land-based work and are being pushed into unskilled and marginalized forms of labour, which are considered socially degrading. Numerous women have been relegated from pompous cultivators to daily wage labourers. The change in responsibility has increased the workload of women. This is clearly due to an overall change in the occupational pattern. Cultivation, farm labour as well as grass cutting activities have severely suffered due to displacement. Tribal women are the main caretakers of livestock like cow, goat, sheep, and poultry which had provided at least some income to women and also provided nutrition for families; but after displacement their control over livestock is declining day by day.

The UCIL took some initiatives to impart training to local and tribal women on subjects like mushroom cultivation, chalk-making, nail polish remover, vermiculture, tailoring, terracota, dress-making, machine embroidery, herbal product, beauty culture, health care and cottage industries (making of candles, incense sticks, greeting cards, etc.). This training programme has been primarily conducted for the women of *Bhatin* village. The training programme has been concluded recently and it will facilitate the trained women to set up a production centre for these items. The UCIL has initiated this programme in view of the Government of India's declaration of the year 2001 as the 'women empowerment year' in order to highlight their rightful place in the main stream of national development.

The UCIL has also started a training centre for tribal women at *Rajdoha* village. Presently, this centre is imparting training to women for glove-making. The material made by the people is sold in market. The UCIL also has a plan to impart training to village women in jute bag-making so as to get more money from handicraft material (UCIL, 2009: 173). It can also assist women to form self-help groups in new resettlement areas to restore their economic freedom lost due to the shifting. It has been reported to researcher by JOAR members that due to decline in source of livelihood as well as joblessness and increased poverty, displaced families were forced to stop their children's education and convert students into child workers, particularly girl child who now are required to help at home. Families are often compelled to seek work in local cities due to decline in source of livelihood. These temporary migrations interrupt the schooling of children. The decline in access to education obviously has long term effects in that it produces a workforce that is less skilled than earlier (Dewan, 2008: 137).

Acceleration of Domestic Violence

Violence against women is rooted in unequal power relations between men and women in society and can be understood within a gender framework. While gender roles prescribed a strict division of labour, women are expected to perform largely reproductive functions like maintenance of the household, child care, etc. The construction of gender roles implies that women have far lesser access to productive resources and decision-making as compared to men, resulting in unequal balance of power. Violence against women is not a myth, but a reality. It is an act of illegal criminal use of physical force and it also includes exploitation, discrimination, upholding of unequal economic and social structures, and the creation of an atmosphere of terror, threat or reprisal. This terror can be seen in domestic violence.

It has been found that the displaced families suffer from different types of adjustment problems between the sexes within family. As men faces powerlessness, women become scapegoats. Displacement has brought anxiety, idleness and insecurity. All these have led to increase in drinking, wife-beating and domestic violence. In some cases, cash received in compensation had led to increase in alcohol intake by men, resulting in domestic violence.

Table 2

Reasons for Increasing Domestic Violence

Reasons for Increasing Domestic Violence	*Number*	*Percentage*
Land acquired by UCIL	20	17.54
Loss of livelihood	10	8.77
Loss of house	11	9.64
Lack of employment	35	30.70
Poverty	6	5.26
Migration	3	2.63
Alcohol drinking	15	13.15
Injustice in society	0	0
Unknown	14	12.28
Total	114	100

The data in Table 2 shows that 114 out of 260 women have stated that there is an increase in the rate of domestic violence after displacement and they have identified various reasons for this. The important among them are: land acquisition (17.54%), loss of livelihood (8.77%), lack of employment (30.70%), poverty (5.26%), migration (2.63%), alcohol drinking (13.15%) and loss of house (9.64%). Due to the trauma of displacement, drinking has increased considerably among men, so have wife-beating and quarrel in the family. Tribal society has the culture of drinking and merry-making. But displacement makes it worse, as men did not find jobs and wasted money on drinking. This has been found in most of the displaced family cases.

Breakdown of Lifestyle

Displacement alienates tribal women from their land and destroys their means of livelihood. Displacement has destroyed their custom, dialects, lifestyle and values. Being deprived of their land, tribal women along with their husband migrate to urban centre in search of work. But migration disrupts harmonious family and village life. There are little opportunities for improving the quality of life like participation in literacy courses, women's group and village meetings. These migrant families are not able to utilize the opportunity offered by various schemes of the tribal development departments.

Majority of women interviewed responded that displacement has brought many transformations in their customs, beliefs and ritual practices. Young tribal girls are giving up their traditional lifestyle and going out to work in small companies to supplement the family income. Mingling with other communities has led to mixed marriages but there are cases where non-tribal men have deserted tribal women and have taken control of her land and property.

The new structural economy (new economic reforms) has created challenges to the tribal society as a whole. Previously, tribals were linked with the regional society only through weekly markets. These markets were places where the tribals not only had economic interaction with others, including non-tribals, but it also facilitated social and cultural linkages. But now, such weekly markets have died a natural death. Instead, markets in new locations have extended beyond regional and state boundaries. Consequently, tribal artefacts, traditional dresses and utensils are hardly sold in these cosmopolitan markets. With the coming of new consumerism, the tribal folk culture – with its oral traditions and indigenous nuances – is fast dying.

Psychological Pressure

When displacement is involuntary, it forces families to displace from their traditional land, snatching away the source of livelihood and eroding cultural fabric. This results in a kind of psychological pressure which was observed during the field survey. Such a situation has affected women more adversely. Perpetual anxiety has left them short-tempered. When the husband or a son is not getting a job or not working properly, they too share the frustration and become tense. Table 3 shows the reasons for stress and post-traumatic stress disorder among women.

During the field survey, it was found that some women were suffering from psychological abnormality. Out of 260 women who have stated to have undergone stress and post-traumatic stress disorder, the dominating reasons were loss of land and loss of livelihood. Among the remaining causes, migration in search of better jobs, financial problems, division of families, less income, debt, alcohol drinking and gambling by husband were identified. For the menfolk, cash in hand, mental stress and pressure made them vulnerable and, hence, the indulgence in alcohol. Shock and trauma of losing everything they had has a frustrating impact on mental health causing disruptive behaviour. Women members of the family also often lost their cool in the face of such disruptive behaviour of male members

Table 3

Reasons for Stress and Post-traumatic Stress Disorder

Reasons	*No.*	*Percentage*
Land acquired by UCIL	145	55.76
Loss of livelihood	55	21.15
Migration	20	7.69
Financial problems to meet minimum needs	10	3.84
Division in family	5	1.92
Number of earning members reduced	3	1.15
Debt increased	12	4.61
Husbands' alcohol drinking habit increased	8	3.07
Gambling increased	2	0.76
Total	260	100

leading to repeated conflicts between them. The younger generation has to face paucity of employment and gives vent to their own resentments by becoming violent with their parents. This has led to regular quarrel between the parents and their children.

Health Risks

Malnutrition, especially among women and children, is one of the most significant fallouts of displacement (Srinivasan, 1996: 13). In Jaduguda, women and child constitute the majority of those whose health and nutrition has been negatively affected due to displacement. In this region, the incidence of several diseases like tuberculosis, chronic lung diseases, cancer, prevalence of spontaneous abortion, still birth, among married women are more vulnerable and to the health of women living around uranium mining areas. Half of the Chatikocha village's women have problem in delivery and miscarriages.

Table 4

Health Risks of Displaced Women

Health Problems	*No. of Person*	*Percentage*
Problem in Menstrual Cycle	117	45
Miscarriage	43	16.54
Still Born	26	10
Fertility Problem	74	28.46
Total	260	100

People in seven villages within one kilometre radius of the tailing dams were interviewed. It was found that 117 (45%) women out of 260 reported about disruptions of their menstrual cycle, 43 (16.54 %) had suffered from miscarriages, 26 (10%) had given birth to stillborn babies in the last five years and 74 (28.46%) reported some sort of fertility problems. Nearly all women complained of fatigue, weakness and depression. So there is a high incidence of miscarriage, fertility problems and disruptions of menstrual cycle.

Maternal Health Care

Maternal health care includes the antenatal, delivery related and post-partum care. But the available information on maternal health in Jaduguda region suggests that situation is satisfactory among displaced family. It has been found during field survey that the *Anganwadi* programme is going on with the help of UNICEF in villages like Mechua, Taliatand, Dungridih, Ichra, and Bhatin, where displaced families are living. Under this programme, if registered medical practitioner doctor declare woman as pregnant then *Anganwadi* programme will provide food grains and cash assistance throughout pregnancy period and even after delivery. *Anganwadi* workers (*sebika and sahayeka*) also extend health care services to the resettlers at their doorstep. According to women respondents, such services help pregnant women and children in particular. They articulated their satisfaction with programme for vaccination, concern of pregnant mother and creation of consciousness about disease like malaria, etc.

Infant and child mortality are considerably high among displaced family. Some cases reveal that child bearing have occurred among mothers in early age (below 18), exposing them to sex and pregnancy before they are physically or emotionally prepared for it. It has been found during interviews that women are less aware of modes of transmission and prevention of HIV than men.

Consultation and Right to Information

It is argued that the displacing agency, i.e. project management, should organise *Jan Adalat* (Public Hearing) and inform people in advance of its coming project and mentally prepare the people in the area for the upcoming changes. The public hearing shall be arranged in a systemic, time bound and transparent manner ensuring the widest possible public participation at the project site. Yet, in almost all displacement situations, the formal consultation did not take place and the affected people were not provided with proper information by the project management. Whether it is regarding the project, land acquisition, compensation or rehabilitation, the project management has rarely taken the initiative to consult the local people to explain the costs and advantages of displacement in the area. The public consultation is the only formal way for local communities to voice their opinion.

Obviously, the right to information was denied more particularly to women on two counts. First by the displacing agency and second by the male members of the family. The belief that men are better equipped and shall tackle the situation outside the four walls of house is ingrained. A vast majority of women have mentioned during household survey that they had no access to information on project and resettlement plans meant for them; they were excluded also because the officials thought that women do not understand complex things.

Women and Law

Tribal customs excluded women from inheriting land and property. Men have mostly determined the control over land in terms of its management, use and disposal. Women seldom enjoy the resources generated from the productive use of these assets such as income accruing from land or rent of property. So deep is the association of the notion of male control over land, that women do not even perceive the absence of claims vis-à-vis such assets as the denial of right. The lack of ownership, however, has made women innocuously vulnerable forever and made them dependent with greater risk of being excluded from their home and livelihood.

Gender biases are evident in the Land Acquisition Act of 1894. Under Section 42 of the Act, the notice for land acquisition to a person with an interest in that land can be served only to an adult male. If, for some reason, the notice cannot be served to an adult male, the law requires that it be pasted on front door of the landowner's house, or at another conspicuous place (for example at the premises of the collector's court). The notice is deemed legally served only when it is handed to an adult male or is acknowledged by him. Women are not treated as 'owners of land' and are, therefore, not considered worthy of receiving this notice.

In a displacement situation where ownership leads to entitlement, women are often disadvantaged when it comes to claiming compensation and other forms of support. Gaining access to compensation requires knowledge of rights and entitlements which women lack. Typical cases are of women left on their own to deal with a system, to which they do not have an access and also suffer from a lack of understanding of the existing rules and regulations (Basu, 2006: 216). The entire process of displacement, including rehabilitation, rightly targets the family as a unit, and within the family the women is the mother, sister or daughter. Her identity does not go beyond these stated dependent relationships. Laws and policies that are based on a dominant role for men tend to relegate women to the background. In such an environment, women hesitate to come forward to make the most of whatever new economic opportunities the project may present. Gender-insensitive policies only lead to negative outcome for women, thereby further widening the existing gender division (Mathur, 2009: 174). Women were rarely consulted by officials or by male members in decision-making processes concerning the land. Their participation was next to nothing. They were not even consulted about decisions concerning food, water, wood-fuel or hand pump. Men, in fact, admitted that had women been consulted and involved in the process of site selection, many of the hardships in the new sites might have been averted (Mehta, 2000: 278).

Women and Protest Movement

Women see the process of displacement as dispossession that pushes them into pauperization. Despite a shared commonality of experience with men, women do understand and experience displacement differently, possibly because of the differing status of their roles and rights in the economy of production and reproduction (Palit, 2009: 284). Women's role in protest movement is linked to their familial responsibilities, their relationship with their children and their attachment to their ancestral lineage and land. There are also other reasons which encourage them to participate in protest movement namely imagination and courage. By 'imagination' it can be said that their capacity to understand and foresee development of events are argued to be sharper than men. Women are quick to grasp the harmful impact of displacement. They too have imagination to understand the future problems of displacement in the form of shortage of food, fodder, cash and so on. This imagination also makes them realize what they are capable of achieving. And courage indicates that women have courage to challenge project management, district authority and state government who are involved in applying Land Acquisition Act, 1894 on their land and forcefully acquired land in the name of 'public purpose'. In Jaduguda, the protest movement gave women an opportunity to organize themselves so that they were better informed about displacement and rehabilitation. They also got an opportunity to discuss among them and make strategy for future action.

Conclusion

Thus, women suffer double discrimination by virtue of being a woman because she is positioned the lowest in the social hierarchy with no control over the resources and the decision-making process. Now they are left with degraded options like casual and informal worker, prostitution or are simply reduced to the status of 'idle' housewives confined to four walls of the house. The impact of displacement has, thus, meant a complete transformation, marginalization and degradation in both the economic and social status of women. The disruption of a close-knit community structure can have several ramifications. Women are socially, emotionally and culturally the worst affected. Their position is worsening due to gender insensitive and biased rehabilitation policies. To bring about a gender sensitive approach, it is essential to give consideration to the anxiety of the displaced women. Management should also undertake gender sensitive planning so that women's issues can be addressed in wider perspective. Improvement of health services by providing training for village-midwives, primary health care centres, family planning counselling, clean water supply and sanitation training, enhancing educational opportunities are also to be taken into consideration by management.

References

Ahmad, M. Shakul. 2004. *Five Decades of Planning and Tribal Development: A Study of Uttaranchal and Jharkhand*, New Delhi: Gyan Publishing House.

Ahmad, Nesar. 2003. *Women, Mining and Displacement: Report of a Pilot Study in Jharkhand*, New Delhi: Indian Social Institute.

Areeparampil, Mathew. 1989. 'Industries, Mines and Dispossession of Indigenous People: The Case of Chotanagpur', in Walter Fernandes and E. Ganguly Thukral (eds), *Development, Displacement and Rehabilitation*, New Delhi: Indian Social Institute, pp. 13–33.

——. 1996. 'Development Due to Mining in Jharkhand', *Economic and Political Weekly*, 15 June, pp. 1524–28.

Banerjee, Souparno. 2008. *Rich Lands, Poor People: Is 'Sustainable' Mining Possible?*, New Delhi: Centre for Science and Environment.

Basu, Malika. 2006. 'Gender Focus in Resettlement Planning', in Hari Mohan Mathur (ed.), *Managing Resettlement in India*, New Delhi: Oxford University Press, pp. 214–28.

Baxi, Upendra. 2008. 'Development, Displacement, Resettlement: A Human Rights Perspective', *India Social Development Report 2008*, New Delhi: Council for Social Development and Oxford University Press, pp. 17–26.

Bhatt, S.C. 2002. *The District Gazetteer of Jharkhand*, New Delhi: Gyan Publishing House.

Cullet, P. 2000. 'Narmada Dam and Human Rights', *Frontline*, 8 July, p. 95.

Das, Sukumar. 2006. 'The Land Acquisition Laws in India: An Overview with Some Suggestions for Amendment', in Hari Mohan Mathur (ed.), *Managing Resettlement in India*, New Delhi: Oxford University Press, pp. 137–72.

Desai, Mihir. 2011. 'Land Acquisition Law and the Proposed Changes', *Economic and Political Weekly*, 46 (26 and 27), pp. 95–100.

Dewan, Ritu. 2008. 'Development Project and Displaced Women', in Hari Mohan Mathur (ed.), *India Social Development Report 2008*, New Delhi: Oxford University Press, pp. 127–38.

Dhagamwar, Vasudha. 1989. 'Rehabilitation: Policy and Institutional Change Required', in Walter Fernandes and Enakshi Ganguly Thukral (eds), *Development, Displacement and Rehabilitation: Issues for a National Debate*, New Delhi: Indian Social Institute, pp. 171–84.

Dharmadhikary, Shripad, Swathi Sheshadri and Rehmat. 2009. 'The First Development Caused Displacement in India: The Forgotten People of Bhakra Nangal', in Renu Modi (ed.), *Beyond Relocation: The Imperative of Sustainable Resettlement*, New Delhi: Sage Publications, pp. 133–53.

Ekka, Alexius and Mohammad Asif. 2000. *Development-Induced Displacement and Rehabilitation in Jharkhand 1951–95: A Database on its Extent and Nature*, New Delhi: Indian Social Institute.

Emberson-Bain, Atu. 1994. 'Mining Development in the Pacific: Are We Sustaining the Unsustainable?', in Wendy Harcourt (ed.), *Feminist Perspectives on Sustainable Development*, London: Zed Book Ltd., p. 46.

Fernandes, Walter. 1998. 'Development-Induced Displacement in Eastern India', in S.C. Dube (ed.), *Antiquity to Modernity in Tribal India, Vol. 1: Continuity and Change among the Tribals*, New Delhi: Inter-India Publications, pp. 217–301.

——. 2008. 'India's Forced Displacement Policy and Practice: Is Compensation up to its Functions?', in Michael M. Cernea and Hari Mohan Mathur (eds), *Can Compensation Prevent Impoverishment?*, New Delhi: Oxford University Press, pp. 180–201.

Ghosh, Biswajit (ed.). 2011. *Interrogating Development: Discourses on Development in India Today*, Jaipur: Rawat Publications.

Herbert, Tony and Kuntala Lihiri-Dixit. 2004. 'Coal Sector Loan and Displacement of Indigenous Population: Lessons from Jharkhand', *Economic and Political Weekly*, 5 June, pp. 567–71.

Hussain, Monirul. 2008. *Interrogating Development*, New Delhi: Sage Publications.

Karlesson, Bengt G. 2009. 'Nuclear Lives: Uranium Mining, Indigenous Peoples and Development in India', *Economic and Political Weekly*, XLIV (34), 22 August, pp. 43–48.

Levien, Michael. 2011 'Rationalising Dispossession: The Land Acquisition and Resettlement Bills', *Economic and Political Weekly*, XLVI (11), 12 March, pp. 66–70.

Lobo, Lancy and Shashikant Kumar. 2009. *Land Acquisition, Displacement and Resettlement in Gujarat*, New Delhi: Sage Publications.

Mahalingam, Ashwin and Aditi Vyas. 2011. 'Comparative Evaluation of Land Acquisition and Compensation Processes across the World', *Economic and Political Weekly*, XLVI (32), 6 August, pp. 1476–85.

Mathur, Hari Mohan. 2008. 'Introduction and Overview', *India Social Development Report 2008*, New Delhi: Council for Social Development and Oxford University Press, pp. 3–13.

——. 2009. 'Gender Biases in Resettlement Planning', in Lyla Mehta (ed.), *Displaced by Development*, New Delhi: Sage Publications, pp. 166–94.

Mehta, L. 2000. 'Women Facing Submergence: Displacement and Resistance in the Narmada Valley', in V. Damodaran and M. Unnithan Kumar (eds), *Postcolonial India: History, Politics and Culture*, New Delhi: Manohar.

Mehta, Lyla (ed.). 2009. *Displaced by Development*, New Delhi: Sage Publications.

Mies, M. 1997. 'Gender and Global Capitalism', in Leslie Sklair (ed.), *Capitalism and Development*, New York: Routledge.

Oommen, T.K. 2004. *Development Discourse: Issues and Concerns*, New Delhi: Regency Publications.

Palit, Chittaroopa. 2009. 'Displacement, Gender Justice and People's Struggles', in Lyla Mehta (ed.), *Displaced by Development*, New Delhi: Sage Publications, pp. 282–84.

Parida, Jayanta. 2006. *Development, Displacement and Rehabilitation: A Case Study of Orissa*, New Delhi: Classical Publishing Company.

Ramanathan, Usha. 2008. 'Eminent Domain, Protest and the Discourse on Rehabilitation', in Michael M. Cernea and Hari Mohan Mathur (eds), *Can Compensation Prevent Impoverishment?*, New Delhi: Oxford University Press, pp. 208–26.

Rebbapragada, Ravi and Bhanumathi Kalluri. 2009. 'The Samantha Judgment: Upholding the Rights of Adivasi Women', in Lyla Mehta (ed.), *Displacement by Development* New Delhi: Sage Publications India Pvt. Ltd., pp. 249–69.

Sahoo, Sarbeswar. 2005. 'Tribal Displacement and Human Rights Violations in Orissa', *Social Action*, 55 (2), April-June, pp. 153–66.

Serageldin, Ismail. 2006. 'Involuntary Resettlement in World Bank-Financed Projects: Reducing Impoverishment Risks for the Affected People', in Hari Mohan Mathur (ed.), *Managing Resettlement in India*, New Delhi: Oxford University Press, pp. 45–66.

Seymour, Frances J. 2008. 'Conservation, Displacement, and Compensation', in Michael M. Cernea and Hari Mohan Mathur (eds), *Can Compensation Prevent Impoverishment?* New Delhi: Oxford University Press, pp. 286–306.

Shiva, V. 1997. 'Development, Ecology and Women', in Rajani Kanth (ed.), *Paradigm in Economic Development: Classic Perspectives, Critiques and Reflections*, Jaipur: Rawat Publications, pp. 224–52.

Srinivasan, Bina (ed.). 1996. *In Defence of the Future: Women Testify against the Tyranny of Displacement*, Mumbai and Baroda: Vikas Adhyan Kendra and Swashraya.

Thukral, Enakshi Ganguly. 2009. 'Displacement and Protecting the Rights of Children', in Lyla Mehta (ed.), *Displaced by Development*, New Delhi: Sage Publications, pp. 82–104.

Trembath, Barry P. 2008. 'Can Improved Resettlement Reduce Poverty?', in Michael M. Cernea and Hari Mohan Mathur (eds), *Can Compensation Prevent Impoverishment?* New Delhi: Oxford University Press, pp. 394–410.

2

Ability to Take Health Care Decision

A Case of Rural Women of Vaishali District of Bihar

RAJEEV K. KUMAR AND TUKARAM N. KHANDADE

Health is one of the important factors of women development and emancipation. In general parlance, health means proper functioning of the body, i.e. a person is able to carry out the routine work without any stress. The WHO has defined health as a state of complete physical, mental and social well-being and not merely the absence of disease or infirmity. But the concept of health and diseases varies from one culture to another and from one geographical region to another. The need for a combined strategy of health and development is suggested in different studies. Good health and well being of women play a great role in the development and emancipation of women. It also contributes to the development of family and society. Good health is a fundamental goal of development and it has been realized that targeting health as part of development is an effective way of improving the welfare of people including the women (Kumar and Kapoor, 2009). Ahuja (2002) in his study relates health to economy. He says that majority of population remain dependent for medical amenities on those places, which are quite far from their village and thus they are not able to avail the proper medical facility. This delays their treatment and consequently, the economy also suffers. Banerji (1982) said the health access is not equal to all the classes of society. It varies between the privileged and the less privileged classes and between the rural and the urban areas of the country.

Women have a different relationship to the health care system than men. Women are more likely to use health care services than men because of their health status, higher incidence of chronic health problems, and lifetime need for reproductive and related services. There are also considerable differences in how different groups of women use the health care system that are driven by economic factors, age and health status and health needs. Many women experience a range of barriers to care that are logistical and economic in nature (Salganicoff, Ranji and Wyn, 2005). It has been observed that most of the rural people are dependent on the public health facilities of the area, but its utilization by the women depends on several factors such as awareness level, proximity of the health facility, educational level, working status, etc. Educated women are likely to have proper knowledge and information on modern medical treatment and have greater capacity to recognize specific illness (Caldwell, Reddy and Caldwell, 1983). Similarly, working women are expected to have greater control over resources in the household. They are likely to have greater knowledge about pregnancy and childbirth due to greater freedom of movement. However, it is also argued that women's work in developing countries is poverty induced and, therefore, likely to have negative impact on the use of their health care services (Berman et al., 1997).

The rural poor are exposed to greater risks because of unhealthy and dangerous conditions and they also suffer from various diseases and malnourishment. The ecology, physical environment like drinking water, housing, sanitation, etc. and health are interrelated (Kumar and Kapoor, 2005). The better health services should be provided to all the people for better growth and development. The accessibility and utilization of health services by the rural women are equally important. To utilize the available health services at the government health facility, the women have to be proactive and conscious towards their health needs. Usually it is found that when it comes to making the health related decision, women do not come forward and take the decision. They have lesser say as compared to their men counterpart in the family. Rao and Somayajulu (2004) observed that though the urban areas, compared to the rural, are better equipped for providing the health services but in spite of this, the urban poor especially women and adolescent girls do not have the access. They attributed the poor health status of the women to several factors such as unhygienic practices, childbearing practices, unavailability of toilets, drainage system, less awareness and women enjoying moderate level of autonomy in view of their role in decision-making. They also found that in spite of universal awareness about the contraceptive methods, only half of the studied women reported to be using any method.

Health is one of the important indicators of development. The economic well being of the family and society also depends on the health of the people. The present study is carried out in two block PHCs of Vaishali district of Bihar state. The main objective of this paper is to understand the women's role in the health decisions, as ability to take the health decision also shows women's emancipation and level of autonomy enjoyed by the women in the family and society. Since the women's ability to make health decisions depends upon several background factors such as age, place of residence, education, occupation, family income, etc. these were also studied and their correlation was also analysed.

Methodology

The present study is carried out in two block Primary Health Centres (PHCs), namely Rajapakar PHC and Patepur PHC of Vaishali district of Bihar. Vaishali is one of the 38 districts of Bihar and it is one of the developed districts of the state as it is located closely to the State capital. The district was selected randomly while the PHCs were chosen on the basis of proximity from the district head quarter. Rajapakar is closest to the district headquarter while Patepur is farthest from the headquarter. Also the first PHC is better managed in terms of the services provided and the quality of HMIS data and reports than the latter, but the number of OPDs is more in the second PHCs as it caters to more population (approx. 3 lakh).

The fieldwork for the primary data collection was carried out in the month of October 2012 by the study team members. The Block Programme Management Units (BPMUs) also helped in the data collection. A total of 140 respondents were interviewed consisting of 70 respondents each from both the PHCs. After editing and cleaning of the data, 10 schedules were removed from the study sample and thus the responses of 130 respondents were analysed. All the respondents were female patients who had come to these PHCs to avail health care services. All the respondents were asked the questions one by one, so that the study team may get fair and unbiased responses.

The data was collected through a structured schedule. Most of the questions in the interview schedule were closed ended and focused on the respondents' socio-economic profile, awareness about the government health facilities and their ability to take health-related decisions. Special attention was given to the quality of data by assigning codes to all the filled interview schedules and questions. After the data collection, the data were fully validated in terms of internal consistency checks before it was analysed. The data were analysed using SPSS software, version–17.

Results and Findings

Socio-Economic Profile of the Respondents

The socio-economic development of the women is one of the important criteria of women empowerment. It has been observed that women belonging to better socio-economic background have more say in the family and the society. They are able to make the decisions about themselves and also have greater stake in the family decision. The following section gives a brief socio-economic profile of the studied respondents.

Since the respondents were drawn from the two Primary Health Centres (PHCs) of Vaishali district, almost all (97%) belong to the rural areas; remaining 3 per cent were not able to respond. The women who come to avail the health services provided by the government facilities are mainly from the adjacent villages. The health needs of urban women are mainly catered by the District Hospital and some of the private hospitals in the town (Table 1).

Table1

Distribution of Respondents by Place of Residence

Place of Residence	*No.*	*%*
Rural	126	96.9
Urban	0	0.0
No Response	4	3.1
Total	130	100.0

Table 2 shows the age profile of the respondents. It could be observed that most of the respondents belong to the young age group of below 30 years (73%) as most of the respondents had come to these PHCs for the ante-natal check-ups and delivery services. The least category of respondents was in the age group of 36–40 years.

Table 2

Distribution of Respondents by Age Groups

Age (in years)	*No.*	*%*
15–20	18	13.8
21–25	46	35.4
26–30	30	23.1
31–35	10	7.7
36–40	10	7.7
41 and above	16	12.3
Total	130	100.0

The marital status of respondents is shown in Table 3. Most of the respondents (89.2%) were married and only a few of them were either unmarried or widow (3% each). A few respondents did not respond to the question.

Table 3

Distribution of Respondents by Marital Status

Marital Status	*No.*	%
Married	116	89.2
Unmarried	4	3.1
Widow	4	3.1
No Response	6	4.6
Total	130	100.0

Education has direct correlation with women empowerment. Higher level of education means more economic avenues for the women and more economic independence to them which is also reflected in the ability to take the decision on their own for their health needs. Table 4 presents the educational status of the respondents. It may be seen that more than half (56%) of the respondents are either illiterate or have education below 10th Class. Only 26.2 per cent have education up to 10th class and very few respondents have completed 12th standard or higher degrees.

Table 4

Distribution of Respondents by Educational Achievement

Education	*No.*	%
Illiterate	19	14.6
Below 10th Standard	54	41.5
Up to 10th Standard	29	22.3
12th Standard and above	4	3.1
No Response	24	18.5
Total	130	100.0

Type of occupation and monthly income of respondents also have a correlation with women empowerment and ability to take health decision. As seen in the following (Tables 5a and b), nearly half of the respondents are housewives (46%). About one-fourth of the respondents are involved in agricultural practices (24.6%) and 13 per cent are involved in daily-wage labour, mostly as landless agricultural labourers. Only a few of them are involved in some petty business. If we see the monthly family income of the respondents, the situation is also not very good as most of the respondents have less than ₹ 4,000 income (almost 56%). Only 13% respondents said their monthly family income was ₹ 5,000 or more, which is also not a very high income as compared to the present day inflation.

Table 5(a)

Distribution of Respondents by Type of Occupation

Type of Occupation	*No.*	*%*
Housewife	60	46.2
Self Business	6	4.6
Agriculture	32	24.6
Daily Labour	17	13.1
No Response	15	11.5
Total	130	100.0

Table 5(b)

Distribution of Respondents by Monthly Family Income

Monthly Family Income (₹)	*No.*	*%*
1,000–2,000	18	13.8
2,001–3,000	15	11.5
3,001–4,000	42	32.3
4,001–5,000	34	26.2
5,000 and above	17	13.1
No Response	4	3.1
Total	130	100.0

Knowledge about Government Health Services

To meet the constitutional obligation of providing free and good quality health services to the people of the state, the government has established the public health system. This is more defined and distinct in the rural areas of all the states, including Bihar. As per the Indian Public Health Standard (IPHS), different levels of health facilities such as District Hospital, Sub-Divisional Hospital/Community Health Centre (CHC), Primary Health Centre and Health Sub-Centre exist on the basis of geography and population of the state. Government has also launched different health schemes such as JBSY (Janani Bal Suraksha Yojana), family planning services, routine immunization, etc. under National Rural Health Mission (NRHM). Besides this, other health facilities are also provided at the government institutions such as free ambulatory services, free medicines, Village Health and Nutrition Day (VHSND), etc. It has been observed that due to these populace measures, the awareness about the government health services among the rural population has increased and they have also started availing these services. These are reflected in the data of increased government institutional delivery and increased rate of immunization in last few years. To motivate the people to avail the services, government has also provided additional human resources in the form of Accredited Social Health Activist (ASHA) and Aanganwari workers (AWWs) on contractual basis.

To know about the level of awareness, the respondents were also asked a few questions relating to the knowledge about the government health facilities in the area, source of information and experience with the government facilities, etc. Since all the respondents were drawn from the government PHCs, most of them (98.5%) were also aware that the facility belongs to the government. None of them said these as private, however only 2 respondents were not able to answer (Table 6). It was also found that more than half of respondents (55.4%) were self-aware about the existence of PHC. For remaining respondents, the source of information was ASHA/ Auxiliary Nursing Midwife (ANM), neighbours or their family members.

Table 6

Respondents by the Awareness of Type of Health Facility

Knowledge about the Type of Health Facility	*No.*	*%*
Government health facility	128	98.5
Private health facility	0	0.0
No response	2	1.5
Total	130	100.0

Table 7

Respondents by the Source of Information Regarding the Government Health Facility

Source of Information	*No.*	*%*
Self	72	55.4
ASHA/ANM	30	23.1
Mother/Father	8	6.2
Neighbours	16	12.3
Husband	2	1.5
No Response	2	1.5
Total	130	100.0

The respondents were also asked whether they have enjoyed the government health facilities in the past or this was their first experience with the facility. On this majority of respondents (85%) said 'yes' and remaining said 'no' (Table 8). The responses reflect the positive attitude of women towards the government health institutions as majority have availed the services previously as well. This may be so because in rural areas there may not be any other good health facility.

Table 8

Respondents by Availing the Government Health Services in the Past

Health Services Enjoyed in the Past	*No.*	*%*
Yes	110	84.6
No	20	15.4
Total	130	100.0

Table 9

Respondents by Reason/s of Choosing Government Health Facility (Multiple Response and N= 130)

Reasons of Choosing Government Facility	*No.*	*%*
Proximity	82	63.1
Free services	48	36.9
Better health services	118	90.8
Rely more on government facilities	48	36.9
Others	2	1.5

When it comes to reasons for choosing the government health facility (Table 9), majority (90.8%) of the respondents chose it because of better health services provided at the government health institutions. Almost two-third women (63%) also chose because of proximity to their houses, and more than one-third chose because of free services and more faith in government facilities (36.9% each).

Women Ability to Take Health Decision

The main purpose of the present study was to assess the women's ability to make the health decisions for themselves and for the family. It also tries to explore the factors associated with the decision-making and barriers in making the decision, if any. It also tries to understand correlation of decision-making to women's health. It may be seen from the Table 10 that almost three-fourth (95/130–73%) respondents were able to make the decision to avail the health services from the government health facility and only one-fourth (33/130 respondents – 25.4%) women said that the decision was made by others. Two respondents were not able to respond to the question (Table 10). This shows that most of the women are able to decide about their own health despite staying in the rural areas.

Table 10

Respondents by Decision Taken to Avail the Government Health Services

Decision Taken	*No.*	*%*
Self	95	73.1
Others	33	25.4
No Response	2	1.5
Total	130	100.0

Usually the decision was either made by the women herself or jointly by family members or head of the family, but in most of the cases the consent of the women is also taken. Of those respondents (Table 11) who said that the decisions were taken by others, 45.5 per cent said that the decision was taken jointly with her and 33 per cent said by the family members. Only 21 per cent said that the decision was taken by the ANM/ASHA. However, the health workers (ANMs/ASHAs) might have encouraged the women and their family members to avail the health services at the government health institutions.

Table 11

Distribution of Respondents on Influencing the Decision by Others to Avail the Health Services (N=33)

Influencing the Decision	No.	%
Joint Decision	15	45.5
Family Members	11	33.3
Others (ANM/ASHA)	7	21.2
Total	33	100.0

Those respondents (Table 12) who said that they have taken the decision on their own (95/130) were also asked about the attitude of the family members towards her at the time of taking the health decisions. On this, most of the respondents (88.4%) said that the family members were positive and supportive and only 4 per cent said that they were neutral about it. A few of respondents (7.4%) also said that they have faced resistance from the family members.

Table 12

Respondents by Attitude of Family Members Towards Decision Taken by Herself (N=95)

Attitude of Family Members	No.	%
Supportive	84	88.4
Neutral	4	4.2
Resistance	7	7.4
Total	95	100.0

Table 13

Respondents by the Type of Relatives who Supported her Decision (N=95)

Family Members Supported the Decision	No.	%
Husband	47	49.5
Mother	15	15.8
Mother/Father in law	7	7.4
Other Family Members	18	18.9
No Response	8	8.4
Total	95	100.0

The respondents (Table 13) were further asked about the family members who have supported her decision on availing the health services. It was encouraging to find that the maximum respondents get the support from their husbands (49.5 %). Rest of them said that they got the support from their mothers and other family members.

In Bihar state, the Community Health Centre (CHC) does not exist and PHCs are established at the block levels which are supposed to function as CHC but unfortunately most of the PHCs in the state provide only basic health services such as Ante-natal Care (ANC), delivery, Post-natal Care (PNC), Out Patient Department (OPD), Family Planning (FP) services but it does not provide c-section or any other specialized services. Table 14 shows the type of services availed by the women. As discussed elsewhere in the study, most of the respondents were married and visited these PHCs either for the ante natal check-up services (56%) or the institutional delivery (37.7%). A good number of the respondents also visited for the OPD services (39%) and only a few of them came to avail the FP services (13%). Of these, nearly half of the respondents decided themselves to avail most of these services except the FP services which were encouraged by others – the front line health workers (ANMs/ASHAs), or family members or government doctors or any others. Since the surgical services were not available in both the PHCs, no woman has responded about this.

Table 14

Respondents by Types of Health Services Availed and Decision Taken by Herself

Type of Services	*Service Availed (Multiple Response N=130)*		*Decision Taken by Herself (Multiple Response N=95)*	
	No.	*%*	*No.*	*%*
Registering for ANC	73	56.2	52	54.7
Institutional Delivery	49	37.7	45	47.4
48 hrs stay in hospital after delivery	9	6.9	5	5.3
OPD Services	51	39.2	39	41.1
Family Planning Services	17	13.1	7	7.4
Surgical Services	0	0.0	0	0.0

Correlates of Women Ability to take Health Decision

To understand the correlation between the women ability to take their health decisions, important factors such as age groups, marital status, educational levels, occupation, monthly income, etc. were also analysed. Table 15 shows the health decision taken by the respondents vis-à-vis their age groups. A total of 128 out of 130 respondents were able to tell about their age. From this we have tried to correlate the decisions made on their health. If we see the table we do not get any clear pattern of the age group on the decision taken, but it may be observed that in the low age group (15–20 years), the health decision was influenced by others, i.e. the respondents did not take self-decision. Maximum self health decisions were made by the women of 21–25 yrs and 31–35 yrs age groups (80% each).

Table 15

Respondents by Age Groups vis-à-vis Decision Taken to Avail the Health Services (N=128)

Age (in years)	*Decision Taken by Themselves*		*Influenced by Others*		*Total*	
	No.	*%*	*No.*	*%*	*No.*	*%*
15–20	11	61.1	7	38.9	18	100.0
21–25	37	80.4	9	19.6	46	100.0
26–30	21	70.0	9	30.0	30	100.0
31–35	8	80.0	2	20.0	10	100.0
36–40	7	70.0	3	30.0	10	100.0
41 and above	11	78.6	3	21.4	14	100.0
Total	95	74.2	33	25.8	128	100.0

Table 16

Respondents by Marital Status vis-à-vis Decision Taken to Avail Government Health Services (N=124)

Marital Status	*Decision Taken by Themselves*		*Influenced by Others*		*Total*	
	No.	*%*	*No.*	*%*	*No.*	*%*
Married	89	76.7	27	23.3	116	100.0
Unmarried	0	0.0	4	100.0	4	100.0
Widow	3	75.0	1	25.0	4	100.0
Total	92	74.2	32	25.8	124	100.0

Table 16 shows the health decision taken by the respondents vis-à-vis their marital status. A total of 124 out of 130 respondents

(95.4%) answered this question. Of this 116 responded about their married status, 77.4 per cent respondents have taken the health decision on their own and remaining was influenced by others. All the unmarried categories of respondents were influenced by others while the health decisions were more taken by married respondents (77%) and widows (75%).

Table 17

Respondents by Educational Status vis-à-vis Decision Taken to Avail Government Health Services (N=106)

Educational Status	*Decision Taken by Themselves*		*Influenced by Others*		*Total*	
	No.	*%*	*No.*	*%*	*No.*	*%*
Illiterate	10	52.6	9	47.4	19	100.0
Below 10th Std	37	68.5	17	31.5	54	100.0
Up to 10th Std.	25	86.2	4	13.8	29	100.0
12th Std. and above	4	100.0	0	0.0	4	100.0
Total	76	71.7	30	28.3	106	100%

Table 17 shows the health decision taken by the respondents vis-à-vis their educational attainment. Only 106 respondents (81.5%) were able to tell about their educational status and rest among them (18.5%) did not respond on this. It can be seen from the table that the ability to take the health decisions by the respondents increases with their educational attainment. Overall 72 per cent respondents have taken self-decisions and the remaining 28 per cent respondents took decision with the help of others. In the illiterate category, only 53 per cent respondents have taken self-decision, while 69 per cent respondents belonging to category below 10th std. and 86 per cent respondents having 10th std. education have taken self-decision. All four respondents of 12th and above std. have taken health decisions themselves.

A total of 115 (out of 130) respondents were able to answer about their occupations. It can be observed from Table 18 that almost 74 per cent respondents have taken their own decision for availing the health services at government institutions. Overall, a good number of women was able to take self-decisions for health services; however, the percentage of self-decision was less in case of housewife (68%) as compared to the women who are involved in any other occupation such as self-business (83%), agriculture (78%), and daily labour (82%).

Table 18

Respondents by Occupational Status vis-à-vis Decision Taken to Avail Government Health Services (N=115)

Occupational Status	*Decision Taken by Themselves*		*Influenced by Others*		*Total*	
	No.	*%*	*No.*	*%*	*No.*	*%*
Housewife	41	68.3	19	31.7	60	100.0
Self-Business	5	83.3	1	16.7	6	100.0
Agriculture	25	78.1	7	21.9	32	100.0
Daily Labour	14	82.4	3	17.6	17	100.0
Total	85	73.9	30	26.1	115	100.0

Table 19

Respondents by Previous Experience of Government Health Services vis-à-vis Decision Taken to Avail Government Health Services

Previous Experience of Government Health Services	*Decision Taken by Themselves*		*Influenced by Others*		*Total*	
	No.	*%*	*No.*	*%*	*No.*	*%*
Enjoyed government health services previously	89	80.9	21	19.1	110	100.0
Not enjoyed government health services previously	6	30.0	14	70.0	20	100.0
Total	95	73.1	35	26.9	130	100.0

From Table 19 it is clear that those women who have availed the health services at the government health institutions previously are more likely to come again. Out of total respondents, 73.1 per cent have taken the decision on their own and rest of them were influenced by others. Respondents having previous experience with the heath facility have taken the decision more (89/110–80.90%) as compared to the first timers (6/20–30%).

Conclusion

All the respondents are women belonging to the rural areas and more than half of them are either illiterate or have education below 10th Class. Majority of them were aware about the government facility and enjoyed the facility previously. The main reason of choosing the government health facility is better health services provided at the facility. Regarding the decision-making, almost three-fourth respondents were able to make their own decision. Of those respondents who said that the decisions were taken by others, half said that the decision was taken jointly with her.

Most of the respondents were married and visited these PHCs either for ANC or delivery or OPD. Only a few of them came to avail the FP services (13%). It was found that in low age group (15–20 years), the health decision was influenced by others. Most of the unmarried respondents were influenced by others while the health decisions were more taken by married respondents (77%) and widows (75%). It was also found that the ability to take the health decisions by the respondents increases with their educational attainment. In the illiterate category, only 53 per cent respondents have taken self-decision, while 69 per cent respondents belonging to the category below 10th class and 86 per cent respondents having studied till 10th class have taken self-decision. Similarly, the percentage of self decision was less in case of housewife (68%) as compared to the women who are involved in any other occupation such as self-business (83%), agriculture (78%) and daily labour (82%). It can be concluded safely that while most of the women of the studied PHCs are able to take their health decision, but the ability to take health decision are more among the women who are mature, having better education, better exposure, and engaged in some economic activities.

Acknowledgement

Thanks are due to the District Health Society, Vaishali, for permitting to conduct the study. We also express our gratitude to the PHCs Patepur and Rajapakar for the necessary support in collecting the data and to the patients for providing their valuable time for interview.

References

Ahuja, K. 2002. 'Need for a Modern Health Care System for Tribals', *Bulletin of Tribal Research Institute*, 29 (1 and 2), pp. 99–113.

Banerji, D. 1982. *Poverty, Class and Health Culture in India*, New Delhi: Prachi Prakashan.

Berman, P., J. Zeitlin, P. Roy and H. Khumtakar. 1997. 'Does Maternal Employment Augment Spending for Children's Health Care? A Test from Haryana, India', *Health Transition Review*, 7 (2), pp. 187–204.

Caldwell, J.C., P.H. Reddy and P. Caldwell. 1983. 'The Social Component of Mortality Decline: An Investigation in South India, Employing Alternative Methodologies', *Population Studies*, 37 (2), pp. 185–202.

Kumar, Rajeev K. and A.K. Kapoor. 2005. 'Some Aspects of Health and Role of Public Health Services in a Primitive Tribe of Jharkhand', in K.K.N. Sharma (ed.), *Health Problems in Rural Areas of India*, Delhi: Academic Excellence, pp. 552–67.

——. 2009. *Management of a Primitive Tribe: Role of Development Dynamics*, Delhi: Academic Excellence.

Rao, A. Prakash and U.V. Somayajulu. 2004. 'Health Status of Women Living in the Slums of Bangalore', in P.J. Reddy (ed.), *Women, Health and Development*, Tirupati: Department of Population Studies, S.V. University, pp. 106–21.

Salganicoff, A., Usha R. Ranji and R. Wyn. 2005. *Women and Health Care: A National Profile*, Melona, CA: Kaiser Family Foundation.

WHO. 1946. *Preamble to the Constitution of the WHO* as adopted by the International Health Conference, New York, 19–22 June.

3

Women Emancipation through Watershed Programmes

AYAN HAZRA

Rural development over the past twenty years has been marked by a gradual shift from the intervention-based method to an approach promising rural people's involvement in his or her own development. Current trends suggest an increased awareness of the human dimension, women's role, environmental protection, sustainability and food security. Under these holistic arrangements, the human factor has a vital role in rural systems. Among the social groups in India, scheduled tribes have the highest percentage of the poor. While they account for only 8 per cent of the total population, they comprise mainly of displaced population. Literacy rate among them is only less than half of the general and that of rural tribal women about one-fourth. The tribal women contribute considerably to household income through farm and non-farm activities. To increase human dimensions in natural resource management, information campaigns must be launched to increase awareness and participation (Bonnal, 2004). One such programme is watershed management.

The term *'Watershed'* strictly refers to the divide/separating one drainage basin from another. Watershed management is an interactive process of integrated decision-making with regard to uses and modification of land and water within a watershed. It has social, ecological and economic dimensions. Watershed aims for protection of the ecosystem and results in immediate gains for the people. In a watershed development programme, afforestation and plantation crops play a very significant role.

Holistic approach for integrated farming system development on watershed basis in rainfed areas is the main pursuit of the developmental activities under the National Watershed Development Programme for Rainfed Areas (NWDPRA). It was initiated in the sixth plan and is continuing. Till the end of the Eighth plan, about 16.5 million hectares covering 2,500 micro-watersheds were treated under NWDPRA improving the livelihood of poor farmers. These programmes are aimed to support the resource-poor small and marginal farmers. More emphasis was given to support the scheduled caste and scheduled tribe farmers particularly those below the poverty line. These programmes were also, to some extent, successful to bring back the isolated tribal community in the mainstream of development. The watershed programmes have a direct impact on the living conditions and economy of the tribals especially women as most of them are engaged in agriculture and allied activities. No systematic study has been carried out regarding the socio-economic upliftment of these people as a result of implementation of watershed programmes. The NWDPRA has completed its first phase of development in the Gariyaband and Mainpur blocks of Raipur district. With a need of crucial scientific assessment of the programme in the tribal area, such assessment will be useful for extending the programme, put corrective measures regarding shortcomings and enable management and extension workers to devise methods and improve the planning and implementation procedure. The impact of programme on socio-economic aspects is important from the point of view of the efficiency and suitability of the programme.

Research Methodology

The study area was undertaken in Raipur district of Chhattisgarh state during the year 2008. The various information is gathered through allied agencies, government departments, eminent local personalities in related subject, social workers, NGOs, etc. An Interview Schedule was prepared based on the information provided by these sources. A pilot survey was undertaken in the villages of selected study area. A sample of 50 tribal families from each village was selected for this study of the socio-economic pattern of tribals with different level of adoption of watershed programmes. The nature of adoption of improved watershed technology by the families, especially women was the main focus of the study. Random sampling method was used to collect the samples from the people with varying income levels and occupations. The base data regarding socio-economic condition of the respondents were measured in terms of the material possession, at present and before the start of the project. The impact of NWDPRA was also assessed in terms of performance of various parameters in the adopted villages as compared to non-adopted villages in the neighbouring areas of these blocks.

Results and Discussions

Before NWDPRA, various development programmes were launched by the government, but tribals could not get adequate benefits from such programmes. The watershed development programme is directly connected to their day-to-day activity and livelihood; therefore, it seems to have impresses them much better than earlier programmes.

Impact on Living Conditions

Forest areas are natural habitat of tribes in which they live and sustain their life on different kinds of food obtained from local flora and fauna. For these people, natural streams and springs are sources of water, the prime need of living. The watershed programme either created or facilitated numerous work opportunities to the respondents that provoked them to undertake and participate in various income generation activities either independently or in groups. These activities not only increased their income but also offered more liberty out of this to make expenditure and raised their standard of living. This was possible due to improved socio-economic conditions and purchasing power of the respondents. It was reflected by way of improved living conditions such as housing, education, sanitation, clothing, hygiene and increased means of entertainment, etc. The improvement in living condition of the respondents is shown in Table 1. The overall proportion of respondents who were satisfied with the present living conditions in pre-project period was little over one-fourth (28%) that was increased to more than double (58.0%) in the post-project period.

Table 1

Improvement in Living Conditions (No. of respondents: 50 families)

Age Group Years	*Pre-Project Period*				*Post-Project Period*				*Per cent Change*	
	Satisfied		*Unsatisfied*		*Satisfied*		*Unsatisfied*			
	Freq.	*%*	*Freq.*	*%*	*Freq.*	*%*	*Freq.*	*%*	*%Satisfied*	*%Unsatisfied*
20–40	8	16.0	26	52.0	19	38.0	15	30.0	137.5	–42.30
40–60	4	8.0	9	18.0	8	16.0	5	10.0	100.0	–44.4
> 60	2	4.0	1	2.0	2	4.0	1	2.0	00.0	00.0
Total	14	28.0	36	72.0	29	58.0	21	42.0	237.5	86.7

This amounts to change of 237.5 per cent increase in satisfied respondents. The highest percentage (30.0%), followed by middle age group (10.0%) of 40–60 years and the lowest satisfied respondents were in the young group of 20–40 years. The satisfaction level of tribal women increased substantially after the implementation of watershed project.

Impact on Basic Amenities

The basic amenities include employment opportunity, marketing of agricultural produce, availability of drinking water, availability of medicinal facilities, problems at work place, food availability to family and access to market, etc. The range of basic amenities important in watershed management is enormous and included environmental issues, crop and livestock production, a whole range of social and cultural concerns, infrastructure planning and entire questions of governance and control. The opinion of tribal women on basic amenities is shown in Table 2.

Table 2

Improvement of Basic Amenities (No. of respondents: 50 families)

Basic Amenities	*Pre-Project Period*				*Post-Project Period*				*Per cent Change*	
	Low		*High*		*Low*		*High*			
	Freq	*%*	*Freq.*	*%*	*Freq.*	*%*	*Freq.*	*%*	*Low*	*High*
Employment opportunity	44	88.0	6	12.0	19	38.0	31	62.0	–56.8	416.7
Marketing of agricultural produce	42	82.0	8	16.0	23	46.0	27	54.0	–43.9	237.5
Availability of drinking water	41	82.0	9	18.0	28	54.0	22	44.0	–34.1	144.4
Availability of medicinal facilities	42	84.0	8	16.0	29	56.0	21	42.0	–33.3	162.5
Problems at work place	24	48.0	26	52.0	39	78.0	11	20.0	62.5	–61.5
Food availability to family	26	52.0	24	48.0	16	30.0	34	68.0	–42.3	41.6
Access to market	28	56.0	22	44.0	25	50.0	25	50.0	–10.7	13.7

In rainfed areas, the success of technical inventory often depends on location specific physical and socio-economic conditions and requires collective action by watershed area people, while farmers pursue complex strategies for producing food and earning their livelihoods. The situation of rural women was characterized by overlook, low productivity, little access to credit, land and training and the use of rudimentary technology. Women had to increasingly make up for the family's food deficit by working as casual hired labour or large farms, or by starting up income generating activities in addition to continuing their farming activities as well as other household tasks.

Impact on Income Level of Tribal families

Table 3 presents the distribution of annual income of respondents. In general, the income level of respondents was very poor before the project period. Majority of the tribal families (76.0%) had annual income less than ₹ 60,000. The economic conditions of respondents improved adequately after the project period. Majority of the respondents (82.0%) had annual income less than ₹ 1, 00,000.

Table 3

Improvement in Annual Family Income (No. of Respondents: 50 families)

Watershed	*Annual Family Income, in Thousands ₹*						
	<20	*20–40*	*40–60*	*60–80*	*80–100*	*100–120*	*120–140*
			Pre-Project				
Frequency	12	13	13	9	1	0	0
Percentage	24.0	26.0	26.0	18.0	2.0	0.0	0.0
			Post-Project				
Frequency	6	8	9	10	8	7	1
Percentage	12.0	16.0	18.0	20.0	16.0	14.0	2.0
			Change/Improvement				
Frequency	–6	–5	–4	+2	+7	+7	+1
Percentage	–12.0	–10.0	–8.0	+4.0	+14.0	+14.0	+2.0

The percentage of respondents with annual income up to ₹ 60,000 was decreased from 26 to 18 per cent with the implementation of watershed programme that improved their economic conditions. No one in the pre-project period had annual income above ₹ 1 lakh, after the completion of project 14 per cent respondents had annual income more than ₹ 1 lakh. The proportion of respondents decreased by 8 per cent (up to ₹ 60,000 annual income), whereas the same percentage of respondents increased in higher income group (> ₹ 60,000 annual income).

Impact on Personality Development of Female Child

Mother is the first teacher of a child. Her teachings/guidance/encouragement greatly contribute to the future course of action and consequent personality development of female child. Tribal women can do this job amicably by encouraging, creating interest and enthusiasm in female child to participate in extracurricular activities that will contribute to her personality development and will lead to make her good citizen of the country. This aspect was covered in the study and is shown in Table 4.

Table 4

Improvement in Education and Extracurricular Activities of Female
(No. of Respondents: 50)

Particulars	*Pre-Project*		*Post-Project*		*Improvement*	
	Frequency	*%*	*Frequency*	*%*	*Frequency*	*%*
Female child education	8	16.0	14	28.0	+6	+75.0
Higher education	1	2.0	3	6.0	+2	+200.0
Sports	4	8.0	14	28.0	+10	+250.0
Dropout cases	30	60.0	11	22.0	–19	–63.3
Cultural programme	24	48.0	27	54.0	+3	+12.5

Impact on Changes in Social Customs

Tribals not only retain their separate ethnic and cultural identity from the non-tribal population, but each of the tribal group also conserves and nurtures its distinct socio-cultural and linguistic tradition. *Kamar* language is a mixture of *Dravidian* and *Aryan* language. In some areas, mixture of *Chhattisgarhi, Halbi* and *Oriya* languages has been seen. Despite *Chhattisgarhi* influence they still speak *'Kamari'* dialect. The tribal women also do not use elaborate dress. Generally, they wear only a *'lugda'*, which they tie round their waist and carry it up to the shoulders across the breasts. The *'lugda'* covers only up to the knees. The lower portion of legs is left uncovered. The women do not use bodice or blouse. Both men and women generally do not have much fascination for ornaments. It is customary for men and women to put on metal chain or head necklaces. Besides, the women put on bracelets on their wrists. Usually women wear wooden or brass *'khilwa'* in their ears. The women are tattooed and usually have figures of a peacock on the shoulders, a scorpion on the back of the hand and dots. On the arms and legs, they have circular lines representing the ornaments usually worn. Now with the advancement of civilization, the women wear saris, blouse and various under garments available in the local market. The girls have started wearing skirts and blouse to attend schools. There is always difference of opinion in tribal women in different age groups, particularly in an individual family it is more pronounced between a mother-in-law and a daughter-in-law. There is always communication gap between these two. The daughter-in-law does not appreciate the rigidity in the prevalent customs which her mother-in-law wants to follow strictly. The opinion expressed by respondents about this rigidity and flexibility in adoption of social customs is shown in Table 5.

Table 5

Improvement in Flexibility of Social Customs (No. of Respondents: 50 families)

Para-meters	*Pre-Project Period*				*Post-Project Period*				*Per cent Change*	
	Rigid		*Flexible*		*Rigid*		*Flexible*			
	Freq.	*%*	*Freq.*	*%*	*Freq.*	*%*	*Freq.*	*%*	*Rigid*	*Flexible*
20–40	23	46.0	10	20.0	14	28.0	20	40.0	39.13	100.0
40–60	9	18.0	3	6.0	6	12.0	7	14.0	33.0	133.3
> 60	3	6.0	2	4.0	2	4.0	1	2.0	33.3	50.0
Total	35	70.0	15	30.0	22	44.0	28	56.0	105.43	283.3

Majority of the respondents (70%), on an average, were rigidly adopting social customs before the project period in the study area; their proportion was reduced to 44 per cent after the project period. This amounts to reduction in rigidity (–26%) in adoption of social customs by the respondents in the study area. Majority of them wanted flexibility in social customs. Similarly, the proportion of respondents who wanted flexibility in social customs reduced with the increased age of the respondents in the study area (40% in the age group of 20–40 years, 14% in the age group of 40–60 years and 2% in the age group above 60 years). This amounts to percentage increase in flexibility in social customs in the various age groups (100% in 20–40 years, 133.3% in 40–60 years and 50.0% in >60 years) after the project period.

Seasonal Schedule of Engagement

The respondents throughout the year remained busy in domestic works and animal care. Religious activities formed an integral part of their culture, besides being engaged in agricultural and the related work in her own field, as well as working as waged labour in plantations and forest departments. Whenever possible, the respondents supplement family's income by raising poultry, weaving and gathering various forest products. New agricultural technologies under watershed programme usually incur opportunities cost by competing with one or more of the many components of the farm household economy, effectively reducing the net benefits of project inventories.

Fruit-bearing trees namely *tendu*, *char* and *mahua* are found in the forests of study area. The tribals eat these fruits as a supplement to diet. *Amla,* tamarind tress, various kinds of edible roots, tubers and leafy vegetables are found in the forests of study area. Tribals used them as food items. They thatch their roofs using the '*khadar* or *khar* grass'. The '*phool bahari*' grass is collected for making brooms. The fruits of '*chind*' tree are used for eating purposes and its leaves are used for preparing brooms. Gums and *lac* are also gathered from some trees. These forests are the sources of valuable materials such as fuel; timber, bamboo and minor forest produce like *mahua, tendu-leaf, lac,* gums, grass, etc. The details of seasonal engagement period under different activities, in the study area, have been worked out and are shown in Table 6.

Table 6

Seasonal Engagement Period under Different Activities

Engagement Period (average man-days)		*Monsoon Season (Jun-Nov)*		*Rabi Season (Dec-Mar)*		*Summer Season (Apr-May)*		*Annual Average*	
		Freq	*%*	*Freq*	*%*	*Freq*	*%*	*Freq*	*%*
Pre-project Period									
Agriculture	< 20	44	14.7	58	19.3	111	37.0	71.0	23.7
	20 to <40	38	12.7	61	20.3	88	29.3	62.3	20.8
	40 to < 60	86	28.7	74	24.7	82	27.3	80.7	26.9
	> 60	132	44.0	107	35.7	19	6.3	86.0	28.7
Forest	< 10	122	40.7	81	27.0	132	44.0	111.7	37.2
	10 to <20	62	20.7	92	30.7	88	29.3	80.7	26.9

Cont'd...

...Cont'd

	20 to < 30	58	19.3	77	25.7	41	13.7	58.7	19.6
	30 to < 40	35	11.7	26	8.7	25	8.3	28.7	9.6
	> 40	23	7.7	24	8.0	14	4.7	20.3	6.8
Domestic +Animal	< 40	19	6.3	30	10.0	233	77.7	94.0	31.3
	40 to <60	17	5.7	149	49.7	61	20.3	75.7	25.2
	60 to <80	52	17.3	119	39.7	5	1.7	58.7	19.6
	> 80	212	70.7	2	0.7	1	0.3	71.7	23.9
Watershed Works	< 10	48	16.0	40	13.3	224	74.7	104.0	34.7
	10 to <20	155	51.7	120	40.0	70	23.3	115.0	38.3
	20 to <30	80	26.7	100	33.3	5	1.7	61.7	20.6
	>30	17	5.7	40	13.3	1	0.3	19.3	6.4
Religious/Cultural + Community	< 10	179	59.7	239	79.7	267	89.0	228.3	76.1
	10 to 20	121	40.3	61	20.3	33	11.0	71.7	23.9
Cottage Industry	< 10	133	44.3	110	36.7	214	71.3	152.3	50.8
	10 to 20	167	55.7	190	63.3	86	28.7	147.7	49.2
Post-Project Period									
Agriculture	< 20	17	5.7	16	5.3	40	13.3	24.3	8.1
	20 to <40	28	9.3	20	6.7	86	28.7	44.7	14.9
	40 to < 60	89	29.7	91	30.3	135	45.0	105.0	35.0
	> 60	166	55.3	173	57.7	39	13.0	126.0	42.0
Forest	< 10	107	35.7	79	26.3	120	40.0	102.0	34.0
	10 to <20	89	29.7	89	29.7	83	27.7	87.0	29.0
	20 to < 30	47	15.7	70	23.3	44	14.7	53.7	17.9
	30 to < 40	30	10.0	30	10.0	30	10.0	30.0	10.0
	> 40	27	9.0	32	10.7	23	7.7	27.3	9.1
Domestic +Animal	< 40	26	8.7	26	8.7	178	59.3	76.7	25.6
	40 to <60	33	11.0	155	51.7	81	27.0	89.7	29.9
	60 to <80	46	15.3	106	35.3	26	8.7	59.3	19.8
	> 80	195	65.0	13	4.3	15	5.0	74.3	24.8
Watershed Works	< 10	16	5.3	12	4.0	67	22.3	31.7	10.6
	10 to <20	80	26.7	88	29.3	106	35.3	91.3	30.4
	20 to <30	101	33.7	112	37.3	63	21.0	92.0	30.7
	>30	103	34.3	88	29.3	64	21.3	85.0	28.3
Religious/Cultural + Community	< 10	130	43.3	177	59.0	165	55.0	157.3	52.4
	10 to 20	170	56.7	123	41.0	135	45.0	142.7	47.6
Cottage Industry	< 10	90	30.0	53	17.7	103	34.3	82.0	27.3
	10 to 20	210	73.7	247	82.3	197	65.7	218.0	72.7

The respondents in the study area were found busy in six different activities throughout the annual cycle consisting of monsoon season (June to November), winter season (December to March) and summer season (April and May). The season-wise time schedule of the tribal women in terms of the average number of man-days (bifurcated into suitable ranges) during pre-project and post-project period is worked out.

Agriculture

The respondents perform almost all agricultural operations either solely or jointly with their male counterpart and other family members. Starting from field preparation, bund making, sowing and harvesting to threshing, processing, value addition and marketing of agricultural produce, they remained busy all over the cropping season. Besides, they were also engaged in other allied agricultural activities such as vegetable growing, processing, value addition and marketing it in the local market. There are three cropping seasons, viz. *monsoon season* (Jun-Nov), *rabi season* (Dec-Mar) and *summer season* (Apr-May). Previously they were growing only rice crop during *monsoon season* but with the implementation of watershed programme and water resource generation they are taking crops in *rabi season* and at some places in *summer season* also. As a result of increased activities, they remained busy throughout the season and most part of the year. On an average, majority of them (42%) are spending more then 60 man days annually in agricultural activities, followed by 35 per cent respondents in the range of 40–60 man days after the project period. The proportion of respondents in the above annual range of engagement period was comparatively less, viz. 28.7 and 26.9 per cent, respectively during pre-project period, when they remained ideal in most part of the year.

Among the three cropping seasons, *monsoon* is the busiest season (with 44% and 55.3% of respondents engaged in pre and post project period respectively) under the engagement period >60 man days. The mix trend was found in the other groups of annual engagement. Before the initiation of watershed project, Urmal Nala watershed shows highest proportion of respondents (25.7%) engaged in agricultural activities spending less than 20 man days annually (Appendix-III). This was closely followed by Pairi Nala watershed (25%) as per Appendix-IV. With the completion of project, the highest proportion of respondents (48.2%) in Sati Nala watershed were found to spend more than 60 man-days annually in agricultural activities. This was closely followed by Urmal Nala watershed (43%). In general, the proportion of respondents under low range of annual engagement period declined and that under higher range was increased during post-project period.

Forest

Tribal women live in fragile eco-regions – forests and hills – and are heavily dependent on agriculture, animal husbandry, forests and other natural resources for their survival. For example, they collect firewood for cooking, fodder for cattle feed, roots, tubers and wild fruits for human consumption. In addition to this, collection and selling of forest produce forms an important source of income to them. In all, tribal women play a central role not only in the gathering, processing and storing but also in utilization, management and marketing of the forest products. They contribute 70 per cent of the work and the rest only is done by men. Tribal women are the primary gatherers and managers of biomass goods in poor rural households. Tribal women's roles and responsibilities are pivotal not only to the management of natural resources but also in the management of domestic economy. Studies have shown that tribal women work longer hours, pool more of their income to the household budgets and manage the day-to-day consumption and cash flow needs. Thus, natural resources provide both subsistence needs and cash incomes, particularly to poor tribal households. The respondents were found to be busy in gathering various types of forest produce in one season or the other. They perform this task either in women's group or jointly with their male counterparts. They gather forest produce; some of it for home consumption and major portion for selling it to middlemen or small forest produce cooperative societies. They were also found engaged in cleaning and value addition of the forest produce in order to get higher values in the market. On an average, highest proportion of respondents (37.2%) were spending less than 10 man days annually followed by 26.9 per cent respondents spending 10 to 20 man days annually in this activity before the initiation of the project, this proportion remained more or less unchanged (34% spending less than 10 man days and 29 per cent spending 20–30 man days annually) after the project's completion.

Domestic Works Including Animal Rearing

Domestic work and animal care is the sole responsibility of respondents, which they cannot avoid; they remained busy throughout the year. They were found to be engaged from early in the morning till the late evening hours in performing various tasks of family works, starting from cleaning and processing of agricultural produce to cooking and serving the food to family members. They also involved themselves in animal and child care in the family, while looking after the ageing and sick members of the family. The majority of the respondents (70.7%) were spending more than 80 man days in this activity during monsoon season before the commencement of the project; this slightly decreased to 65 per cent after the completion of project.

Watershed Works

The participatory approach of watershed management includes, in addition to the technical aspects, the economic, social, political and cultural dimensions of natural resource conservation and management. Besides physical upgradation of the resources, it includes capacity building, expanded educational and training programmes, monitoring and evaluation, field demonstration and improved sharing and dissemination of information on approaches and methodologies so that users can benefit from the lessons learned.

Though the watershed works as per the established norms were started after the initiation of the project, but the farmers practiced some of it since past many years with either self or the assistance in various forms with government agencies. This revealed that the majority of them (monsoon – 51.7%, Rabi – 40%, summer season – 23.3% and annual – 38.3%) were spending 10–20 man days in watershed works (strengthening and maintenance of rice bunds, disposal of excess runoff, watering of rice fields, shallow dug wells, *dabri,* etc.) in pre-project period. The watershed programme was found to generate adequate awareness among the respondents about the importance of different techniques of water conservation against drought that might reduce crop production drastically. As a result of this understanding and water resource generation, majority of the respondents (monsoon – 33.7%, rabi – 37.3%, summer season – 21% and annual – 30.7%) were spending 20–30 man days in watershed works during post-project period.

Religious/Cultural and Community Works

These activities form the cultural heritage of their community. The tribal women take active participation in these activities to maintain their identity. These activities are so deeply embedded in their culture that it is very difficult to divert them from this to other activity. In general, the tribal women are participating in watersheds activities, without much sacrifice. With the impressive economic gains of community activities, this trend is now changing slowly, towards increased involvement in community activities. Majority of the respondents (59–89%) were spending less time (<10 man days) in this activity, during pre-project period. The highest proportion (89%) was found in summer season (April and May), followed by rabi season (79.7%) and the lowest was in monsoon season (59.7%), under the engagement period less than 10 days. The majority of respondents (73–79%) in all the watersheds were devoting less than 10 man days annually for religious/cultural and community works before the commitment of the programme.

Cottage Industry

The respondents were previously engaged in bamboo artwork, basket making, mat making and other rural cottage works before the initiation of project. The watershed officials encouraged them in various income generation activities leading to entrepreneurship development through financial and technical assistance. Some of the these activities and techniques are *dona-pattal* making machine, sewing machine for stitching clothes, women fish cooperative society, women training in micro enterprises, assistance in grocery shop, *tendu patta* collection and dressing, etc. Women self-help groups (SHG) were formed to take up these small-scale income generation activities and sharing the benefits. Various types of training to respondents in the field of bee keeping, mushroom production, sericulture, vegetable production, value addition, packaging, marketing and animal care were imparted to improve their skills and capacity in these activities. The participation of respondents in these micro enterprises in general increased in post-project period. Majority of them were involved in these activities (71.3%, summer season, <10 man days: 67%, rabi season: 63.3% with engagement period: 10–20 man days, monsoon season: 55.7% with engagement period 10–20 man days) during pre-project period.

Gap between Farmer's View and Investigator's View

The investigator's view was recorded in consultation with the well-reputed elder men and women of the villages, sarpanch and village *kotwar* who were well acquainted with the socio-economic conditions of the respondents. This was carried out to check any discrepancy that arose on particular information supplied by the respondent, still some gaps were unavoidable between the respondents' and investigator's views.

Conclusion

India is a home to over one-fifth absolute poor. The government through various programmes focuses on using its limited resources to develop approaches for assisting this vulnerable group. Rural development has been marked by a gradual shift from the intervention-based method to an approach promising rural people's involvement in his or her own development. Current trends suggest an increased awareness of the human dimension, women's role, environmental protection, sustainability and food security. Literacy rate among them is only less than half of the general and that of rural tribal women about one-fourth. The tribal women contribute considerably to household income through farm and non-farm activities. To increase human dimensions in natural resource management, information campaigns must be launched to increase awareness and participation.

Tribal women in Chhattisgarh live in fragile eco-regions and are mostly engaged in subsistence farming, hunting, fishing and collection of forest produce. Only a few of them are engaged in trades. Subsistence farming is, in fact, very toilsome and precarious and the people are, therefore, susceptible to sufferings and food scarcity at the time of natural calamity and crop damage. The work participation is one of the most important indicators of the social and economic status of the women in the society. The structure of the rural economy can greatly be improved when women participate fully and on equal terms with the male counterparts.

The watershed programmes have a direct impact on their living conditions and economy. A meagre research is done particularly in the field of watershed on the socio-economic status. The NWDPRA has completed its first phase of development in the Gariyaband and Mainpur blocks of Raipur district. There is a need of crucial scientific assessment of the programme in the tribal area; such assessment will be useful for extending the programme, put corrective measures regarding shortcomings and enable management and extension workers to devise methods and improve the planning and implementation procedure. The impact of programme on socio-economic aspects is important from the point of view of the efficacy and suitability of the programme. Socio economic upliftment of resource poor farmers through employment and resource generation; particularly empowerment of tribal women through SHG, *Mahila Samiti*, small saving groups and extending support for establishment of micro enterprises, are some of the thrust areas of watershed programme. Besides social awareness among women, the programme was found to be successful in making them self-reliant, economically independent and vigilant about their rights in the society. Health consciousness, educational awareness and access to information further add to their personality development as a consequence of project implementation.

References

Agrawal, S.S., R.S. Bhople and M.A. Sagane. 1993. 'Evaluation of National Workshop on Watershed Management', *Maharashtra Jour. Extn. Edn.*, 12, pp. 145–48.

Babu, T.H. 1991. 'Socio-Economic Appraisal of Agro Forestry Technology in the Rainfed Areas of Maheshwaram Watershed Project', International Conference for Minimizing Risk in Rainfed Agriculture, New Delhi, pp. 6–9.

Barbier, Edward. 1988. 'The Economies of Farm Level Adoption of Soil Conservation Measures in the Uplands of Java', Working Paper, World Bank Environment Department, pp. 11–18.

Bonnal, J. 2004. 'The Sociological Approach in Watershed Management: From Participation to Decentralization', proceedings of the African Regional Workshop on Watershed Management, Chapter 9, Part 4: Social Aspects, pp. 117–22.

Hazra, A. 2008. *Empowerment of Tribal Women through Watershed Development Programme: A Study of Raipur District*, PhD research work submitted to Pandit Ravishankar Shukla University, Raipur.

Hazra, C.R. and D.P. Singh. 1998. 'Efficient Crop Production through Soil and Water Conservation on Watershed Basis at Tejpura, Jhansi', *Jour. of Soil and Water Cons. India*, 31 (3 and 4), p. 22.

Kaushal, R.C. 1994. 'Evaluation Study on Economic Viability of Watershed Management Project in the Degraded Aravali Foothills of Haryana', *Ind. Jour. Agril. Economics*, 49 (4), pp. 210–22.

Khepar, S.D., S.K. Sondhi, J.K. Chawla and Mandeep Singh. 2001. 'Enhancement of Irrigation through Watershed Programme', *Jour. of Soil and Water Cons.*, 45 (1 and 2), pp. 41–49.

Kottakayam, J.J. 1983. *Social Structure and Change among the Tribals*, New Delhi: D.K. Publishing House, p. 53.

Mahnot, S.C., P.K. Singh and Y. Sharma. 1992. 'Socio-Economic Evaluation of Watershed Management Project: A Case Study', *Jour. Rural Dev.*, Hyderabad, 11 (2), pp. 219–27.

Mishra, P.K. and M.H. Hussain. 2001. 'Impact Evaluation on Peddagedda Watershed of Srikakulma District in Andhra Pradesh', *Report – CRIDA*, Hyderabad.

Palta, A., N. Sharma and M. Vishwakarma. 1995. 'Socio-Economic Profile of the Kamar's: A Primitive Tribe of M.P.', *Bull. – Tribal Res. Inst.*, Bhopal, M.P., XXIII (2), pp. 57–62.

Samra, J.S., V.N. Sharda and A.K. Sinha. 2001. 'Water Harvesting and Recycling: Indian Experiences', *CS and WCR and TI*, Dehradun, p. 347.

Seth, S.L. 1991. 'Institutional Adjustments for Participatory Approaches on Watershed-Based Sustainable Farming System Development in Rainfed Areas', *Intl. Conf. for Minimizing Risk in Rainfed Agriculture*, New Delhi, pp. 6–9.

Vishwakarma, M. 2000. *A Study of Food Consumption Pattern and Food Analysis of Rare Foods Eaten by Kamars: A Primitive Tribe of Madhya Pradesh*, PhD Thesis, Government D.B. Girls PG College, Pandit Ravishanakar Shukla University, Raipur.

4

Status of Tribal Women in Modern India

ANIRBAN MUKHERJEE

India is home to a diverse population of indigenous peoples. More commonly known as 'adivasis' or the 'tribal' population, indigenous groups comprise 8 per cent of the total population of India. According to the Census of India (2001), tribes account for 84.4 million people in India. In the Indian context, tribal groups are the earliest known settlers of the land if not autochthonous (Singh and Kaur, 2009: 121). In contemporary India, tribal groups represent ethnic minorities that are highly impoverished and part of the lowest tiers of the Indian class system (Rath, 2006: 16; Sujatha, 2002: 93). Several of their distinguishing characteristics are that the majority live in scattered, inaccessible, small settlements in remote, hilly-forested areas of the country and depend primarily on hunting, agriculture and fishing for their livelihood (Rath, 2006: 34). Most of the tribal dominated areas lack basic infrastructural facilities like roads, transportation, communications, electricity and medical facilities (Sahoo and Das, 2006: 269).

Some of the largest tribal groups in India are the Gonds, Santals, Khasis, Kharia, Lodhas, Angamis, Bhils, Bhutias, Birhors, and Greater Andamanese. These tribal groups have their own distinct cultures, traditions, languages and lifestyles with varying levels of social and economic development. In all, there are 573 tribal groups in India (Sujatha, 2002: 87). The most economically disadvantaged groups are officially recognized by the Indian government as 'Scheduled Tribes' and are eligible for some affirmative action measures.

The status of women in the tribal society is comparatively higher than that of women in the mainstream Indian society (Roy Burman, 2012). The sex ratio of the tribal population in India in 1991 was 971 females per 1,000 males in comparison to 927 females among the mainstream society (ibid.). Further, though some tribes have son preference, yet they don't engage in discriminatory practices like female infanticide or sex determination tests (Bhasin, 2007: 5; Roy Burman, 2012). Tribal women are considered to be assets by their families (Roy Burman, 2012). Hence, in contrast to the mainstream Indian society, the custom of bride price is prevalent among the tribes. In situations where the groom is unable to pay the bride price, he renders physical labour and services at his in-law's place (ibid.).

Tribal women actively contribute to the sustenance of their families (ibid.). They are involved in agricultural production process which includes ploughing, digging, sowing, manuring, transplanting, harvesting, winnowing, etc. (Awais, Alam and Asif, 2009: 2). Moreover, processing of food grains comes within the exclusive domain of tribal women. As Awais et al. (2009: 2) narrate, *'Every morning tribal women dehusk millet and paddy in husking levers and then clean the grains and cooks them. They not only save money, but also earn it, unlike females of other communities.'*

Women are also responsible for collecting minor forest produce and selling them in the market to earn a living. Chaudhary's (2010) research in the tribal areas of Betul in Madhya Pradesh found tribal women to be solely responsible for the collection and marketing of firewood. More importantly, the income that the tribal women procure by selling the firewood is spent on meeting the basic requirements of their families like rice, pulse, edible oil, soap, detergent powder, etc. (Chaudhary, 2010; Roy Burman, 2012). The purpose of this paper is to highlight the status of tribal women in the present Indian society and how their conditions have deteriorated because of one-sided developmental policies of the government. It also attempts to bring out the struggle of the tribal women against top-down developmental strategies of the Indian government that hardly evaluate the ecological consequences of their projects. Tribal women share an intimate relationship to nature and development induced destruction of nature have increased their hardship for sustaining livelihoods. This paper strives to gain some understanding in this direction. The paper is divided into six sections. The first section discusses the educational achievement of the tribal women and also highlights the major hurdles in the path of tribal education in India. The second section portrays the health status of tribal women and the impact of environmental degradation on their deteriorating health conditions. The third section highlights the lop-sided nature of developmental policies of the Indian government and how they contradict the very process of tribal empowerment. The section also describes the biased nature of the developmental policies against tribal women. The fourth section presents the relationship that tribal women share with forest. The fifth section narrates the role of tribal women in ecological sustenance, with special reference to the Chipko movement. Finally, the conclusions of the study are discussed.

Educational Status of Tribal Women

The Indian government has implemented an array of policy initiatives in the post-colonial period for the development of the tribal population. One focus of these initiatives has been extending education to tribal groups by constructing and operating primary and secondary schools in the tribal dominated areas of rural India. Over the past several decades, school enrollment among tribal children has increased (Sedwal and Kamat, 2008: 5). Data suggests that while school enrollments among the tribal children have increased by 25 per cent, enrollment among the scheduled tribe girls recorded a steeper rise of 36 per cent (Awais et al., 2009: 4). Similarly, at the upper primary level of education, the rise of enrollment of the tribal girls (47%) surpassed that of the tribal community (35%) (ibid.).

Despite such increase in enrollment percentage, the literacy rates of the tribals in India remain low. The tribals are reported to have very low literacy rate of 25.9 per cent and more so among the tribal females (14.5%) (NSSO, 1991; Basu, 1993: 25). This is more of a concern because the Indian Census considers a person to be literate if he or she could read and write with understanding any of the Indian languages and most literates in the tribal communities of India are educated till the primary level (Basu, 1993: 25).

In this context, Sujatha (2002: 92) identifies three types of constraints hindering the development of tribal education: external, internal, and socio-economic. A key external constraint is that in India, decisions concerning education policy (e.g. curriculum design, textbook adoption, teacher recruitment) are set at the state level and are uniform for the entire state. These decisions generally fail to take into account the cultural specificities of tribal groups which, in turn, serve to stunt educational development. For example, school vacations and holidays are scheduled in reference to the context of the non-tribal population and do not take into account tribal festivals and other important events, thereby lowering school enrollments and attendance (Sujatha, 2002: 94).

Key internal constraints to educational development include the lack of quality of school provisions, suitable teachers, relevant content and curriculum (ibid.: 93). Schools in tribal areas function with bare minimum facilities and lack proper classrooms, teaching-learning materials, blackboards, drinking water facilities, toilets, and playground (Rathnaiah, 1977: 147; Sujatha, 2002: 93). In addition, it has been found that the pedagogy developed for school children in mainstream Indian society is not well suited for the tribal context because of its rigidity, emphasis on discipline, and teacher-centred instruction (Sujatha, 2002: 93).

A key socio-economic constraint to tribal education identified by Sujatha (2002: 93) is rampant poverty among the tribal population. In response to their impoverished situation, the Indian government has implemented incentive (i.e., subsidy) programmes designed to increase the school attendance of tribal students. These programmes include such benefits as free school uniforms and supplies and free mid-day meals. Sujatha (2002: 93) found that these programmes did not provide full coverage for all students; the supplies provided were of inferior quality, and many of the benefits either did not reach eligible students entirely or did not arrive in time for the beginning of the school year. In many cases, additional educational expenditures were required of tribal families in order that their children attend school, which placed a serious financial hardship on them (Sujatha, 2002: 93).

Health Status of Tribal Women

Basu (1993: 37) identifies nutritional deficiency to be a common problem among the tribal women. Nutritional deficiency adversely affects the ability to resist infections, leads to chronic sickness and permanent brain damage in the post weaning period. Tribal women commonly suffer from maternal malnutrition, which pose a serious health concern for those who have pregnancies closely spaced. Besides, it should be noted that pregnant women's nutrition has a bearing on the survival chances of the infant and its subsequent growth (Basu, 1993: 35).

Basu (1993: 35) highlights that the diet of none of the tribal groups in India is satisfactory and generally lacks in Vitamin A, Vitamin C, riboflavin, and animal protein content. For instance, diets of the tribes of Kerala were found to be deficient in terms of calories and protein content. Similarly, studies conducted by the National Institute of Nutrition (1971) and the Planning Commission of India (Sixth Five Year Plan, Government of India) recorded high protein deficiency in the tribal diet of the rice-consuming belts of the country (Basu, 1993: 35).

In understanding nutritional deficiency among the tribal groups, emphasis should also be laid on their customs and taboos. For example, milk consumption is prohibited among certain tribal groups because milking of cow is considered a taboo (ibid.: 36). Thus, malnutrition suffered by Kannikar tribal women of Trivandrum was due to lack of milk, milk products and pulses in their diet. Pregnant and lactating tribal women were found to be deficient in terms of calorie consumption. There was a widescale prevalence of pyrexia, respiratory complaints, gastro-intestinal diseases and rheumatic diseases among the tribal women (ibid.).

Interestingly, a study conducted by Ali (1980) among the tribal groups of Phulbani, Koraput, and Sundergarh districts of Odisha attributed the cause of malnutrition to rampant deforestation that created food shortages and prolonged droughts. Similarly, Basu (1993: 37) posits that deforestation adversely affects the lives of tribal in terms of increasing their workload and creating food shortages. Extensive deforestation increases the distance to be traversed to collect minor forest produce and firewood. This particularly has bearing for the tribal women, who generally are responsible for collecting and distributing food and often go hungry to feed others in cases of shortage. Coupled with the problems of malnutrition and increased workload among the tribal women, deforestation has also deprived the tribals of the medicinal herbs. Such ecological imbalance has resulted in rapid proliferation of diseases like tuberculosis, stomach disorders, and malaria among the tribals in the recent years (Menon, 1987: 374; Basu, 1993: 38).

Government's Policy towards Tribal Development

The policy of the Indian government towards tribal development could at best be described as 'lop-sided.' Deforestation in the tribals belts have resulted in a shortage of fuel, fodder, food, and foliage which form the very vitals of the tribal economy (Awais et al., 2009: 3). To exemplify with concrete evidence – the government of India in 1995 decided to construct a hydro-power generation plant at Bagmundi, West Bengal. The 900 MW (4 X 225 MW) Puruliya Pumped Storage Project is the largest pump storage project in India and one of its kind in terms of installed capacity and magnitude of underground structure

(Bhattacharyya, 2005: 1). The construction of the dam required the destruction of a substantial portion of the forest. This had a devastating consequence for the poverty-sticken tribals (Santal, Munda, Bhumij, Birhors) of the area, who constitute the majority population of the area. The construction of the dam meant that the tribals could no longer rely on the forest produce for sustaining their livelihood. For example, it hampered the traditional lac cultivation of the tribals because of the deposition of dust particles from crushed stones around tree trunks. Bhattacharyya's (2005: 4) study found that villagers of Bareria are losing an approximate amount of 10–15 moulds of lac annually. The loss poses a serious economic constraint on the tribal sustenance considering that lac used to be sold for ₹ 50–150 and the lac egg for ₹ 200–500 per kilo (Bhattacharyya, 2005: 4).

The project also impaired the tribal livelihood strategy of selling forest wood in the market. The tribals used to collect forest wood worth ₹ 25–30 in a day and their income increased in the rainy seasons due to the scarcity of fuel wood in the market. Bhattacharyya's (2005: 4) interviews with the tribals revealed rampant felling of 'sal', 'kendu', 'mohul', 'piyal', 'ashon', 'dha', 'dumur', 'parurh' trees for the project. To make matters worse, consumer prices is on the rise due to the influx of outsiders in the region (Bhattacharyya, 2005: 4).

Finally, the project caused enormous air and noise pollution in the area. Sound of heavy vehicles and crushing of stones have led to the area being covered by thick dark smog. Considering the devastating impact the project has on the lives of the tribals, it is surprising that the government did not consult with the tribes about the project nor did it create alternative employment opportunities for them (ibid.: 4–5).

Similar evidence of exploitation is witnessed in the displacement-induced scenarios where tribals are often the main victims. One such instance of stark exploitation was the displacement of tribals from the mountains of southern Odisha. The mountains of southern Odisha is a source of good quality of bauxite and the base rocks of these mountains are referred to as Khondalite after the tribal group of 'Khonds,' recognizing the close connection that the tribals enjoy with these mountains (Padel and Das, 2006: 4). In the period 1950–1960, Indal (Indian aluminium), a subsidiary of Alcan (Aluminium Canada), installed an aluminium smelting plant at Hirakud in northwestern part of Odisha and a bauxite processing plant in the northern part of Odisha. The plants drew hydro-electric power and water from the Hirakud dam of Sambalpur area, which displaced a minimum of 1,60,000 people, with tribals constituting 50 per cent of the displaced people. Even worse, few of the displaced people were rehabilitated (ibid.).

The legislations protecting the tribal rights in India are equally ambiguous and have many loopholes in them. While the states prohibit the purchase of tribal land by the non-tribals, yet there is no legislation in place prohibiting the acquisition of tribal lands by the state in 'public interest' (Kurup, 2008: 103). In fact, the Land Acquisition Act of 1894 empowers the state to acquire public property for numerous purposes (ibid.). Kurup (2008) identifies the main cause of the problem in the inability of the tribes to exercise fundamental rights to property. Under Article 300A of the Constitution the tribals are entitled to legal rights to property which is not given the same importance as fundamental rights (Kurup, 2008: 103). Besides, the 'authority of law' found in Section 4 (i) of PESA (Panchayat Extension to Scheduled Areas Act, 1996) explicitly empowers the government to acquire lands in the Scheduled Areas (ibid.).

Similar ambiguity exists in case of forest laws in India. Indian legislation classifies forest into three categories: reserve forests (which should be left untouched), protected forests (where exploitation is not prohibited unless specifically mentioned) and village forests (whose use and management is assigned to the local communities) (ibid.: 106). Thus, the use of a forested region for consumption purposes by the tribal communities depends on the classification of the forest. Even if PESA entitles tribal communities 'the ownership of minor forest produce,' the right becomes meaningless unless the state designates the forested areas to be village forests and not reserve forests. Unfortunately, PESA does not specify the ways in which states should safeguard the rights of the tribal groups to forests (ibid.).

In addition, there is the existence of Joint Forest Management (JFM) programme, which provisions the state to constitute separate village committees supervised by the state's forest department (ibid.). Though such state-controlled committees should ideally be staffed entirely by members of the tribal community as per the Fifth schedule of the Constitution, yet it is entirely up to the state jurisdiction to abide by the recommendation or not. The lack of coordination between the village committees constituted under the PESA and those formed under the JFM recommendation is apparent from the fact that the JFM guidelines released by the federal Ministry of Environment and Forests in 2000 does not highlight upon the PESA's role (ibid., 107).

With rapid depletion of forests and displacements induced by developmental projects, many tribals are forced to work as coolies in the industrial sector (Roy Burman, 2012). In parts of Maharashtra, Madhya Pradesh, Gujarat and Rajasthan, poverty induces them to work in brick kilns and building sectors (ibid.). While both the tribal men and women are heavily exploited in such places, the women suffer more as they are sexually abused and paid less in comparison to the men (ibid.).

Though the government tries to compensate the displaced tribals by offering rehabilitation packages, it is unfortunate that such rehabilitation packages are often biased against tribal women. For instance, the Narmada Water Dispute Tribunal's (NWDT) Award, which administers the rehabilitation of people displaced by the Sardar Sarovar Project, evidences gender bias in its definition of family as *'husband, wife, and minor children and other persons dependent on the head of the family example, widowed mother.'* (I (3) (i), p. 126). Besides, sub-clause I (3) (ii) adds to this gender bias by considering every major son to be a separate family (Ganguly Thukral, 1996: 1501).

Ganguly Thukral (1996: 1501) observes that even though the states of Maharashtra, Gujarat and Madhya Pradesh designed their own rehabilitation package for those adversely affected by the Sardar Sarovar Project, yet they all entailed certain discriminatory clauses. For example, Maharashtra did not consider the daughter of the oustees to be separate families (Revenue and Forest Department, Resolution No. RPN 3188/CR/30/88/R–5 dated June 29, 1989, Clause V; Ganguly Thukral, 1996: 1501). Though Gujarat borrowed the definition of family from the Award and made it comprehensive by including all women widowed after 1980s as separate families, yet it considered women who were widowed before 1980 to be 'dependents' of the head of the family (ibid.).

Discrimination against women is evident in Madhya Pradesh's definition of 'family' and 'displaced person' as well. Thus, a family is defined as, *'family in relation to displaced persons means the family of displaced persons consisting of such persons or his or her spouse, minor son, unmarried daughter, minor brother or unmarried sister, father or mother and other members residing with him and dependent on him for livelihood'* (Section 2 (9); ibid.). Likewise, a displaced person is defined as, *'any tenure holder, tenant, government leaser or owner of other property who on account of acquisition of his land … has been displaced from such land or other property'* (Section 2 (8); ibid.).

Ganguly Thukral (1996: 1501) notices similar gender bias in policies aiming to compensate Tehri dam oustees. She notes that even if a woman happens to be the owner of a land, she and her husband are together entitled only to a single plot of land, and compensation is only given to the husband. Thus, Ganguly Thukral (1996: 1501) aptly argues, *'In the absence of any affirmative clauses including them, women are automatically left out, since they seldom possess ownership rights.'* It should also be added that displacement is accompanied with tremendous loss of resources that adversely affects the life of women. This was evidenced in the case of Kohadia villages of Korba in Madhya Pradesh where displaced women had no forest in the vicinity to depend on and hence had to rely on the market for fuel. It was a challenging situation considering the fact that majority of the people was unemployed or underemployed (Ganguly Thukral, 1996: 1501).

Furthermore, women suffer more than men in the transition period between actual displacement and resettlement. In the absence of proper resettlement policy in the Sardar Sarovar Project Resettlement scenario, many displaced people found it difficult to move to a new site. Many resorted to maintaining two families – one in the submerged village and other in the resettled site – which created a fraction within the families. In most cases, it is the women, aged people and children who stayed back (ibid.).

Likewise, Ganguly Thukral (1996: 1502) argues that whenever there is a rise of unemployment, women are the first ones to lose jobs. This has to do with the fact that women often sacrifice their careers for men when employment is scarce. In the displacement-induced scenarios, the compensatory projects have very limited number of jobs to offer to the affected and in most cases it offers one job for every displaced family (Fernandes, 2007: 8). Usually the most eligible male member of the family gets the job and the women suffer without any compensation (Ganguly Thukral, 1996: 1502).

Tribal Women and Forest

The associations of the tribals with forest have been generational and they depend on it for sustaining themselves. According to the Report of the Forest Survey of India, 2003, in districts that constitute 33.6 per cent of the country's geographical area, 60.4 per cent of the 63 per cent of forest cover in the country and 63 per cent of dense forest fall within 187 tribal districts (Awais et al., 2009: 3). Tribal women collect water, fuel, edible fruits, flowers, vegetables, berries, etc. from the forest. Some of the forest produce are used by tribals for securing commercial ends. For instance, by selling natural gums, resins, medicinal plants, plants used in perfumery, and tendu leaves, tribals secure 70 per cent of their total income (ibid.).

Years of experience of sustaining livelihood amidst most untoward situations have given the tribals keen insight about the working of nature and ecological stability. Their intense knowledge of environment is reflected in their water harvesting techniques, agricultural practices, irrigation systems, use of forest plants and herbs for medicinal purposes, etc. (ibid.). For example, a study of the tribes of Madhya Pradesh revealed names of 165 trees, shrubs, and climbers that they rely on for their food (ibid.). Among these 165 varieties of trees and shrubs, 19 provide roots and tubers, petals and leaves of 35 varieties are cooked as vegetables, fruit is obtained from 63 varieties, 17 yield juice, in addition to supplying nuts, figs, honey, etc. (Agarwal, 1989: 55). Likewise, the tribes of Attapadi valley of Kerala rely on approximately 80 varieties of fruits, leaves, barks and flowers for medicine. These forest products have played a critical role in helping the tribals to cope with the seasons of acute food shortages and starvation (ibid.). Hence, the availability of these resources is essential for the sustenance and survival of tribal community in India.

The Role of Tribal Women in Ecological Development

In highlighting the role of tribal women in ecological development, it is of utmost important to focus on the ecofeminist movement. This US-based movement originated when Sherry Ortner observed that women's interest coincide with nature and men's with culture (Awais et al., 2009: 2). Awais et al. (2009: 3) summarize the basic premises of the movement as: (a) women and environment are distinctly related; (b) women's responsibilities make them dependent on nature; (c) women possess an extensive knowledge of natural resources. Ecofeminists contend that the connection between the dominance of nature and women is ideological and it places women and nature under the dominance of men (Agarwal, 1992: 120).

Ecofeminists believe that a woman occupies a mediating role between nature and culture and thus calls for an integrated view of nature, culture and gender issues (Agarwal, 1992: 120; Awais et al., 2009: 3). As Awais et al. (2009: 3) put it, *'An appropriate strategy of development would be one which is not only ecologically sustainable but takes the interests of women into consideration.'* Women can contribute immensely in the creation of sustainable eco-system because they simultaneously play the roles of producers, consumers and educators in their families (Awais et al., 2009: 3).

Vandana Shiva (1992: 207) perceives the violence against nature to be an offshoot of industrial development and colonial imposition. Since women in the third world countries rely on nature for sustaining themselves and their families, destruction of nature is akin to destruction of resources that women require to sustain themselves (Agarwal, 1992: 124). Let us now highlight upon the Chipko movement to understand the involvement and activism of the tribal women about maintaining ecological balance.

The Chipko movement was started in 1972–1973 when the tribal population of Chamoli district in Uttar Pradesh protested against the auctioning of 300 ash trees to a sports good manufacturer, while the government denied permission to the local labour cooperative to cut few trees in order to manufacture agricultural implements for the community (ibid.: 147). This was followed by protests when the forest department declared an auctioning of approximately 2,500 trees in the Reni forest on the banks of Alaknanda river (Jain, 1984: 1792). The protest was led by Gauri Devi, a woman of Bhotia tribe in Lata region. She compared the forest to her mother's home and cautioned the labourers that they can touch the trees only after shooting her. The effort of the tribal women to save the forest did not go in vain, the expert committee set up by the Uttar Pradesh government declared the Reni forest to be a sensitive area and imposed a ten-year ban on cutting of trees in an area covering over 450 square miles at Reni forest (ibid.).

Instance of female participation in the Chipko movement was not restricted only to the above-mentioned incident. For example, in the June of 1977, Sarala Behn protested against the illegal felling of trees and excessive tapping of resin from the Chir pine forest (Shiva and Bandyopadhyay, 1986: 137). Similarly, in the December of 1977, the felling of Adwani forest was vehemently protested by Bachchni Devi, wife of a local village contractor. The activists tied sacred threads to the trees to mark their vows of protection. In the February of 1978, the axe-men arrived with huge numbers of armed police with the plan that the latter would encircle the forest during the felling of trees (Shiva and Bandyopadhyay, 1986: 137). However by the time the contractors arrived, each tree was embraced and guarded by three volunteers. Encountered with such resistance, the police withdrew before sunset (ibid.).

There are several unique features of the involvement of tribal women in the Chipko movement. *First,* besides protesting the commercial exploitation of the Himalayan forest by non-local contractors alongside with men, women also differed from village men in terms of difference of priorities about resource use (Agarwal, 1992: 147). Tribal women have repeatedly strived for saving the forest and the environment sacrificing the shallow gains from development projects with high environmental costs. Agarwal (1992: 147), for instance, highlights the awareness of tribal women about the potential consequence of lop-sided government policies when it proposed the establishment of potato-seed farm by felling the oak forest in Dongri Paintoli village. While the men supported the programme for its promise of cash income, the women opposed it on the grounds that it would deprive them of the only source of fuel and fodder in the locality and thereby increase the distance to be travelled to collect fuel (Agarwal, 1992: 147).

Secondly, Agarwal (1992: 147) notes that tribal women were actively involved in protecting trees, and prohibited tree auctioning and illegal cutting of trees. Thus, in Gopeshwar town, local women's group appointed a watchman who guarded the surrounding forest and regulated the collection of forest produce. Twigs were allowed to be collected freely, but felling of trees was strictly prohibited (Agarwal, 1992: 147).

Thirdly, Agarwal (1992: 147–48) observes replanting trees to be an essential part of the Chipko movement. However, men and women differed on the choice of trees to be planted. While the women preferred trees that provided fuel, fodder, and daily necessities, the men supported the plantation of trees that served commercial purpose. Thus, it can well be induced that tribal women made more responsible choice as far as the subsistence of their families is concerned (Agarwal, 1992: 148).

Fourthly, Agarwal (1992: 148) aptly considers the Chipko movement to be much more than an ecological movement as it addressed issues relating to male alcoholism, domestic violence and irresponsible expenditure by men. It was an empowering movement for the women and it changed their self-perception.

Finally, another standout feature of the movement was that it encompassed a holistic understanding of the environment. Women recognized that forests do not comprise merely of trees, but soil, vegetation and water constitute an integral part of the ecosystem as well. Thus, the women identified the interdependence between different components of nature and the role such interdependence play in the creation of a sustainable environmental condition (Agarwal, 1992: 148).

However, it should be noted that Chipko movement is not the only instance where tribal women protested against injustice meted out to them. There are several evidences of opposition of tribal women against ill-conceived developmental policies. Tribal women, for instance, protested when Balco (Bharat Aluminium Company) attempted to set up bauxite mines in the Gandhamardhan hills of western Odisha (Padel and Das, 2006: 4). The project was opposed on the ground that tribes of the area depended on the forest cover of the hill for their livelihood. Tribal women took an active part in the movement and when their husbands were jailed, women stopped the way of the police and company vehicles by placing their babies. The situation was such that Ministry of Environment and Forests had to call off the project in 1987 (ibid.).

Conclusion

Women in tribal societies enjoy a comparatively higher status than that of women in the mainstream Indian society. Moreover, they are actively involved in securing sustenance for their families. In the recent years, though the school enrollment among the tribal girls have increased, yet their literacy rate has remained rather low. Nutritional deficiency is a common problem among the tribal women and their diet often lacks essential nutrients.

Tribal women share a close relationship to forests and they depend on forests for securing their livelihoods. However, deforestation and development-induced forcible displacement have destroyed the symbiotic relationship that tribals share with nature. It has led to shortages of food, fuel, fodder and foliage, which constitute the very vitals of the tribal economy. Such exploitation of tribals in the modern society is augmented due to the existence of ambiguous legislations that protect tribal rights. For instance, while there are legislations prohibiting the acquisition of tribal lands by non-tribals, but there is no legislation restricting such acquisition by the state. Further, rehabilitation packages offered to the displaced tribals often include discriminatory clauses and are evidenced to be biased against women. Nonetheless, tribal women have not passively accepted their fate and have time and again protested against the injustice meted out to them and their community.

Tribal women have the potential to become the harbingers of empowerment and progress of their community. It is an irony that the independent and industrious nature of tribal women has rarely caught attention of the administrators. This aptly raises the question: What is the real purpose of policies aiming at tribal development? Das and Das (1992: 1373) answer the question as follows: *'Perhaps it should be apparent to all and sundry that the government wants to put up no more than a facade of concern for tribal development.'* In other words, such policies provide one means used by Indian elites to generate mass acceptability and political legitimacy among tribal groups while incorporating them into Indian society in a dependent and marginal position. I strongly believe that the remedy lies in designing holistic developmental strategies that take into account the grassroots realities of the tribal community and by adopting Das and Das (1992) recommendation of offering systemic support to tribal initiatives and struggles.

References

Agarwal, Bina. 1989. 'Rural Women, Poverty and Natural Resources: Sustenance, Sustainability and Struggle for Change', *Economic and Political Weekly*, 24 (43), WS46-WS65.

——. 1992. 'The Gender and Environment Debate: Lessons from India', *Feminist Studies*, 18 (1), pp. 119–58.

Ali, A. 1980. 'Health and Genetic Problems of Khutia Khonds of Bulubaru Village, Phulbani District, Orissa', *The Newsletter*, 1 (2), pp. 103–14.

Awais, Mohammad, Tosib Alam and Mohd. Asif. 2009. 'Socio-Economic Empowerment of Tribal Women: An Indian Perspective', *International Journal of Rural Studies*, 16 (1), pp. 1–11.

Basu, S.K. 1993. 'Health Status of Tribal Women in India', *Social Change*, 23 (4), pp. 19–39.

Bhasin, Veena. 2007. 'Status of Tribal Women in India', *Studies of Home and Community Science*, 1 (1), pp. 1–16.

Bhattacharyya, S. 2005. 'The Puruliya Pump Storage Project: People, Environment Suffer for the Uncertain Peaking Power', *South Asia Network on Dams, Rivers and People*, 3 (8 and 9), pp. 1–5.

Census of India 2001. New Delhi: Government of India.

Chaudhary, S.N. 2010. *Tribal Economy at Crossroads*, Jaipur and New Delhi: Rawat Publications.

Das, Achyut and Vindhya Das. 1992. 'Development and Tribal Women', *Economic and Political Weekly*, 27 (27), pp. 1372–73.

Fernandes, Walter. 2007. 'Development-Induced Displacement: The Class and Gender Perspective', paper presented at the International Conference on the Emerging Woman in the Indian Economy, Christ University, Bangalore, 26–27 November, pp. 1–13.

Ganguly Thukral, Enakshi. 1996. 'Development, Displacement and Rehabilitation: Locating Gender', *Economic and Political Weekly*, 31 (24), pp. 1500–03.

Jain, Shobhita. 1984. 'Women and People's Ecological Movement: A Case Study of Women's Role in the Chipko Movement in Uttar Pradesh', *Economic and Political Weekly*, 41 (13), pp. 1788–94.

Kurup, Apoorv. 2008. 'Tribal Law in India: How Decentralized Administration is Extinguishing Tribal Rights and Why Autonomous Tribal Governments are Better?', *Indigenous Law Journal*, 7 (1), pp. 89–126.

Menon, Geeta. 1987. 'Tribal Women: Victims of the Development Process', *Social Action*, 37 (4), pp. 373–90.

National Institute of Nutrition. 1971. *Annual Report*, Indian Council of Medical Research, Hyderabad.

National Sample Survey Organization. 1991. *A Report on Living Conditions of Tribals and Non-Tribal Areas*, No. 380, Government of India.

Padel, Felix and Samarendra Das. 2006. 'Anthropology of a Genocide: Tribal Movements in Central India against Over-Industrialization', presented at South Asia Anthropology Group, UK.

Rath, Govinda (ed.). 2006. *Tribal Development in India: The Contemporary Debates*, New Delhi: Sage Publications.

Rathnaiah, E.V. 1977. *Structural Constraints in Tribal Education*, New Delhi: Sterling Publishers.

Roy Burman, J.J. 2012. 'Status of Tribal Women in India', *Mainstream Weekly*, L (12).

Sahoo, P.K. and B.C. Das. 2006. 'Primary Education in the Tribal Belt of Orissa', in Govinda Rath (ed.), *Tribal Development in India: The Contemporary Debate*, New Delhi: Sage Publications, pp. 258–78.

Sedwal, Mona and Sangeeta Kamat. 2008. *Education and Social Equity: With a Special Focus on Scheduled Caste and Scheduled Tribes in Elementary Education*, New Delhi: National University of Educational Planning and Administration, pp. 1–43.

Shiva, Vandana. 1992. 'Women's Indigenous Knowledge and Biodiversity Conservation', *India International Centre Quarterly*, 19 (1/2), pp. 205–14.

Shiva, Vandana and Jayanta Bandyopadhyay. 1986. 'The Evolution, Structure and Impact of the Chipko Movement', *Mountain Research and Development*, 6 (2), pp. 133–42.

Singh, Rattan and Gagandeep Kaur. 2009. 'Human Rights of Indigenous People: A Reflection of Reality', *Asia-Pacific Journal of Social Sciences*, 1 (1), pp. 117–26.

Sujatha, K. 2002. 'Education among Scheduled Tribes', in Govinda Rath (ed.), *India Education Report: A Profile of Basic Education*, New Delhi: Oxford University Press, pp. 87–95.

Part II

Violence Against Women

5

Rape and Indian Society

SADHNA GUPTA

> Rape is not a crime against the person of a woman, it is a crime against the entire society ... Rape is, therefore, the most hated crime. It is a crime against basic human rights and is also violative of the victim's most cherished of all the Fundamental Rights, namely the Right to Life contained in Article 21.
>
> — Bodhisattwa Gautam vs. Subhra Chakraborty[1]

Definition

The word 'rape' is derived from the Latin term 'rapio', which means to seize. Rape literally means a forcible seizure and that is the essential characteristic of the offence. It means the violation of one's esteem. Rape is a crime not only against the person of a woman but a crime against society, being the worst kind of social menace. It is viewed as a crime against the 'honour' of not just the girl who is raped but also of her family. Apart from being regarded as a dehumanizing act it is an unlawful intrusion on the right of privacy and sanctity of female. It is violative of the victim's most cherished of the Fundamental Right that is the Right to Life contained in Article 21 of the Constitution.[2] In common parlance it can be defined as sexual assault which includes any sexual activity carried out against the will of the victim through the use of violence, coercion or intimidation even if it did not end in penetration. It is not necessary to prove the completion of sexual intercourse by the emission of seed; intercourse is deemed complete upon proof of penetration only. The slightest degree of penetration is enough. If penetration cannot be satisfactorily proved, the defendant may be convicted of attempted rape; if the intent is not proved, he may be convicted of indecent assault.[3] In *Pani Bhusan*

Behera vs. State of Orissa,[4] the Orissa High Court has held: ... the rupture of hymen is by no means necessary to constitute the offence of rape. Even a slightest penetration in the vulva is sufficient to constitute the offence of rape. Vulva penetration with or without violence is as much rape as vaginal penetration.

Rape has existed invariably with time and place. In year 1999, it was said that rape takes place once in every 54 minutes.[5] Another study conducted by the Centre for Development of Women's Studies gives even more disturbing statistics. It states that 42 women are raped everyday in India that is one in every 35 minutes.[6] Within the span of two year it is said that rape takes place once in 29 minutes.[7] In 2004, there were 18,233 reported rape cases in the country but the victims of rape cases were 18, 239. Of the total victims of rape, 8.9 per cent (1,622) were girls under the 15 years of age, while 11.0 per cent (2,004) were teenaged girls (15–18 years). Nearly two-third, 62.2 per cent (11,343) were women in the age group 19–30 years, 17.5 per cent (3,189) were in the age group of 31–50 years, while only 0.4 per cent (81) were over 50 years of age. Offenders were known to the victims in as many as 85.6 per cent cases. Of these, parents/close family members were involved in 3.2 per cent cases, neighbours were involved in 34.3 per cent cases and relatives were involved in 6.6 per cent cases.[8] Despite gender equality and women empowerment being the buzzword of the 21st century, their hollowness and futility is apparent in the face of rape cases total figure (18, 233) being an all time high. According to the all-India figures from National Crime Record Bureaus (NCRB), the number of rape cases is spiraling to dizzying heights each year. Table 1, 2, 3, 4 and 5 shows as follows:

Table 1

Incidence of Rape During 1995–2004

Year	*No. of Rape cases*
1995	13,754
1996	14,846
1997	15,330
1998	15,151
1999	15,468
2000	16,496
2001	16,075
2002	16,373
2003	15,847
2004	18,233

Source: National Crime Records Bureau 2004.

Rape cases have reported mixed trends over last five years with a decrease of 2.5 per cent in 2001 over 2000, an increase of 1.8 per cent in 2002 over 2001, a decrease of 3.2 per cent in the year 2003 over 2002 and substantial increase of 15 per cent in 2004.

Table 2

Incidence of City-wise Number of Rapes and Rapes with Murders in India during 2000–2002

City	*2000 (Up to Nov)*		*2001 (Up to Nov)*		*2002 (Up to Nov)*	
	Rape	*Murder*	*Rape*	*Murder*	*Rape*	*Murder*
Ahmedabad	16	99	75	10	9	209
Bangalore	28	201	203	33	28	192
Bhopal	80	64	55	98	94	59
Kolkata	32	43	62	19	30	50
Chennai	5	57	84	27	21	86
Hyderabad	41	104	96	32	55	110
Jaipur	32	38	34	25	41	59
Lucknow	19	158	100	24	18	130
Mumbai	95	273	260	101	102	223
Patna	12	208	172	15	16	227
Delhi	436	4	382	8	386	7

Source: Centre for Social Research.

Table 2 shows the rising incidence of rape and rape with murder in the metro cities likes Chennai, Delhi, Mumbai and Kolkata during 2000 to 2002. There was decrease in number of rape cases during 2001 but again it increased in 2002 as compared to 2000.

Table 3

Incidence of Rape in West Bengal Districts–2003

Name of Districts	*Custodial Rape*	*No. of Gang Rape*	*No. of Other Rape*	*Total Person Arrested*
Bankura	–	1	42	46
Birbhum	–	4	44	38
Bardhaman	–	9	60	97
Cooch Behar	–	3	50	48
Darjeeling	–	2	22	27
Hooghly	–	2	35	34

Cont'd...

...Cont'd

Howrah	–	20	15	13
Jalpaiguri	–	4	56	52
Pashim Medinipur	–	4	46	37
Purba Medinipur	–	6	27	31
Murshidabad	–	8	98	104
Malda	–	4	53	63
Nadia	–	7	101	107
24 Parganas (N)	–	15	76	86
24 Parganas (S)	–	9	80	96
Purulia	–	2	23	36
Uttar Dinajpur	–	4	20	17
Dakshin Dinajpur	–	1	30	33
Total	–	105	878	965

Source: W.B. Commission for Women, *Sexual Violence and Law,* Annexure II, p. 48–51.

Table 3 shows the rising incidence of rape against women in West Bengal districts, including gang rape, together with the number of persons arrested. According to the information available for 2003, prevalence of crime against women (rape) was more pronounced in the districts of Nadia, North and South 24 Parganas, Murshidabad, Bardhaman, Jalpaiguri and Cooch Behar.

Table 4

Age-Group-Wise Victims of Rape Cases (Total) (Sec. 376 IPC) During 2011

State/UT	*No. of Reported Victims*	*Up to 10 Years*	*10–14 Years*	*14–18 Years*	*18–30 Years*	*30–50 Years*	*Above 50 Years*	*Total Victims*
Andhra Pradesh	1,442	99	147	400	652	136	8	1,442
Arunachal Pradesh	42	6	13	1	22	0	0	42
Assam	1,700	4	9	27	1,114	538	8	1,700
Bihar	934	23	18	50	757	86	0	934
Chhattisgarh	1,053	33	100	344	377	186	13	1,053
Goa	29	3	6	11	7	2	0	29
Gujarat	439	16	45	69	263	39	7	439
Haryana	733	9	15	42	550	115	2	733

Cont'd...

...Cont'd

Himachal Pradesh	168	7	12	53	73	20	3	168
Jammu & Kashmir	277	2	3	15	201	56	0	277
Jharkhand	784	0	7	42	591	142	2	784
Karnataka	636	21	24	59	471	60	1	636
Kerala	1,132	59	98	284	422	260	21	1,144
Madhya Pradesh	3,406	67	309	886	1573	546	27	3,408
Maharashtra	1,701	136	175	534	724	169	7	1,745
Manipur	53	4	8	11	23	6	1	53
Meghalaya	130	25	30	15	47	16	1	134
Mizoram	77	21	13	15	17	10	1	77
Nagaland	23	5	6	4	4	4	0	23
Odisha	1,112	2	44	119	758	172	17	1,112
Punjab	479	20	32	115	278	32	3	480
Rajasthan	1,800	26	73	295	1,052	342	12	1,800
Sikkim	16	3	3	5	4	0	1	16
Tamil Nadu	677	45	46	181	365	39	2	678
Tripura	205	22	22	1	141	18	1	205
Uttar Pradesh	2,042	150	305	633	816	138	0	2,042
Uttarakhand	129	1	9	13	83	23	0	129
West Bengal	2,363	1	34	217	1,671	439	1	2,363
Total (States)	23,582	810	1,606	4,441	13,056	3,594	139	23,646
Union Territories								
A & N Islands	13	2	2	5	4	0	0	13
Chandigarh	27	6	1	9	6	5	0	27
D & N Haveli	4	0	0	1	2	1	0	4
Daman & Diu	1	0	0	0	1	0	0	1
Delhi	572	57	97	185	194	37	2	572
Lakshadweep	0	0	0	0	0	0	0	0
Puducherry	7	0	1	5	1	0	0	7
Total (UTs)	624	65	101	205	208	43	2	624
Total (All-India)	24,206	875	1,707	4,646	13,264	3,637	141	24,270

Source: National Crime Record Bureau.

Table 4 shows that there were 24,270 victims of rape out of 24,206 reported rape cases in the country. Nearly 10.6 per cent (2,582) of the total victims of rape were girls under 14 years of age, while 19 per cent (4,646 victims) were teenage girls (14–18 years). As many as 54.7 per cent (13,264 victims) were women in the age-group 18–30years. However, 15 per cent (3,637 victims) victims were in the age-group of 30–50 years while 0.6 per cent (141 victims) were over 50 years of age. Delhi has earned the odium of 'rape capital' with an incidence of 572 rape cases in 2011. But in the same year, it was Madhya Pradesh that reported the highest number of cases for rape (3,406). After MP the states reporting the highest incidence of rape cases in 2011 were West Bengal (2,363), UP (2,042), Rajasthan (1,800), Maharashtra (1,701), Assam (1,700) and Andhra Pradesh (1,442). According to the National Crime Records Bureau, the number of rape cases registered in India increased by a startling 873.3 per cent, from 2,487 in 1971 to 24,206 in 2011.

Table 5

Offenders Relation and Proximity to Rape Victims 2011

State/UT	*No. of Cases in Which Offenders Were*				
	No. of Cases in which Offenders were Known to the Victims	*Parents/ Close Family Members*	*Relatives*	*Neighbours*	*Other Known Persons*
States					
Andhra Pradesh	1,442	0	29	362	1051
Arunachal Pradesh	42	0	0	5	37
Assam	1,700	0	72	418	1,210
Bihar	934	2	18	408	506
Chhattisgarh	1,053	39	135	392	487
Goa	28	1	1	7	19
Gujarat	438	2	29	74	333
Haryana	733	8	43	393	289
Himachal Pradesh	168	8	7	25	128
Jammu & Kashmir	276	0	18	77	181
Jharkhand	784	8	117	306	353
Karnataka	352	1	42	81	228
Kerala	1,119	38	56	244	781
Madhya Pradesh	3,406	10	301	1,849	1,246
Maharashtra	1,699	43	97	566	993

Cont'd...

...Cont'd

Manipur	53	0	0	16	37
Meghalaya	117	6	14	24	73
Mizoram	77	3	16	32	26
Nagaland	16	9	0	4	3
Odisha	1,112	0	92	302	718
Punjab	467	6	61	156	244
Rajasthan	1,689	43	134	502	1,010
Sikkim	16	1	0	1	14
Tamil Nadu	675	2	96	249	328
Tripura	205	1	14	99	91
Uttar Pradesh	2,042	2	79	452	1,509
Uttarakhand	112	4	6	35	67
West Bengal	1184	7	20	540	617
Total (States)	21,939	244	1,497	7,619	12,579
Union Territories:					
A & N Islands	13	0	3	1	9
Chandigarh	27	0	0	2	25
D & N Haveli	4	0	0	0	4
Daman & Diu	1	0	1	0	0
Delhi	558	23	59	211	265
Lakshadweep	0	0	0	0	0
Puducherry	7	0	0	2	5
Total (UTs)	610	23	63	216	308
Total (All-India)	22,549	267	1,560	7,835	12,887

Source: National Crime Record Bureau.

Table 5 shows that offenders were known to the victims in as many as in 22,549 (94.2%) cases. Parents/close family members were involved in 1.2 per cent (267 out of 22,549 cases) of these cases, neighbours were involved in 34.7 per cent cases (7,835 out of 22,549 cases) and relatives were involved in 6.9 per cent (1,560 out of 22,549 cases) cases. So, the data indicates that in most of the rape cases the victims were victimized either by neighbours or relatives.

Rape is the gravest crime against human dignity. It is difficult to find any eye witnesses as the crime done is hidden. Rape, as defined under Section 375[9] of the Indian Penal Code, has its origin in the laws of 1,736 as applicable in Britain. That year, Sir Mathew Hale, in his history of the Pleas of the Crown (1786: 629) presented common law rape doctrines which were immediately noticed to be hostile to the interests of women*. One of the requirements was to inform the jury during trial that rape charges were easy to bring but difficult to defend.[10] Consequently, with changing times, reforms were introduced and the above requirement was removed. In contemporary times, rape is found in different form, i.e. child rape, marital rape, custodial rape, gang rape and date rapes.

Child Rape: Rape by itself is one of the most obnoxious crimes but child rape is the most reprehensible bestiality, which requires special provisions for penalization in law. Ironically, rape laws make no distinction between rape of minor and that of an adult. In *Sudhesh Jhaku vs. KCJ,*[11] although it was painfully evident that the minor, aged six, had been brutally abused by her father, purely on account of deficiency in law, the judge was left with no option but to drop charges of rape and retain only the less serious charge of outraging the modesty of the minor. In case of *Sakshi vs. Union of India,*[12] it was held that Section 375 cannot be altered as to include all forms of penetration. An exercise to alter the definition of rape, as contained in Section 375 of IPC by process of judicial interpretation and that too when there is no ambiguity in provisions of the enactment is bound to result in good deal of chaos and confusion, and will not be in the interest of society at large. Recently, in the case of *State of Madhya Pradesh vs. Balu,*[13] a girl of thirteen years was raped by a villager. The accused was guilty of rape under Section 376 of the IPC. He was given an imprisonment of ten months on the ground that the accused was seventeen years old at the time of the incident and was illiterate villager coming from rural area.

Marital Rape: The term 'marital rape' refers to unwanted intercourse by a man on his wife obtained by force, threat of force or physical violence or when she is unable to give consent.[14] Unwanted intercourse refers to all sorts of penetration whether anal, vaginal or oral. Marital rape has been kept out of purview of criminal law due to the presumption that the husband can exercise his right on the wife. But in 1983, Section 376A, was incorporated in the IPC whereby sexual act with a legally separated unwilling wife recognized as a criminal offence. There are three kinds of marital rape, namely:

- *Force-only Rapes:* The husband uses enough force to coerce the wife to intercourse
- *Battering Rapes:* Women are raped and simultaneously battered by their husbands experiencing both physical and sexual violence.

---

* He emphasized – 'The husband cannot be guilty of rape committed by himself upon his Lawful wife for by their mutual matrimonial consent and contract'.

- *Sadistic/Obsessive Rape:* These involve torture and/other perverse sexual acts. Pornography is frequently involved in sadistic form of rape.[15]

In India the exception to Section 375 of the IPC explicitly says that sexual intercourse by a man with his own wife, not being under fifteen years is not rape. Thus, if the wife is above fifteen then forcible intercourse even without her consent is not rape.

Custodial Rape: Custodial rape is a particularly important category of rape since it represents a flagrant abuse of the authority of the government, the very institution which is bound to promote and protect the rights of women.[16] Single women, widows with young children and women belonging to the lower strata of society become easy prey to custodial rape because they are already deprived of the supportive mechanism. Custodial rape did exist before 1980s but did not find itself in the glare of media spotlight. It was a Supreme Court Judgment in *Mathura rape case*[17] that shocked people out of their complacency and brought the crime of custodial rape in the limelight.

The Criminal Law (Amendment) Act, 1983, has resulted in some welcome changes for the rape victims. Sections 375 and 376 of the IPC have been substantially changed and several new sections have been introduced, viz. Sections 376A, 376B, 376C, and 376D, IPC. These sections deal with crimes which, strictly speaking, do not come under the definition of rape but are equally heinous and brutal. The amendment introduced in 1983 has catered for this anomaly. Now, sexual intercourse in a custodial situation, though it does not amount to rape, is a serious crime even if the woman has consented to it. These new sections were introduced with a view to stop sexual abuse of women in custody, care and control by various categories of persons which not amounting to rape were nevertheless considered highly reprehensible.

Gang Rape: When a woman is raped by one or more in a group of persons acting in furtherance of their common intention, each of them is deemed to have committed gang rape which is the crudest and the most extreme form of male chauvinism and is treated as an aggravated form of rape under Penal Code.[18] In *Uttam Kumar vs. State,*[19] the Bombay High Court held that rape by two persons will be sufficient to constitute the offence of gang rape. In case of gang rape there shall be 10 years of rigorous imprisonment.

Date Rapes: In the West, there are date rapes acknowledged by law, wherein a boy dates a girl and forces a physical relation on her. The situation is not the same in India and judicial attitudes differ. In *Prem Chand vs. State of Haryana,*[20] it was argued before the court by the defence counsel that the prosecutrix was a consenting and willing party as she was going around with the appellant of her own free will and, therefore, the question of commission of offence did not arise. Again, in *Nana Ram Chanda vs. State of Maharashtra,*[21] it was observed that since the prosecutrix was a willing and consenting party, the court opined that a lenient view should be taken. Date rape may be recognized as rape, or it may involve coercive sex that has left the victim feeling confused and traumatized. It is not a legal term but it may be referred as 'relationship rape'. Now-a-days, we find that friendship is made through telephone and later through e-mail, contacts are called on dates where one is victimized by force rape.[22]

Law Relating to Rape

Section 375 of the IPC states that a man is said to commit 'rape' who, except in the case hereinafter excepted, has sexual intercourse with a woman under circumstances falling under any of the six following descriptions: *First* – Against her will … .[23]

Section 376 of the IPC provides punishment for rape in which the rapist shall be punished with imprisonment for not less than seven years but which may extend to life imprisonment.

Section 377[24] of the IPC can be applied to other forms of penetration. It has frequently been used to address adult sexual abuse of children, including male children, as the current law on rape is inapplicable to such cases. The New Delhi High Court in dealing with a finger penetration of a six-year old child in 1996[25] barred the creative interpretation of Section 377 to include non-penile abuse of children and said it amounted to an offence under Section 354, 'violation of modesty'[26].

The Criminal Law (Amendment) Act, 1983 made a significant change related to procedural law by adding *Section 114A*[27] to the Indian Evidence Act which allows drawing a conclusive presumption as to the absence of consent in certain prosecutions for rape involving custodians.

Another significant procedural change was the amendment of *Section 327* of the CrPC in Criminal Law (Amendment) Act, 1983 which added Sub-sections 2 and 3. Sections 327 of the CrPC deals with the right of the accused to an open trial but taking into account problems faced by rape victims in open court, the new Sub-sections were inserted.[28]

In case of rape, there was tendency of the courts to go into past character of the victim, to arrive at the conclusion, whether or not consent to the act was given and also while awarding punishment to the accused. The legislature brought about an amendment in 2003 by inserting a Proviso to *Section 146* of the Indian Evidence Act, 1872 that in a prosecution for rape, it shall not be permissible to put questions in the cross examination of the prosecutrix with respect to her general moral character.[29] This led to the deletion of *Section 155 (4)* of the Indian Evidence Act, 1872 in 2003, whereby the 'generally immoral character' of the prosecutrix cannot be a ground raised by the accused for rape.

Right to Live with Human Dignity

India being signatory to the Universal Declaration of Human Rights 1948, the framers of the Indian Constitution thought of incorporating those provisions in the Constitution which could be benefited to the Indian society. The Preamble to the Constitution of India assures, among other things, 'dignity of the individual'. Article 21 guarantees the right to life and personal liberty. The Supreme Court of India, through its inimitable judicial activism, added to the fundamental right to life and personal liberty a variety of positive dimensions and significant humanitarian contours basically to enhance the dignity and quality of the guaranteed right to life and to make 'life' something more than 'mere animal existence'.[30] In this context, it is evident that Article 21 guarantees the rape victim to live with dignity who has been subjected to non-consensual violence attack.

The main objective and concern of the International Bill of Human Rights and the Protection of Human Rights Act, in the ultimate analysis, is the right to live with human dignity. The Charter of United Nations not only exhibits reaffirmed faith of the international community in fundamental human rights and human dignity but it also obliges every State to promote universal respect for, and observance of, human rights.

The Sexual Assault Bill

The Criminal Law (Amendment) Bill 2012, replacing the word 'rape' by the phrase 'sexual assault' and seeking to widen the scope of the offence, was introduced by Home Minister Sushil Kumar Shinde on 4 December 2012. The amendment bill expands the definition so that cases of sexual assault where victims were male would fall under the same law along with cases where victims were women. At present, the offence is defined under Section 375 of the Indian Penal Code as per which a man is said to commit 'rape' in case he has sexual intercourse with a woman against her will. Under the bill, an offender can be jailed for life in cases of sexual assault, irrespective of the victim's gender. The term 'sexual assault' has also been widened to include forced unnatural sex. The bill lays down strict provisions under which persons below 18 making a complaint will not have to face the accused in court or police stations. It has raised the age of consent from 16 to 18 years. The bill also carries provisions that make acid attacks a separate offence punishable by a maximum of 10 years in jail. An attempt to do so could send the accused the jailed for five to seven years.

Anti-Rape Ordinance

The President of India has accorded his assent to the Criminal Law (Amendment) Ordinance, 2013, on 3rd February. The ordinance, which replaced the word 'rape' with 'sexual assault' to expand the definition of crime against women, entails changes in the criminal law by amending Indian Penal Code (IPC), Code of Criminal Procedure (CrPC) and the Evidence Act. It includes key recommendations of the Justice J.S. Verma committee, the government had set up, after the 16 December 2012 gang rape to suggest ways to strengthen laws on sexual crime against women. The government, however, went beyond the panel's recommendations that stopped short of proposing death penalty for rapists. It includes the provision for capital punishment in cases where rape leads to death or leaves the victim in a persistent 'vegetative state'. In such cases, the minimum punishment will be 20 years in jail which can be extended to the natural life of the convict or death, adding discretion will be with the court.

In a bid to make the law women friendly, the ordinance suggests that only a woman police officer will take the statement of the victim of the sexual crime. Women under 18 years will not be confronted with the accused but provision of cross examination has been retained. There will be no personal appearance of witnesses before police officers. The IPC allows the court to impose a lower sentence. The ordinance takes away the power of the court to lower the sentence.

Penalty in term of years in jail has been recommended for a government servant if he does not cooperate on sexual offence case or harms the process of law. The panel had recommended five years in jail. While accepting the recommendation to record the statement by police officers of the person reporting the crime at his or her residence, the government has made optional suggestion to videograph the proceedings. The ordinance says if a person facing acid attack kills the accused in the process of self-defence, then she will be protected under the 'right to self defence'. The ordinance has accepted some of the recommendations made by the Justice Verma Committee such as making voyeurism, stalking and acid attacks punishable offenses.

The government has rejected a recommendation of the Verma panel on Armed Forces (Special Powers) Act that no sanction would be required if the armed forces personnel are accused of a crime against woman. The ordinance also did not accept the suggestions of the Verma Committee that dealt with sexual violence among members of the armed forces and police personnel. The committee had asked for a removal of the Armed Forces Special Powers Act that gives the armed forces immunity from prosecution and proposed that the senior police or army officer would be held responsible for a sexual offense committed by a junior officer.

Other issues in which the government ordinance rejected the suggestions of the Verma committee are; the incorporation of marital rape as a punishable criminal offense, the payment of compensation to victims of sexual violence and the lowering of the juvenile age from 18 to 16 years. The ordinance has also made the definition of rape gender-neutral, rather than keeping it gender-specific to women as suggested by the Verma Committee.

The Criminal Law (Amendment) Act, 2013

New definition of rape is included in The Criminal Law (Amendment) Act, 2013. 32 Under Section 375 of the Penal Code stated that a man is said to commit 'rape' if he:

1. penetrates his penis, to any extent, into the vagina, mouth, urethra or anus of a woman or make her to do so with him or any other person; or
2. inserts, to any extent, any object or a part of the body, not being the penis, into the vagina, the urethra or anus of a woman or makes her to do so with him or any other person; or
3 manipulates any part of body of a woman so as to cause penetration into the vagina, the urethra or anus or any part of body of such woman or makes her to do so with him or any other person; or
4. applies his mouth to the vagina, anus, urethra of a woman or make her to do so with him or any other person, under the circumstances falling under any of the following seven descriptions:

First: Against her will.

Second: Without her consent.

Thirdly: With her consent, when her consent has been obtained by putting her or any person in whom she is interested, in fear of death or of hurt.

Fourthly: With her consent, when the man knows that he is not her husband and that her consent is given because she believes that he is another man to whom she is or believes herself to be lawfully married.

Fifthly: With her consent when, at the time of giving such consent, by reason of unsoundness of mind or intoxication or the administration by him personally or through another of any stupefying or unwholesome substance, she is unable to understand the nature and consequences of that to which she gives consent.

Sixthly: With or without her consent, when she is under eighteen years of age.

Seventhly: When she is unable to communicate consent.

Under Section 376 (1) Whoever, except in the cases provided for in Sub-section (2), commits rape, shall be punished with rigorous imprisonment of either description for a term which shall not be less than seven years, but which may extend to imprisonment for life and shall also be liable to fine.

Whoever:

1. being a police officer, commits rape
   (i) within the limits of the police station to which such police officer is appointed; or
   (ii) in the premises of any station house; or
   (iii) on a woman in such police officers' custody or in the custody of a police officer subordinate to such police officer; or
2. being a public servant, commits rape on a women in such public servant's custody or in the custody of a public servant subordinate to such public servant; or
3. being a member of the armed forces deployed in an area by the Central or a State Government commits rape in such area; or
4. being on the management or on the staff of a jail, remand home or other place of custody established by or under any law for the time being in force or of a woman's or children's institution, commits rape on any inmate of such jail, remand home, place or institution; or
5. being on the management or on the staff of a hospital, commits rape on a woman in the hospital; or
6. being a relative, guardian or teacher of, or a person in a position of trust or authority towards the woman, commits rape on such woman; or
7. commits rape during communal or sectarian violence; or
8. commits rape on a woman knowing her to be pregnant; or

(i) commits rape on a woman when she is under sixteen years of age;

9. commits rape on a woman incapable of giving consent; or
10. being in a position of control or dominance over a woman, commits rape on such woman; or
11. commits rape on a woman suffering from mental or physical disability; or
12. while committing rape causes grievous bodily harm or maims or disfigures or endangers the life of a woman; or
13. commits rape repeatedly on the same woman,

Shall be punished with rigorous imprisonment for a term which shall not be less than ten years, but which may extend to imprisonment for life, which shall mean imprisonment for the remainder of that person's natural life, and shall also be liable to fine.

Section 376A whoever, commits an offence punishable under Sub-section (1) or Sub-section (2) of Section 376 and in the court of such commission inflicts an injury which causes the death of a woman or causes the woman to be in a persistent vegetative state, shall be punished with rigorous imprisonment for a term which shall not be less than twenty years, but which may extend to imprisonment for life, which shall mean imprisonment for the remainder of that person's natural life, or with death.

Section 376D where a woman is raped by one or more persons constituting a group or acting in furtherance of a common intention, each of those persons shall be deemed to have committed the offence of rape and shall be punished with rigorous imprisonment for a term which shall not be less than 20 years, but which may extend to life which shall mean imprisonment for the remainder of that person's natural life, and with fine: Provided that such fine shall be just and reasonable to meet the medical expenses and rehabilitation of the victim, provided further that any fine imposed under this section shall be paid to the victim.

Suggestion

- Universities should introduce gender sensitization modules in their curriculum and involve faculty and student in regular discussions on women's issue, in which girls and women could be an integral part which can probably lay the foundation for the creation of healthy mindset. There should be a dedicated task force in university campus which monitors women's safety and

security. Plainclothes police should be placed in and around university and women's college.
- Rising rape cases across the country should be tried in 'Dedicated Courts'. Dedicated courts will mean faster trials, meaning reduction of the time lag between crime and punishment; this will be a strong deterrent against rape cases.
- In each district, presence of Dedicated Court where only rape cases are tried can be an effective tool to bring down the crime graph by cutting backlog, ensuring speedy trials and time bound justice to the victim.
- Such courts would enable a judicial infrastructure that is sensitized towards rape victims and trained to handle these trials more effectively. Women lawyers to prosecute rape cases, special judges to be appointed, training ought to be imparted to better understand the advancement in forensic evidence as evidence alone could be enough to nail a rapist.
- Special court should not mean each trial ends in conviction but it will ensure a fair and fast trial where sound evidence still has to be produced in court and conviction are on merit.
- The police also have to be trained in handling rape investigations in better way. CCTVs in public places should be installed to identify those who harass women.
- Government should pay all medical expenses of rape victims and help them for proper rehabilitation.

Conclusion

Rape is a crime not only against the person but against the entire society. It affects a woman psychologically and pushes her into deep trauma. When a woman is ravished what is inflicted is not physical injury but a deep sense of deathless shame. It is crime against basic human right to live with human dignity as contained in Article 21 of the Indian Constitution. According to it, the right to life with human dignity is the fundamental right of every citizen and the State is under constitutional duty to provide at least minimum conditions ensuring human dignity.[31] Rape laws are covered under Section 375 and 376 of the IPC. Under these sections, rape is seen only in times of penile-vaginal penetration. It does not include, for instance, anal or oral penetration. It does not include penetration by objects. As a result of these loopholes, very often judges find themselves trying rape cases under more watered down sections; 'outraging the modesty of a woman', for instance. The Indian

Penal Code makes no distinctions between rape of a minor, and that of an adult. Child abuse should be recognized as an offence against innocence and therefore, the law against child rape should be made more stringent. Though the founding father of India Constitution after great deliberation, incorporated certain provisions in favour of women; the ground reality lies in the fact that how many women have been benefited. The answer is not much encouraging, so the society must come forward to see that the goals of the Constitution are achieved. Justice J.S. Verma Committee concludes by saying 'The nation has to account for the tears of millions of women'. Delay in conviction may be a factor behind the rise in crime against women because it dilutes the deterrent power of punishment, for this delay. Chief Justice of India Altamas Kabir, on 7 January 2013, directed all high courts to immediately set up fast track courts to deal exclusively with rape and other crimes against women. This is one of the progressive steps which will provide justice to victims. There is need to sensitize policemen in dealing with rape cases. The new 'anti-rape law' will not help in checking such crimes without police reforms. As opined by Swami Vivekananda, if the nation wants to reach the pinnacle of glory, the women folk who are the incarnation of the goddess, should not be neglected and thrown into insignificance. The nation which relegates the seat of the women in the back is bound to decline.

Notes

1. 1996 (1) SC 490 at 500.
2. No person shall be deprived of his life or personal liberty except according to procedure established by law.
3. *Halsbury's Laws of England*, 4th Edition, para 1228, p. 653.
4. 1992 (3) SCC 204.
5. *The Tribune*, Chandigarh Edition, 15 April 1999.
6. Cover Story: 'Sexual Crimes', *India Today*, 9 September 2002, p. 50.
7. National Crime Record Bureau Report 2004.
8. Ibid.
9. A man is said to commit 'rape' who, except in the case hereinafter excepted, has sexual intercourse with a woman under circumstances falling under any of the six following descriptions:

   First: Against her will.

   Second: Without her consent.

Third: With her consent, when her consent has been obtained by putting her or any person in whom she is interested in fear of death or of hurt.

Fourth: With her consent, when the man knows that he is not her husband and that her consent is given because she believes that he is another man to whom she is or believes herself to be lawfully married.

Fifth: With her consent, when, at the time of giving such consent, by reason of unsoundness of mind or intoxication or the administration by him personally or through another of any stupefying or wholesome substance, she is unable to understand the nature and consequences of that to which she gives consent.

Sixth: With or without her consent, when she is under sixteen years of age.

Explanation: Penetration is sufficient to constitute the sexual intercourse necessary to the offence of rape.

Exception: Sexual intercourse by a man with his own wife, the wife not being under fifteen years of age, is not rape.

10. Advani Poornima, Lina Gonslaves and J.K. Mittal, *Rape: A Legal Study*, New Delhi: National Commission for Women, 2000, p. 29.
11. 62 (1996) DLT 563.
12. 2004 Cri. L.J. 2881 (S.C.).
13. AIR 2005 SC 222: 2005 Cri. L.J. 335.
14. R. Revathi, *Law Relating to Domestic Violence*, Hyderabad: Asia Law House, 2004, p. 51.
15. R. Julia and Herman Schewendinger, *Rape and Inequality*, California: Sage Publications, 1993, p. 95.
16. Thomas B. Jeyaseelan, *Women Rights and the Law*, 2nd Edition, New Delhi: Indian Social Institute, 2005, p. 188.
17. Tukaram and Another vs. State of Maharashtra AIR 1979 SC 185.
18. Section 376 (2) (g) of Indian Penal Code 1860.
19. 1991 Cr. L.J. 1644 Bom.
20. 1982 (2) CLR 82.
21. 1884 Cr.L.J. 85.
22. Aaj Tak News dated 7 October 2006, Time: 16.52.
23. Supra note 9.
24. It states that 'whoever voluntarily has carnal intercourse against the order of nature with any man, woman or animal shall be punished with imprisonment of either description for a term which may extend to ten years, and shall also be liable to fine'.
25. S.J. vs. K.C.J. and Others, 62 (1996) Delhi Law Times 563.
26. 'Whoever assaults or uses criminal force to any woman, intending to outrage or knowing it to be likely that he will thereby outrage her modesty,

shall be punished with imprisonment of either description for a term which may extend to two years, or fine or with both'.

27. In a prosecution for rape under Cl. (a) or Cl. (b) or Cl. (c) or Cl. (d) or Cl. (e) or Cl. (g) of Sub-section (2) of Section 376 of the Indian Penal Code (45 of 1860), where sexual intercourse by the accused is proved and the question is whether it was without consent of the woman alleged to have been raped and she states in her evidence before the Court that she did not consent, the Court shall presume that she did not consent.
28. After renumbering the old section as Sub-section (1), Sub-section 2 now reads: '(2) Notwithstanding anything contained in Sub-section (1), the inquiry into and trial of rape or an offence under Section 376, Section 376-A, Section 376-B, Section 376-C or Section-D of the Indian Penal Code (45 of 1860) shall be conducted in camera; provided that the presiding judge may, if he thinks fit, or on an application made by either of the parties, allow any particular person to have access to, or to remain in, the room or building used by the court; (3) where any proceedings are held under Sub-section (2), it shall not be lawful for any person to print or publish any matter in relation to any such proceedings, except with the previous permission of the court'.
29. The Evidence Act 1872, Section 146:

    Questions lawful in cross-examination:

    When a witness is cross-examined he may be asked any question ... (Provided that in prosecution for rape or attempt to commit rape, it shall not be permissible to put questions in the cross-examination of the prosecutrix as to her general immoral character.)
30. Francis Corallie Mullin vs. Administrator, Union Territory of Delhi, AIR 1981 SC 746.
31. Vikram Deo Singh vs. State of Bihar, AIR 1988 SC 1782.
32. The Criminal Law (Amendment) Act, 2013.

6

Cruelty and Dowry Death

SADHNA GUPTA

> Marriages are made in heaven, is an adage. A bride leaves her parental home for the matrimonial home; leaving behind sweet memories, with a hope that she will see a new world full of love in her groom's house. She leaves behind not only her memories, but also her surname, gotra and maidenhood. She expects not only to be a daughter-in-law, but a daughter in fact. Alas! The rise in the number of cases involving harassment of newly wedded girls for dowry shatters the dreams. In-laws are characterized to be outlaws for perpetrating terrorism which destroys the matrimonial home. The terrorist is dowry, and it is spreading its tentacles in every possible direction.
>
> — Kamesh Panjiyar vs. State of Bihar[1]

Dowry, in Hindu society, was originally a symbol of parents love and affection for the daughter, expressed by way of gifts at the time of her marriage, which also helped the newly weds to start their life together. As per the ancient custom *kanyadan* was followed by the ritual of *Vardakshina,* which was a nominal amount, decided unilaterally by the girl's father according to its financial position, *yathashakti*. It did not comprise any evil motive of extracting money or gifts from the bride's parents.[2] But today dowry has degenerated into a sordid commercial transaction and a vehicle of harassment and torture of married women and extortion from their parents. This system of dowry has ruined many families and created many unhappy homes. Of late, it has been seen that not only brides but prospective teenaged girls, out of sheer frustration, seeing the worried look on the face of their parents all the time, are driven to commit suicide. Some cannot reconcile themselves to the unbearable trauma of making an exhibition of themselves and parading before the prospective in-laws only to be rejected because the demands of dowry are too high.[3] An article on *Status of Women in India – A depressing scenario* points out that dowry death takes place once in every 1,000 minutes.[4] Previously, dowry was seen only under the Hindu society but now it is prevalent in all sections of the society, from the poor to the affluent and the illiterate to the highly educated.

Dowry means any property or valuable security given or agreed to be given either directly or indirectly by one party to a marriage to the other party to the marriage or by the parents of either party or by any other person to either party to the marriage. It may be given at or before or any time after the marriage in connection with the marriage of the said parties. But it does not include dower or 'mahr' in case of person to whom the Muslim Personal Law (Shariat) applies.[5]

The Legislature has, in its wisdom while providing for the definition of 'dowry', emphasized that any money, property or valuable security given, as a consideration for marriage, 'before, at or after' the marriage would be covered by the expression 'dowry'.[6] Meaning of the expression 'dowry' as commonly used and understood is different than the peculiar definition thereof under the Act. Under Section 4 of the Act, mere demand of dowry is sufficient to bring home the offence to an accused. Thus, any 'demand' of money, property or valuable security made from the bride or her parents or other relatives by the bridegroom or his parents or other relatives or vice-versa would fall within the mischief of 'dowry' under the Act where such demand is not properly referable to any legally recognized claim and is relatable only to the consideration of marriage. Marriage in this context would include proposed marriage also more particularly where the non-fulfillment of the 'demand of dowry' leads to the ugly consequence of the marriage not taking place at all. The expression 'dowry' under the Act must be interpreted in the sense which the statute wishes to attribute it.[7]

According to the National Crime Records Bureau of the Ministry of Home Affairs, the number of crimes against women reported was 53,860 in 1987. It rose to 74,903 in 1991. For the same years, the numbers of dowry death cases were 1,912 and 5,157, respectively. In the category of 'cruelty by husband and his relatives' the rise was from 11,603 to 15,949. However, the bureau claimed that there was a decline in dowry death in recent years. In 2001, the figure was 6,851; in 2002 it declined to 6,822 and in 2003 it was 6,285. Similarly, complaints of

Table 1

Incidence of Crimes Committed against Women During 2011

State/UT	**Population (In Lakhs) #*	*Rape (Sec. 376 IPC)*			*Kidnapping and Abduction (Sec. 363–369, 371–373 IPC)*			*Dowry Deaths (Sec. 304B IPC)*			*Cruelty by Husband and relatives (Sec. 498A IPC)*		
		I	*R*	*P*	*I*	*R*	*P*	*I*	*R*	*P*	*I*	*R*	*P*
States													
Andhra Pradesh	846.65	1,442	1.7	6.0	1,612	1.9	4.5	599	0.7	7.0	13,376	15.8	13.5
Arunachal Pradesh	13.83	42	3.0	0.2	60	4.3	0.2	0	0.0	0.0	18	1.3	0.0
Assam	311.69	1,700	5.5	7.0	3,192	10.2	9.0	121	0.4	1.4	5,246	16.8	5.3
Bihar	1038.04	934	0.9	3.9	3,050	2.9	8.6	1,413	1.4	16.4	2,607	2.5	2.6
Chhattisgarh	255.40	1,053	4.1	4.4	365	1.4	1.0	104	0.4	1.2	834	3.3	0.8
Goa	14.58	29	2.0	0.1	17	1.2	0.0	1	0.1	0.0	18	1.2	0.0
Gujarat	603.83	439	0.7	1.8	1,442	2.4	4.1	30	0.0	0.3	6,052	10.0	6.1
Haryana	253.53	733	2.9	3.0	733	2.9	2.1	255	1.0	3.0	2,740	10.8	2.8
Himachal Pradesh	68.57	168	2.5	0.7	191	2.8	0.5	4	0.1	0.0	239	3.5	0.2
Jammu & Kashmir	125.49	277	2.2	1.1	1,023	8.2	2.9	11	0.1	0.1	286	2.3	0.3
Jharkhand	329.66	784	2.4	3.2	660	2.0	1.9	282	0.9	3.3	659	2.0	0.7
Karnataka	611.31	636	1.0	2.6	715	1.2	2.0	267	0.4	3.1	3,712	6.1	3.7

Cont'd...

...Cont'd

Kerala	333.88	1,132	3.4	4.7	221	0.7	0.6	15	0.0	0.2	5,377	16.1	5.4
Madhya Pradesh	725.98	3,406	4.7	14.1	1,088	1.5	3.1	811	1.1	9.4	3,732	5.1	3.8
Maharashtra	1123.73	1,701	1.5	7.0	1,252	1.1	3.5	339	0.3	3.9	7,136	6.4	7.2
Manipur	27.22	53	1.9	0.2	116	4.3	0.3	1	0.0	0.0	39	1.4	0.0
Meghalaya	29.64	130	4.4	0.5	37	1.2	0.1	1	0.0	0.0	21	0.7	0.0
Mizoram	10.91	77	7.1	0.3	0	0.0	0.0	0	0.0	0.0	9	0.8	0.0
Nagaland	19.81	23	1.2	0.1	3	0.2	0.0	0	0.0	0.0	1	0.1	0.0
Odisha	419.47	1,112	2.7	4.6	1,008	2.4	2.8	465	1.1	5.4	2,320	5.5	2.3
Punjab	277.04	479	1.7	2.0	517	1.9	1.5	143	0.5	1.7	1136	4.1	1.1
Rajasthan	686.21	1,800	2.6	7.4	2,713	4.0	7.6	514	0.7	6.0	12,218	17.8	12.3
Sikkim	6.08	16	2.6	0.1	10	1.6	0.0	0	0.0	0.0	4	0.7	0.0
Tamil Nadu	721.39	677	0.9	2.8	1,743	2.4	4.9	152	0.2	1.8	1,812	2.5	1.8
Tripura	36.71	205	5.6	0.8	116	3.2	0.3	30	0.8	0.3	702	19.1	0.7
Uttar Pradesh	1995.81	2,042	1.0	8.4	7,525	3.8	21.2	2,322	1.2	26.9	7,121	3.6	7.2
Uttarakhand	101.17	129	1.3	0.5	283	2.8	0.8	83	0.8	1.0	307	3.0	0.3
West Bengal	913.48	2,363	2.6	9.8	3,711	4.1	10.4	510	0.6	5.9	19,772	21.6	19.9
Total (States)	11,901.11	23,582	2.0	97.4	33,403	2.8	93.9	8,473	0.7	98.3	97,494	8.2	98.3

Cont'd...

...Cont'd

Union Territories													
A & N Islands	3.80	13	3.4	0.1	12	3.2	0.0	0	0.0	0.0	5	1.3	0.0
Chandigarh	10.55	27	2.6	0.1	46	4.4	0.1	2	0.2	0.0	46	4.4	0.0
D & N Haveli	3.43	4	1.2	0.0	8	2.3	0.0	0	0.0	0.0	3	0.9	0.0
Daman & Diu	2.43	1	0.4	0.0	2	0.8	0.0	0	0.0	0.0	2	0.8	0.0
Delhi	167.63	572	3.4	2.4	2,085	12.4	5.9	142	0.8	1.6	1,575	9.4	1.6
Lakshadweep	0.64	0	0.0	0.0	0	0.0	0.0	0	0.0	0.0	0	0.0	0.0
Puducherry	12.44	7	0.6	0.0	9	0.7	0.0	1	0.1	0.0	10	0.8	0.0
Total (UTs)	200.82	624	3.1	2.6	2,162	10.8	6.1	145	0.7	1.7	1,641	8.2	1.7
Total (All-India)	12,101.93	24,206	2.0	100.0	35,565	2.9	100.0	8,618	0.7	100.0	99,135	8.2	100.0

Source: National Crime Records Bureau of the Ministry of Home Affairs.
Total population including women
I – Incidence R – Rate of Crime P – Percentage share
* Actual Census–2011 Population (Provisional)

dowry harassment and related atrocities declined from 7,000 in 2002 to 5,700 in 2003. NCRB report explained that the cases of dowry deaths have increased by 2.7 per cent during the year 2011 over the previous year (8,391 cases). 26.9 per cent of the total such cases reported in the country were reported from Uttar Pradesh (2,322 cases) alone followed by Bihar (1,413 cases) (16.4%). The highest rate of crime (1.4) was reported from Bihar as compared to the national average of 0.7.

Table 2 would explain the position of crime against women in respect of dowry-death in the State of West Bengal.

Table 2

District-wise Incidence of Crime against Women (CAW)

	Total CAW Under IPC		*Torture/cruelty by Husbands/Relatives*			*Dowry Death*		
	2000	*2003*	*1995*	*2000*	*2003*	*1995*	*2000*	*2003*
Bankura	194	264	59	112	153	9	17	20
Birbhum	353	367	115	201	219	6	11	13
Bardhman	727	739	223	482	107	8	34	30
Cooch Bihar	336	369	111	189	209	0	3	11
Darjeeling	133	156	28	64	69	0	1	3
Hooghly	583	567	320	453	457	4	7	14
Howrah	267	237	107	175	168	5	22	17
Jalpaiguri	297	376	108	158	210	1	3	4
PashminMedinipur	904	530	558	598	376	28	56	18
Purba Medinipur	–	402	–	–	276	–	–	37
Murshidabad	440	814	78	245	468	0	4	17
Malda	213	275	43	89	119	1	5	4
Nadia	595	600	226	370	363	11	22	23
24 Parganas (N)	843	1,128	546	589	784	3	21	24
24 Parganas (S)	975	1,214	469	692	884	2	49	44
Purulia	259	187	107	139	94	0	4	8
Uttar Dinajpur	225	170	74	113	85	1	5	14
Dakshin Dinajpur	242	227	37	126	113	–	4	8
Total (excluding cases registered by Government Rly. Police)	7,586	8,872	3,319	4,785	5,609	89	268	312

Source: NCRB, Crime in India and Special Inspector General of Police, State Crime Records Bureau, Kolkata.

Existing Laws

In order to curb the evil of dowry, the *Dowry Prohibition Act* was passed in 1961. Certain states passed amendments to this Act. Despite statutory prohibition of dowry, the menace continued more, because the law was absolutely ineffective and in view of its language it was very difficult to apprehend and convict anybody under the Act. There were various loopholes in the statute. The offence was not cognizable and, hence, the culprit could not be arrested without a warrant. The complaint had to be made within one year from the date of the offence.

As a result of the increase in certain regions in what are euphemistically called dowry deaths, but are in reality murder or cases of women driven to suicide, women's organizations and members of Parliament demanded that stringent laws to be passed to fight the growing dowry menace. The Parliament appointed a Joint Committee of both houses to review the working of the Act in early 1981. The report was submitted in August 1982, and again in November of the same year. Parliament debated the question of dowry and was assured by the Home Minister that stringent measures would be taken against police officers found guilty of dereliction of duty in registration and investigation of dowry deaths and a bill to make the Dowry Prohibition Act more effective would be introduced at the earliest. The amendment was enacted in August 1984.[8]

The Dowry Prohibition (Amendment) Act, 1984 has made far reaching changes in the Act so as to make it more effective. Now the presents etc. given by a party to the other need not be by way of consideration for the marriage and it is enough if they have been given in connection with the marriage. This Act has amended the definition of dowry by substituting the words, 'in connection with the marriage' (for the original words as 'consideration of marriage'). Another significant change which has been brought under the Dowry Prohibition (Amendment) Act, 1986 in the definition of dowry is that it now includes the property given at any time after the marriage.

Unfortunately, despite modifications to the Act in 1984 (Act 63) and 1986 (Act 43), to make it more effective, the Dowry Prohibition (Amendment) Act has remained more or less a dead letter, as evident from the following figures of registration of cases there under:

Table 3

Incidence of Cases Under Dowry Prohibition Act, 1961

	1990	*1995*	*1996*	*1997*	*1998*	*1999*	*2000*
All India	2,155	2,814	2,647	2,685	3,578	3,064	2,876
Delhi	4	10	4	10	10	8	9
Haryana	0	0	0	1	8	2	1

Source: National Crime Records Bureau.

The number of cases under the Act has been falling during the last two years, with a decrease of 20 per cent in 2000 as compared to 1998. (More than 30% of the cases are registered in Bihar alone, other states with comparatively better registration being Odisha, Andhra Pradesh, Karnataka, Tamil Nadu and Uttar Pradesh; use of the Act in other states and union territories, including both Delhi and Haryana, is only negligible).

Before the amendment of inserting Section 304-B and 498-A of the Indian Penal Code, dowry death was only actionable by police only if it resulted in 'grievous hurt' in terms of Section 320 of the IPC, or worse making it cognizable offence. Moreover, what we find in the Indian society is that the husband was considered to have more or less a proprietary right over the wife. When any matters related to dowry death were reported to the police, it was thought to be family disputed matter which they would seek out within four corners of their house, thus leaving the problem unsolved. In order to combat with such evil the legislature introduced these two sections under the Indian Penal Code.

A new offence, the offence of cruelty to wife by her husband and in-laws have been created by inserting a new chapter XX-A and a new section – Section 498-A in the Indian Penal Code. In 1983, Section 498-A of the Indian Penal Code defined a new cognizable offence, namely, 'cruelty by husband or relatives of husband'. This means that once such a complaint is registered by the victim or any of her relatives, the police have no option but to take action. This law takes particular cognizance of harassment, where it occurs with a view to coercing the wife or any person related to her, to meet any unlawful demand regarding any property or valuable security or occurs on account of failure by her or any person related to her, to meet such a demand. The offenders are punishable with imprisonment which may extend to three years as well as a fine.

Another amendment was also made under the Indian Penal Code naming the crime as 'dowry-murder' or 'dowry death' under Section 304-B. The section states that if the death of a woman is caused by burns or bodily injury, or occurs under abnormal circumstances, within seven years of her marriage and if shown that prior to death she was subjected to cruelty by her husband or his relatives, in connection with demands for dowry, such a death would be called 'dowry-death' and the husband or relative would be deemed to have caused her death.

By inserting a new Section 113-B in the Indian Evidence Act, the lawmakers stipulated that in cases that are registered by the police as those of 'dowry-death', the court shall presume that the accused is guilty unless he can prove otherwise.

Role of Sections 498-A and 304-B

Section 498-A of the IPC is a step towards ensuring that the unlimited privileges of a husband in the holy relationship of marriage are rendered unjustifiable by criminal courts when his inhuman behaviour jeopardize the mental and physical well-being of the wife. Section 498-A is integral to offences under Section 304-B and 'cruelty' is a common ingredient to both the sections. In fact, the Supreme Court held in *Shanti vs. State of Haryana*[9] that the two Sections (304-B and 498-A of Indian Penal Code) are not mutually exclusive and, in cases of 'dowry-death', both from the point of view of practice and procedure and to avoid technical defects, charges under both the sections should be framed. The Supreme Court further held that in the absence of any explanation under Section 304-B about the meaning of cruelty, the meaning of cruelty and harassment has to be taken as the same as in the explanation to Section 498-A of the IPC.

In *Baldev Krishnan vs. State of Punjab*[10], the Apex Court held that 'taunts to the deceased by the accused saying that better proposals were received for the groom who were willing to give more dowry and making humiliating remarks about the low quality of gifts brought in by her during the marriage, amounted to harassment on account of insufficient dowry', and that even if there was proof of no physical torture, proof of mental torture was sufficient for conviction.

Role of Judiciary

Judiciary from time to time, through judicial interpretation, has explained the meaning of term 'mental cruelty' under Section 498-A. Thus, repetitive taunting of the bride by calling her *ugly,*[11] *forcing to leave the matrimonial home,*[12] *refusal to send to parents house,*[13] *non-return or depriving of Istridhan,*[14] etc., have been held to amount to mental torture, by words and deeds, even without any physical torture/cruelty.

In the case of *Kunhiabdullah vs. State of Kerela,*[15] the Supreme Court said that menace of dowry cut across caste, religion and geographical location. Both husband and mother-in-law stood for Section 304-B.

In *Joint Women's Programme vs. State of Rajasthan,*[16] a social organization took up a few cases of alleged dowry deaths in Rajasthan and Haryana. The Supreme Court took a path-breaking step directing state governments to set up special dowry cells at the state level to investigate into such unnatural deaths.

In *Kundala Bala Subramanyam vs. State of Andhra Pradesh,*[17] dealing with a cases of 'bride-burning' the Supreme Court has expressed the view that mostly older women in the family are worst perpetrators of crime like bride burning and urged men to stop being 'mute spectators'.

In the case of *State of Karnataka vs. Devaraj,*[18] where a young woman was brutally murdered and her in-laws misled the authority that it was a suicide, the Karnataka High Court regretted that the quality of police investigation in the dowry death of a poor village woman 'was downright shameful' and resulted in grave failure of justice.

The Allahabad High Court, in *Dev Prasad vs. State of UP,*[19] observed that young girls are killed for dowry as could be seen from the large number of FIRs under Section 303-B of the IPC being filed all over the country. 'We are surprised that while an ordinary murder can be punished by death sentence under Section 302 of the IPC, a dowry death, which is a much worse offence, has a maximum punishment of life imprisonment. A dowry death is not just an ordinary crime. It is a social crime. It outrages the modern conscience; it makes the whole society revert to feudal barbarism. Hence, we recommend to Parliament to amend the law and provide for death sentence in dowry death cases.' In this case, a girl of 23 years was harassed for dowry and burnt after three years of marriage. No post-mortem examination was done. The husband was convicted under Section 303-B of the IPC. He moved the High Court to quash the FIR.

In *State vs. Maregowda,*[20] the Karnataka high court dealt with a husband who used to come drunk and harass his wife for money. Ultimately she hanged herself. She left a suicide note implicating him. The Sessions Judge acquitted the husband of charges under the Dowry Prohibition Act and under Sections 498-A and 304-B of the IPC. On appeal, the high court stated that the suicide note could be treated as dying declaration. It could not be rejected, as the Sessions Judge did, merely because it was written in red ink on the reverse side of the electoral card.

In *Shaik China Buda vs. State of Andhra Pradesh,*[21] case, husband and relatives harassed deceased for additional dowry and the medical evidence proved that deceased died due to consumption of poisonous pesticide. At the same time, there is a categorical admission by parents of the deceased that the accused husband had a liking for the deceased and evidence of all witnesses are full of inconsistencies. There is no specific evidence against main accused for offence under Section 498-A, further all other accused persons were acquitted; therefore Court held that appellant also entitled to get benefit of doubt.

In *Satvir Singh and Others vs. State of Punjab,*[22] Court held that with regard to demand for dowry the burden of poof is on prosecution. The word dowry in Section 304-B of the IPC should be any property or valuable given or agreed to be given in connection with the marriage. The customary payment in connection with birth of child or other ceremonies are not enveloped within the ambit of 'dowry'.

Conclusion

From time immemorial, women have been placed on a pedestal 'mother of mankind'. Paradoxically, the most horrendous cruelties are inflicted on her, often without reason and mostly without just cause. Incidents of dowry death are a blot on civilized society but they occur frequently despite various legal measures existing. Although geographically men and women share the same space, they live in different worlds. The mere fact that women hold up half the sky does not appear to give them position of dignity and equality. Though we have entered into the new millennium yet, women have been discriminated all these years. The discrimination cannot be explained as legislative insufficiency but from the attitudinal bias of the society. Through various provisions in the UN Charter, the members of the United Nations reaffirmed their faith in fundamental rights and in the dignity and the worth of human person.[23] Further, this Charter contains a provision for international cooperation in solving international problems including promoting and encouraging respect for human rights and fundamental freedoms for all without distinction as to race, sex, language and religion.[24]

The need of the day is now to be collectively conscious and bring about a change of heart and attitude. The legislature has realized and amended the laws, providing stringent punishments in dowry-death cases and even permitted the raising of presumptions, against an accused in cases of unnatural deaths of the brides within the first seven years of their marriage.

The Dowry Prohibition Act was enacted in 1961 and has been amended from time to time but this social piece of legislation, keeping in view the growing menace of the social evil, also does not appear to have served much purpose as dowry seekers are hardly brought to book and convictions recorded are rather few. Laws are not enough to combat the evil. A wider social movement of educating women of their rights, to conquer the menace, is what is needed particularly in rural, where women are still largely uneducated and less aware of their rights and fall an easy prey to their exploitation. The role of courts, under the circumstances assumes greater importance and it is expected that the courts would deal with such cases in a more realistic manner.

Time and again the Supreme Court of India has extended the ambit of Article 21 of the Constitution of India and held that mere existence is not the right to live – it is the right to live with dignity. But unfortunately, such has been the social conditions and have been the prejudices in the man's society that even personal liberty guaranteed to woman under Article 21 of the Constitution has no meaning to her. Thus, wherever crimes are committed against women the same should be viewed in the context of violation of her right under Article 21 of the Constitution and not merely as a crime against society.

Notes

1. 1 February 2005.
2. Shoba Saxena, *Crimes against Women and Protective Laws*, New Delhi: Deep and Deep Publications Pvt. Ltd., 1995, p. 116.
3. Reference to the photograph published in newspaper and magazines three sisters, namely, Mamta, Alka and Poonam Sahu in Kanpur committed suicide by hanging themselves from ceiling fan and other incidents which keep happening.
4. *The Tribune*, Chandigarh Edition, 15 April 1999.
5. Section 2 of the Dowry Prohibition Act, 1961.
6. This definition as contained in Section 2 of the Dowry Prohibition Act has to be read wherever the expression 'dowry' occurs.
7. S. Gopal Reddy vs. State of Andhra Pradesh AIR 1996 SC 2184, Criminal Appeal No. 231 of 1994 (From the Judgement and Order dated 16

October 1990 of Andhra Pradesh High Court in Crl. R.C. No. 446 of 1990), decided on 11 July 1996.

8. Ashima Sahu, *Women's Liberalization and Human Rights*, Jaipur: Pointer Publishers, 2000, pp. 185–87.
9. AIR 1991 SC 1226.
10. AIR 1997 SC 1666.
11. Pawan Kumar and Others vs. State of Haryana 1998, SCC (Cri) 740.
12. Anjali Sharma vs. Government of NCT Delhi and Others, 2000 (1) JCC (Delhi) 142.
13. Kodadi Srinivas Lingam and Others vs. State of AP, 2001 Cri. L.J. 602.
14. Surinder Kumar Yadav and Others vs. The State, 2000 (1) JCC (Delhi) 245.
15. AIR 2004 SC 1731.
16. AIR 1987 SC 2060.
17. 1993 (1) Crimes 1169: 1993 Cr. L.J. 1635.
18. 2002 Cr. L.J. 2299.
19. 2002 Cri. L.J. 4291.
20. 2001 Cri. L.J. 4491.
21. 2002 Cr. L.J. 256.
22. AIR 2001 SC 2829.
23. For reference see the Preamble of the United Nations Charter.
24. Article 1(3) of the United Nations Charter.

7

Domestic Violence on Married Women in India

An Overview

SUDARSANA MUKHOPADHYAY

> Domestic violence or violence in the family has been an age old problem. This was never discussed openly and was thought to be a very personal problem occurring behind the closed doors.
>
> — Pradeep Agarwal[1]

Today domestic violence on married women is a universal problem. It is a great social and legal problem in India also. Every day in India many women are burnt alive, beaten to death and forced to commit suicide due to different kinds of domestic violence. Some of these cases are highlighted by the media. Domestic violence cuts across all cultural, socio-economic, educational, religious and ethnic boundaries in India. So we find this violence in rural or urban areas, among educated and uneducated women, in all sectors of the society. Now a days with growing urbanization and increasing stress and strains in daily life, family violence on married women have been increasing and also recognized as an important health problem in India. Many married women victims of domestic violence in India are unable to leave this abusive situation due to psychological and socio-economic factors and continue to be victims of such violence putting their lives and health in jeopardy. In this context, it is also mentioned that family is the basic unit of the society and the safest place for women, but now this unit, the family which is a secure place for women, is no more a safe and comfortable place for them due to domestic violence. Therefore, domestic violence on married women is a heinous crime for a society that is operating in a severe form of oppression against women and which has been increasing in India with alarming proportion.

According to National Crime Record Bureau, 2007–2012 domestic violence is widespread in India. As per the rate of domestic violence in the family, Andhra Pradesh (AP) is occupying the first position in India and West Bengal is in second position. As per the rate of dowry deaths, Uttar Pradesh (UP) is occupying the first position, Bihar is in the second position, Madhya Pradesh (MP) is in third position and West Bengal is in the fourth position in India. According to West Bengal Commission for Women, domestic violence incidents have increased by 45 per cent in 2007 years. But more than 44 per cent cases are going unreported due to poverty, lack of manpower, etc. Therefore, in India there is scarcity of reliable statistics relating to the prevalence of domestic violence. In this context, I would like to mention the historical background of domestic violence on married women in their matrimonial homes.

Historical Background of Domestic Violence on Married Women in their Matrimonial Homes

History tells us about the position of women in their matrimonial homes from Vedic period to modern period. In *Vedic period* there was no instances of domestic violence in the family. Vedic era was the golden era, so far as the personal freedom of women and their equality of status in the family and society were concerned. In that period, married women were treated as queens of their household and monogamy was practiced by the general people. Thus, women were treated as equal partners, friend and equal sharer in joys and sufferings of her husband's life in Vedic era.

The seeds of domestic violence were first sown in *post-Vedic* period by Manu Smriti and other dharmashastras. The status and honourable position of a married woman was gradually deteriorated and various restrictions were put on the woman's rights and privileges by Manu. So woman was regarded as subservient to man and confined to household works and child bearing only. Thus, in post-Vedic period, women lost their individuality and high status in the society. They were suppressed and oppressed by their husbands and their existence and happiness were dependant on that of their husbands' decree of fates.

After that, in *medieval period,* women were treated as chattels by their husbands and in-laws. Social evils like *satipratha,* child marriage and female infanticide were rampant. The evil of dowry had become deep rooted in many parts of India. Polygamy and system of *devdasi* were widespread. So in that time women were totally dominated by the feudal social order and the rules and regulations of the patriarchal families. Pardah system was very popular in those days. In that dark-age many inhuman practices, including domestic violence, prevailed in the society in the name of social custom and religion.

In *British period* also domestic violence on married women was very common in the society. Early marriage, enforced widowhood, female infanticide, *satipratha*, *devdasi* system, *purdah* system, dowry system, caste system, polygamy, etc. were prevalent in the society. But during the British rule some awareness was created for the removal of those social malaises by many Indian social reformers like Raja Ram Mohan Roy, Ishwar Chandra Vidyasagar, M.G. Ranade, Mahatma Gandhi, Lokmanya Tilak, Rishi Arobindo, Swami Vivekananda, Dadabhai Naoroji, etc. who had received English education and began to think about the injustice done to the women.

After that in *post-Independent period*, the social status of married women was gradually improved by the Hindu Marriage Act 1955, the Indian Penal Code 1973, the Indian Evidence Act 1872, etc. For example, polygamy was legally prohibited. The Hindu Marriage Act enforced strict monogamy and bigamy, child marriage, etc. were also prohibited by that Act. The Section 498A of the IPC (i.e. punishment for cruelty by husband and in-laws), Section 304B of the IPC (dowry death), Section 306 of the IPC (i.e. abetment to commit suicide), Section 494 and 495 of the IPC (i.e. punishment for bigamy) were also introduced to stop the crimes and Section 113A and Section 113B of Indian Evidence Act were to help the victimized married women to fight with that heinous crime.

In this context I would also like to mention that several other laws were introduced for protecting married women from violence behind the closed door of their matrimonial homes. As for example – Dowry Prohibition Act 1961, Medical Termination of Pregnancy Act 1971, The Commission of Sati (Prevention) Act 1987, The Pre-Natal Diagnostic Technique (Regulation and Prevention of Misuse) Act 1994, etc. At that time, the framers of the Constitution were also conscious of the discrimination and unequal status of the married women in their matrimonial homes and they included certain general as well as specific provisions in the Constitution under part III as Fundamental Rights, i.e. (Art 14–17, Art 19–25), etc. part IV as Directive Principles of State policy, i.e. (Art 39, 39A, 42) and 51A as Fundamental Duties to improve the status of women.

But unfortunately it has been noticed that at that time though constitutionally as well as legally, women in India enjoyed a unique status of equality with men but in reality the position of married women in their matrimonial homes were deteriorated and domestic violence was treated as the normal wear and tear of their everyday lives.

Now it is nearly 65 years since the independence of our country but still the position of married women in their matrimonial homes has not improved. Only 23 per cent married women have rights to speak in their family matters in India.[2] Different kinds of domestic violence, i.e. *satipratha*, female infanticide, forced abortion, forced prostitution, marital rape, dowry death, bride burning, bride beating, cruelty, bigamy, desertion of innocent wife, etc. are still very prevalent in our country. These incidents of domestic violence have been regularly reported and highlighted by the press, media, National Commission for Women (NCW), Non-governmental Organisations (NGOs), etc.

Though there are plethora of progressive and protective legislations favouring women and we have 73 per cent literate women in India, but we failed in our aims to uplift the social status of married women.[3] A recent survey pointed out that almost every six hours somewhere in India a young married woman is tortured by domestic violence. Not only that, 45 per cent of Indian married women are slapped, kicked or beaten by their husbands and also that 75 per cent of battered women contemplate suicide. There is an annual increase of 9.2 per cent cases of domestic violence, of which a large number of cases are going unreported due to some socio-economic reasons.[4] Now it can be mentioned that before 2005 there was no specific civil law on domestic violence in India and married women have been compelled to use matrimonial remedies like judicial separation, divorce, etc. to obtain reliefs. So the Government of India on 13 September 2005 introduced a new civil law for the protection of the victim women of domestic violence and the act came on the statute book as 'The Protection of Women from Domestic Violence Act, 2005 (43 of 2005)'.

Definition of Domestic Violence

Generally domestic violence is a violence that occurs within the family between the persons who are related through intimacy, blood and law. Majority of perpetrators of the domestic violence are men and majority of victims are women, specially married women. Domestic violence differs with households, individuals and situations. According to Section 3 of the Protection of Women from Domestic

Violence Act 2005, domestic violence means: 'Any act, omission or commission or conduct of the respondent which constitutes harms or injuries or endangers the life, health, safety and well-being of the aggrieved person. It also includes causing physical abuse, sexual abuse, verbal abuse, emotional abuse and economic abuse'. The perpetrators often harasses, harms or injures the aggrieved person or any other person related to her for dowry or any valuable security. According to Section 2 (q) of the protection of women from Domestic Violence Act, 2005: Respondent means any adult male person who has been in a domestic relationship with the aggrieved person and against whom the aggrieved person has sought any relief under this Act. The Act also provides that an aggrieved wife can file a complaint against her husband or relatives of her husband who are torturing her mentally or physically. According to Section 2 (a): Domestic relationship means a relationship between two persons who live together in a shared household when they are related by consanguinity, marriage, etc. and other family members are living together as a joint family. According to Section 2 (f) of the protection of women from Domestic Violence Act, 2005: Aggrieved person means any woman who is or has been in a domestic relationship with the respondent and who is tortured by the respondent. It also includes women who live together with their male partners.

Today domestic violence is a universal phenomenon. Around the world, one out of three women is suffering from domestic violence silently. So, universally recognized concept of domestic violence is: Domestic violence is a range of abusive and threatening behaviours, including physical abuse, sexual abuse, verbal and emotional abuse, economic abuse as well as intimidation, isolation and coercion. It is perpetrated by one partner upon the other to gain and maintain control. It happens in the family, home and sometimes the children and other members of the family are involved into it.

In India there are different forms of domestic violence, such as:

1. Cruelty on woman by husband and in-laws.
2. Dowry death or murdering a wife for insufficient dowry.
3. Marital rape and sexual harassment by husband.
4. Wrongful confinement of a woman within her matrimonial home.
5. Forcing a wife to abort her female foetus or female foeticide.
6. Driving out a woman from her matrimonial home.
7. Abetting the victim woman to commit suicide.
8. Deserting the wife and living with another woman without any reason.

9. Forcing a widow to commit sati, etc.
10. Not allowing the bride to visit her parents or to talk with the neighbours.
11. Wife beating or physically torturing the wife or causing grievous hurt to the wife.
12. By forcing the working wife to leave her job while denying her food and basic amenities.
13. Economically crippling the woman by misappropriating her property and *stridhan*.
14. Putting excessive household work upon a woman and denying her privacy.
15. Abusing the children for torturing the wife mentally, etc. are common forms of domestic violence in India.

    According to Section 3 of The Protection of Women from Domestic Violence Act, 2005 – Domestic Violence can be of four types:

    (i) *Physical abuse*: Any act or conduct which is of such a nature that causes bodily pain, injury of the victim woman. Physical violence also leads to irritable bowel syndrome, gastrointestinal disorder and chronic pain. These health consequences become complexes when women fail to have access to timely health care due to various reasons.

    (ii) *Sexual Abuse:* Any conduct of sexual nature which humiliates, degrades or otherwise violates the dignity of victim woman. Women who experiences sexual abuses are more likely to suffer from Sexually Transmitted Disease, AIDS and so on. Generally, women are afraid to raise the issue of contraceptives, as they are afraid of experiencing violence by their husband.

    (iii) *Verbal and Emotional Abuse:* Insult, ridicule, humiliation of the victim woman specially with regard to not having a child or a male child and repeatedly threatening any person in whom the aggrieved woman is interested. Emotional abuse has far more psychological implications, as it erodes self-esteem and brings personality breakdown and total loss of functioning of an otherwise normal human being.

    (iv) *Economic Abuse:* Misappropriation of the property and *stridhan* of the aggrieved woman by her husband for economically crippling the woman is called economic abuse. Domestic violence can push economically fragile households into an economic crisis.

Theoretical Perspective of Domestic Violence

There are some theories relating to domestic violence which try to explain why family violence may occur?

1. *Conflict Theory:* As per the conflict theory, when a husband receives little prestige or income from his job, he cannot influence the persons around him then he tries to dominate his wife through domestic violence.

   Similarly, where a woman has more prestigious job than her husband, the husband feels jealous and tries to dominate his wife through domestic violence. Thus, here the use of domestic violence is a recourse of domination.
2. *Conservative Theory:* According to conservative thecrists family is a social institution, the patriarchal nature of family and traditional division of labour allows men to think himself superior than a woman and then they treat women inferior to them which is the cause of family conflict.
3. *Cyclical Theory:* According to walker's cyclical theory of violence, the interaction between the husband and the wife is changed in a cyclical pattern:
   (i) Tension building phase
   (ii) Acute phase
   (iii) Tranquil phase
4. *Marxian and Radical Feminists Theory:* According to this theory the property and economic relation between the spouses are the main causes. Some of them believe that biological factor and male dominance, etc. are also responsible for domestic violence on married women.
5. *Moderates Theory:* According to this theory, in the political and economic field the position and prestige of men and women are not same. To eradicate this difference we must modify the families in such a way that men and women can share and enjoy equal responsibilities and attention within and outside their families.
6. *Coercive Theory:* According to William Goode, the male members of the family use physical abuse against their female life partners to suppress and oppress them because in the family it is a coercive form of social control.
7. *Exchange Theory:* As per this modern theory domestic violence is nothing but the cultural tolerance of women in a society and the costs and rewards of those behaviours. So if the legal and social sanctions are very violent then the perpetrators must think twice before using that crime on their wives.

8. *Behaviorist System Theory:* The violent family background specially in the joint families are highlighted in this theory. Perpetrators, mainly the husband and in-laws, are viewed as an agent of patriarchy.

Domestic Violence as Health Hazard

Today domestic violence is a serious health problem in India. According to the WHO report on violence and health, one person dies almost every minute somewhere in the world due to domestic violence. In India, many deaths due to domestic violence are explained as accidents or attributed to natural or unknown deaths. Often domestic violence like physical and mental abuses, cruelty, marital rape, female foeticide, etc. causes severe physical injuries and mental trauma among the victim women. The physical effects of marital rape may include injuries to private organs, lacerations, soreness, bruising, torn muscles, fatigue and vomiting.

Women who have been battered by their husbands may suffer physical consequences including broken bones, black eyes, bloody noses, knife wounds, etc. Due to marital rape, some specific gynaecological complications may arise, i.e. miscarriages, still birth, bladder infection, infertility and the potential construction of sexually transmitted disease including HIV. These married women also suffer severe mental and psychological traumas including fear psychosis due to domestic violence and loose their self-confidence totally and confine themselves behind the closed door of the houses of their husband and in-laws.

Domestic Violence as a Human Rights Issue

Human rights are some basic rights which are inherent in our nature and without which we cannot live as human beings. The human rights of women generally include rights to equality before law, right against gender discrimination, right against harassment, right to abortion, right to privacy, right to economic empowerment. Today domestic violence is recognized as a gross human rights violation by different International Women's Conventions. The UN Conference documents, i.e. Vienna declaration and Programme of Action 1993 and Beijing Declaration and Platform for Action 1995, recognized domestic violence as a human right issue. The UN convention on elimination of all forms of discrimination against women 1979, recognized domestic violence as a gender-based violence. Article 17 of this convention creates a committee on the elimination of discrimination against women which recognized domestic violence as a human right issue.

In India, domestic violence violates Article 21 of the Constitution of India. According to Article 21 'No person shall be deprived of life or personal liberty except according to the procedure established by laws. This right to life includes right to live with human dignity, right to shelter, right to privacy, etc. Right to live with dignity and prestige is one important human right because without this human right, other human rights cannot be enforced. Domestic violence attacks the very dignity of women and considers women as a chattel. Domestic violence also undermines self respect and dignities of the victim women. Not only that, female foeticide, marital rape, *satipratha*, etc. are also attacking the very dignity of a woman and violates the human rights of women. Therefore, domestic violence is a gross human right violation.

Indian Law Relating to Domestic Violence on Married Women

Domestic violence is a barbarous attitude towards women in India. Its existence was first shown in post-Vedic period. From that time to British period, there was no law relating to this crime. After independence there are five kinds of laws which are dealing with domestic violence offences:

1. Constitutional law relating to domestic violence.
2. Criminal law relating to domestic violence.
3. Civil law relating to domestic violence.
4. Statutory law relating to domestic violence.
5. Remedies available under law of torts.

Constitutional Law Relating to Domestic Violence

In the 21st century, domestic violence on married women is an issue that can be sorted out within the four walls of the house and some amount of violence is considered as a part of normal wear and tear of marital life. After independence of India, the framers of the Constitution of India were conscious about the discrimination towards and unequal treatment of women in every field of their lives and violence against women, including domestic violence. So they included certain general as well as specific provisions in the Constitution of India under Part III as 'Fundamental Right' and Part IV as 'Directive Principles of State Policy' for the uplift of the status of women and also to eradicate the violence against women from the society. Article 14 to 19 and 21 of the Indian Constitution deals with this crime to uplift the status of the victim married women.

Criminal Law Relating to Domestic Violence

There are three criminal laws relating to domestic violence:

1. Indian Penal Code 1860
2. Criminal Procedure Code 1973
3. Indian Evidence Act 1872

Civil Law Relating to Domestic Violence

After independence there was no specific civil law relating to domestic violence. After the long standing demand by NCW and different women NGOs for specific civil law against domestic violence, in September 2001, Government of India passed 'The Protection of Women from Domestic Violence Act 2005'. In this Act Sections 3, 8, 9, 10, 12, 18, 19, 20, 31 (i) are very important sections which try to protect women from this type of crime.

Statutory Laws Relating to Domestic Violence

There are many statutory laws relating to domestic violence such as the Dowry Prohibition Act 1961. This Act which was amended twice, once in 1984 and then in 1986, is an attempt to abolish giving or taking dowry as a social custom at the time of marriage and has made it punishable. The commission of Sati Prevention Act 1981, Medical Termination of Pregnancy Act 1981, Prenatal Diagnostic Techniques (Regulation and Prevention of Misuse) Act 1994, all are dealing with different types of domestic violence offences, including female foeticide, female infanticide, etc. But despite the plethora of protective laws, dowry death, bride burning and other severe types of domestic violence still exist in our society.

Remedies Available Under Law of Torts

Domestic violence offences which are generally punished under Law of Torts are battery, assault, false imprisonment, etc. In these cases the perpetrator husband physically abuses the victim married women. Violence are in nature of slapping, punching, kicking or physically striking a person. The remedies for these offences are damages i.e monetary compensation for harm caused to the wife by the accused husband. It includes medical and other expenses, compensation for physical pain and suffering, damages for nervous shock, etc. Injunctions and restraining orders are other remedies which are available to the victim wives in these cases. In this context, it can be stated that in spite of plethora of progressive and protective legislations favouring women, India failed to uplift the social status of women. Though the new civil law, i.e. The Protection of Women from Domestic Violence

Act, 2005 is implemented properly by the state machinery, still today domestic violence is common in both urban and rural India but largely ignored and accepted as a way of life in our country.

Role of Indian Judiciary

Today, domestic violence is the greatest human right scandal in India. So, Indian Judiciary comes forward with an aim to eradicate this crime by different valuable judgments and to generate public awareness against such social evil. In India, judiciary usually deals with domestic violence cases like:

1. Cruelty by husband and in-laws under Section 498A, IPC
2. Bride burning, dowry death cases under 304B, IPC
3. Murder under Section 302, IPC
4. Abetment to suicide under Section 306, IPC
5. Bigamy under Section 494, IPC, etc.

There are hardly any cases registered for hurt, grievous hurt, wife beating, marital rape, etc. before the court. Often, the victim married woman of domestic violence is seeking divorce, judicial separation, maintenance from husbands, custody of children, etc. from the court for getting redressal from her accused husband and relatives of her husband who tortured her mentally and physically. Recently, the judges are trying to realize the vulnerable condition of the victim women of domestic violence and trying to give pragmatic judgment relating to domestic violence offences. In these cases, judges are playing a dynamic role in expounding the laws and clarifying the legal norms so that the culprit does not escape punishment due to technical difficulties and inadequacies of law. In domestic violence cases, Indian Judiciary follows strict rules of evidence specially relating to Section 113A and 113B of Indian Evidence Act 1872. In these types of cases, judges prefer to stress on circumstantial evidence where direct evidences are missing and these evidences against the accused should be definite, conclusive in nature and must be consistent with the guilt.

In (1) Wazir Chand Vs State of Haryana. AIR 1989 SC 378, (2) Gurbachan Singh Vs Satpal Singh. AIR 1990 SC 209, (3) Bhupendra Singh Vs State of Punjab. AIR 1988 SC 1011; the Supreme Court relied upon the circumstantial evidences to punish the accused. Sometime in these types of cases judiciary rely upon the dying declaration made by the victim women about the cause of their deaths. But where the husband, because of his brutal behaviour, fears that his wife may blame him or his parents in her dying declaration and due to that reason, he threatens his wife, her children and loved ones with dire consequences if she tells the truth. In this circumstance, threat is so over powering that the victim wife has no courage to speak the truth even in the last moment of her life. In such cases, generally conflicting dying declaration is made, therefore, the judges always read thoroughly and interpret the dying declaration with an eye on the social reality of the life of an Indian Woman. If there are more than one dying declarations than the court scrutinizes all of them to find the truth and all these dying declarations must be consistent on the material particular by before the court can accept and rely upon the same. In Yashoda vs State of MP and others. (AIR 2005 SC), etc. the court relied upon the dying declaration of the victim woman to punish the accused.

In this context, I would like to mention that in these type of cases, generally bail or anticipatory bail shall not be granted by the court till the investigation is completed, because experience shows that the freedom is mostly misused by the accused. The accused tampers with evidence or tries to blackmail the victim and her family or threatens them. So granting bails to the suspect at the stage of investigation creates impediments in the proper investigation of the case. Also, in domestic violence cases, court is always very cautious in cancelling or granting bail or anticipatory bail.

On 14 February 2006, the Supreme Court delivered a landmark judgment that all marriages irrespective of religion must be compulsorily registered.

The Supreme Court observed that if all marriages irrespective of religion are registered as mandatory, then it would:

1. help to prevent child marriage.
2. check bigamy and polygamy.
3. help the tortured women to exercise their rights under marriage, maintenance from husband, custody of children, etc. and
4. deter the accused husbands from deserting their wives easily.

Sometimes Judges are trying to reconcile the broken marriage and in many divorce cases they direct several couples to arrive at an amicable settlement for the sake of their children. By this way the judges are successful in bringing these couples together again. In 2003, the Hon'ble Calcutta High Court had given a remarkable instruction that – 'the husband would be compelled to live separately from his family with his wife only, if his wife so desires. The husband can not force his wife to live with his parents because law does not permit such right to a husband.' Kakali Ghosh vs. Asis Ghosh (Division bench of Hon'ble justice Ajoy Roy and Prodipto Roy).[5]

In 2004, in another case, the High Court of Calcutta stated that – if the victim wife who has been abandoned by her husband without any reason is unable to bear the expenses to continue her proceeding of court case, against her husband, then she is entitled to get extra money from her husband for her court proceedings.[6] By this way Indian judiciary always try to help the victim women and their families to get proper justice.

Role of National Commission for Women

In January 1992, the National Commission for Women was set up as a statutory body under the National Commission for Women Act, 1990, to review the Constitutional and legal safe-guard for women, recommend remedial legislative measures for women, facilitate redressal of grievances and advise the government on all policy matters affecting women. The NCW is constantly fighting against violence against women, including domestic violence. Everyday many domestic violence cases are coming from different parts of India to NCW. The National Commission for women is divided into four departments or units for the purpose of its smooth functioning. These units are –

1. Complaints and Counselling Cell
2. Legal Cell
3. Public Relation Cell
4. Research and Study Cell

In domestic violence cases complaints, either oral or written, are received from the victim women or their relatives by the Complaints and Counselling Cell of the National Commission for Women. These cells usually receive domestic violence cases like dowry death, dowry harassment, cruelty, bigamy, desertion, maintenance, divorce, custody of children, matrimonial dispute, female infanticide, female foeticide, misappropriation of property, etc. Ordinary family dispute cases are settled by counselling of both the parties which takes place in presence of the counsellors of the Complaints and Counselling Cell of the commission. The complaints of domestic violences which are received by the commission are investigated by the police whenever necessary and these cases are monitored by this commission for expeditious action. An inquiry committee is constituted to look into serious domestic violence cases and also to make spot inquires, examine various witnesses, collect evidence and submit the report with recommendation. After that, it is monitored by them to provide immediate relief and justice to the victim of domestic violence.

Legal cell of NCW finds the lacunae among the existing laws which are dealing with domestic violence and provide valuable suggestions to the government. It gives valuable advice in making government policies to uplift the status of women. It provides free legal aid to the distressed women if required. Recently NCW took an innovative step to provide speedy justice to the victim married women through Parivarik Mahila Lok Adalat which is organized by NGO in association with District Legal Aid and Advisory Board, social activist, advocates and others with the commission's financial assistance. NCW by its Public Relation Cell is launching many legal awareness programmes relating to domestic violence against married women for the public. Often, NCW conducts workshops, campaigns, seminars relating to domestic violence to make public aware about this social evil by this cell. It also launches sensitization programmes for police, NGOs, judiciary and government officials for implementation of safeguard and laws for the benefit of women who are victims of domestic violence offences. NCW by its Research and Studies Cell promote many research projects relating to domestic violence against married women and suggests action plan and remedial measures to resolve this problem. By this way NCW is earnestly fighting to combat domestic violence with its commendable sincerity but still domestic violence is prevalent in our country.

Suggestions

Some pragmatic suggestions for combatting the domestic violence offences are:

1. *Legal Aid Cells and Shelter Homes:* Domestic violence against women is a barbarous crime. So Indian Government must set up legal aid cells and shelter homes in all the districts of our country to create legal awareness about the legal rights of women and emergency shelter homes for victim married women after they are deserted by their husbands and other family members.
2. *Compulsory Education for Girl Child:* Education for girl child should be mandatory and legal awareness and legal rights of women should be a mandatory reading in every school and college.
3. *Public Awareness:* The people of India should be aware about the proper meaning of domestic violence against married women and the harmful sides of the crime should be explained to them by the media, press, etc.
4. *Role of Bridegroom's Family and Role of Parents of the Accused Husband:* The bridegroom's family should be sympathetic, liberal and kind hearted towards the family of the bride. They should accept the newly wedded bride whole heartedly. The in-laws,

specially the mother-in-law, should treat newly wedded bride as their daughter and help her to adjust in the new environment.

On the other hand, sometimes male children who in their childhood have experienced domestic violence are usually found to become perpetrators of domestic violence in their later lives. So, if they are properly guided by their parents from childhood to respect every woman then, they should love their wives and treat them as their friends, partners and better halves.

5. *Setting up more Family Courts:* Generally in our country majority of women in domestic violence cases are seeking divorce and judicial separation. Therefore, to provide speedy and easily available justice in domestic violence cases, more Family Courts should be created by the Indian Government.
6. *Pre-marital Counselling:* In India, pre-marital counselling centres must be set up by every Family Counselling Centre and counsellors should be directed to offer premarital counselling among youths and elders about the evils of dowry, female foeticide, marital rape, goodness of the Section 498A of the IPC and its misuse, importance of other protective laws of domestic violence, danger of wife-beatings, necessity of HIV test report and thalassemia test report before a healthy marriage, etc.

   Because here premarital counselling is a preventive measure, family counselling is a remedial measure.
7. *Role of the People:* In India, due to patriarchal dominance in the society, girl children are still unwanted in the family. So to reduce the rate of female-foeticide and female-infanticide, people should treat men and women as equals for a developed society as it is envisaged under our Indian Constitution.
8. *Religious Belief:* Religious belief is an instrument which helps people to obey the path of reasoning, rights and rectitude and their noble attitude helps us to show respect toward our wives as friends and better halves.

Conclusion

The menace of domestic violence on married women is a crime which is not created in a day nor will it be removed from the society in a year. It is a deep-rooted crime in India in spite of many non-implemented progressive and protective laws and landmark judgments of Supreme Court and different High Courts for removing this crime from our traditional Indian society. Majority of the people think that domestic violence is the basic marital right of husbands and their families. In the present century, it would increase due to change in lifestyle. It is considered as a slow poison which is swallowing the ingredients of the family life as it strikes in various forms like physical, sexual, emotional and psychological, destroying completely the personality of a human being.

Notes

1. Pradeep Agarwal, *The Medical Profession and Domestic Violence on Women*, New Delhi: Butterworths India, 2000.
2. *The Times of India*, 26 September 2012.
3. Ibid.
4. 'Thrush it Out Again', *The Hindustan Times*, http://www.hindustantimes.com/news.
5. *Ananda Bazar Patrika*, 16 September 2003.
6. *Ananda Bazar Patrika*, 14 January 2004, Krishna Adhikari vs. Anal Adhikari.

References

Agarwal, Pradeep. 2000. *The Medical Profession and Domestic Violence on Women*, New Delhi: Butterworths India.

Bhattacharya, Rinki. 2004. *Behind the Closed Doors: Domestic Violence in India*, New Delhi: Sage Publications.

Gupta, Sadhna and Pankaj Kumar. 2006. 'Domestic Violence: Some Socio-Legal Aspects', *Legal News and Views*, 20 (4).

Jaising, Indira. 2001. *Law of Domestic Violence*, Delhi: Universal Law Publishing Co. Pvt. Ltd.

Majumder, Maya. 2007. *Protecting Our Women*, New Delhi: Dominant Publishers.

Mukherjee, Roma. 1998. *Legal Status and Remedies for Women in India*, New Delhi: Deep and Deep Publications.

Saxena, Shobha. 1999. *Crimes against Women and Protective Law*, New Delhi: Deep and Deep Publications.

8

Crime against Women in Sikkim

SWATI AKSHAY SACHDEVA

Women are regarded as the providers of care and love in their families. In every society there are indicators which are used to define equality; some of these are education, occupation, etc. But various studies have shown that a social biasness and inequality prevails against the women. In Sikkim, however, the situation is very different; women in this part of the country are not subjected to the same inequalities as their counterparts in rest of the country. However, there is no mention of the crime committed against women in Sikkim. There are reported cases of extreme atrocities against women in Sikkim establishing the fact that the state, although relatively peaceful and prosperous, is not immune to the social trend of crime against women. This paper highlights some of the crimes committed against the women in Sikkim and aims to fill some of the existing gaps in this context.

Definition

Violence is an act carried out with the intention or perceived intention of physically hurting another person (Gelles and Straus, 1979). Gender violence is defined as 'any act involving use of force or coercion with intent of perpetuating promoting hierarchical gender relations' (APWLD, 1990; Schuler et al., 1996). To this definition was added: 'violence perpetrated or condoned by the State'. Adding gender dimension to the definition amplifies it to include violent acts perpetrated on women because they are women. Manifestations of violence include physical aggression, such as blows of varying intensity, burns, attempted hanging, sexual abuse and rape, psychological violence through insults, humiliation, coercion, blackmail, economic or emotional threats and control over speech and actions. In extreme, but not unknown cases, death is the result (Adriana, 1996).

Violence against women has been clearly defined as a form of discrimination in numerous documents. The World Human Rights Conference in Vienna first recognized gender-based violence as a human rights violation in 1993. In the same year, United Nations declaration, 1993, defined violence against women as any act of gender-based violence that results in, or is likely to result in, physical, sexual or psychological harm or suffering to a woman, including threats of such acts, coercion or arbitrary deprivations of liberty, whether occurring in public or private life' (Cited by Gomez, 1996).[1]

Patriarchy, Gender Roles and Violence

A society that expects males to dominate in all family decision-making is called as patriarchy. It describes a political system ruled by men in which women have inferior social and political status, including basic human rights (Kottak, 1994: 198). Sylvia Walby in 'Theorizing Patriarchy' calls it 'a system of social structures and practices in which men dominate, oppress and exploit women' (Walby, 2002). Patriarchy is based on a system of power relations, which are hierarchical and unequal, where men control women's production, reproduction and sexuality. It imposes masculinity and femininity character stereotypes in society, which strengthen the iniquitous power relations between men and women. Patriarchy values male dominance as a natural inalienable right, thereby enforcing the inferiority and subordination of women. Normative behaviour derived from this value includes institutional discrimination against women in education, health and in labour force, resulting in restricted opportunities, lower wages.

In India, the problem of violence against women is a result of a long-standing power imbalance between men and women. Men have access to property and resources and there is also a sexual division of labour in India, which results in female exploitation – physically, mentally and commercially. Radhika Coomaraswamy identifies different kinds of violence against women, in the United Nation's Special Report, 1995.

1. Physical, sexual and psychological violence occurring in the family, including battering, sexual abuse of female children in the household, dowry-related violence, marital rape, female genital mutilation and other traditional practices harmful to women, non-spousal violence and violence related to exploitation.

2. Physical sexual and psychological violence occurring within the general community including rape, sexual abuse, sexual harassment and intimidation at work, in educational institutions and elsewhere, trafficking in women and forced prostitution.
3. Physical, sexual and psychological violence perpetrated or condoned by the state

The family socializes its members to accept hierarchical relations, which are interlinked with cultural and social factors. Culture of many societies does not permit equality between men and women. For, in many cultures gender dichotomization has its genesis in religion (Sarkar, 1999: 205). The different processes of socialization creates different gender roles because of which the man is given the role of domination and control and women the role of submission and obedience.

Position of Women in Sikkim

Sikkim, situated in the Eastern Himalayas, represents a meeting ground of several cultures manifested in distinctive lifestyle of its several tribal communities. According to the 2011 Census, Sikkim has a population of 610,577. Ethnically, the state comprises three groups – the Bhutias (descendants of Tibetan and Bhutanese immigrants who came to Sikkim in the 16th and 17th centuries), the Lepchas (the indigenous people of Sikkim) and the Nepalis (who migrated from Nepal in the 18th and 19th centuries). In addition, others came to Sikkim as businessmen, traders, service providers and labourers.

The women of Sikkim are unique in many ways. 'Like everything else in Sikkim they also truly manifest the influence of the sylvan serenity of the august hills of the Himalayas and the deep pervasive influence of the quintessence of Buddhism. These influences have made their lives free from many discriminatory inequalities from which the women suffer elsewhere' (Bhattacharya, 1994). In Sikkim, women constitute nearly 47 per cent of the total population. There social economic position in the state seems to be better than that in the rest of the country. Under the measurement of HDI (Human Development Index), women of Sikkim have been given special place in GDI (Gender Development Index), GEM (Gender Empowerment Measures) calculations. Women enjoy many freedoms and have recorded significant gains in the race of overall human development. In Sikkim, women enjoy relatively greater freedom than in other parts of the country.

Another striking feature of Sikkim is the absence of gender differentials along many indicators of human development. For instance, in

1998–99, 83.2 per cent of boys and 82.6 per cent of girls between 6–17 years attended school. In contrast to unfavourable sex ratio in population as a whole, the number of women in government employment is greater than man. They are more visible in public sphere in Sikkim than a norm for India and south Asia as a whole. The fact that in 1999–2000 the number of women headed houses in Sikkim rural areas (142 per thousand) was higher than national average, indicates not only the impact of migration but also the status accorded to women in the state (Diyali, 2009).

This paper is an attempt to highlight some of the crimes that are registered against women in Sikkim. The data has been collected from the crime branch of Sikkim, some of the major police stations like the Sadar Police Station of Gangtok and also from some NGOs working in this regard. Interviews have also been conducted with some women who have faced such problems and also, in general, women have been interviewed to find their views and reasons about why violence of such nature is now finding place in a relatively peaceful society like Sikkim also.

Crime Against Women in Sikkim

The status of women in Sikkim, their economic contribution to fabric, autonomy or authority, involvement in the decision-making process in all socio-economic, cultural and most important the political sphere gives them a high social status. In Sikkim, there have also been no reported case of gender discrimination, inequality, sexual harassment at work place, infanticide, foeticide or dowry-related death. However, there are very vague and oblique references when it comes to the crimes reported against them like domestic violence, rape, murder, molestation, eve-teasing, kidnapping, etc.

Domestic Violence

Physical violence as well as explicit forms of aggression is used by the more powerful in the household as methods to ensure obedience of the less powerful and, therefore, related to power dynamics in a household. At every stage in the life cycle, the female body is both the object of desire and of control (Thapan, 1997). Domestic violence includes not only inter-spousal violence, but also violence perpetrated by other family members. Generally, an important part of the power relationship between spouses and their families relates to dowry and its ramifications (Karlekar, 1995). There is a wide societal tolerance for wife-abuse, which is very often even considered justifiable under certain circumstance. Domestic violence includes harassment, maltreatment, brutality or cruelty and even the threat of assault – intimidation. It includes physical injury, as well as 'willfully or knowingly placing or attempting to place a spouse in fear of injury and compelling the spouse by force or threat to engage in any conduct or act, sexual or otherwise, from which the spouse has a right to abstain'. Abuse of wives and wife beating – or in more extreme cases wife battering is the most common form of abuse worldwide irrespective of class, religion, community (Bogards, 1988; Chen, 1922; Hoff, 1990, Strauss, 1980).

In Sikkim, the number of cases reported against domestic violence is very few. As we can see from the Table 1, incidences of such nature almost appear insignificant.

Table 1

Cases of Domestic Violence

Year	*Number of Cases*
2007	6
2008	5
2009	1
2010	4
2011	1

Source: Crime Branch of Sikkim.

SPACE conducted a survey of VAW and D (Violence against Women and Discrimination) in Sikkim in 1999 and the following facts emerged.

- There has been no tangible research undertaken with respect to VAW and D in the sate of Sikkim.
- So far, only one agency, the Women Counselling Cell (WCC) meant to arbitrate in cases of VAW and D as well as domestic violence exist in the state which was till recently run by the Department of Women and Child Welfare.
- Another government agency functioning under the ageis of the High Court of Sikkim and popularly known as *family courts* is mostly a catalytic agency consisting of a bench of senior citizens, enterprising women and statesmen who meet once a week to settle domestic disputes.

- Sikkim's women are basically shy and meek by temperament and can be easily bulldozed into humble submission by their husbands, in-laws, brothers and even their parents.
- The subject of VAW and D has been accepted as preordained by fate and direct consequences of one's actions in past lives.

Every woman who stays in a violent relationship will have her own reasons to do so. Her abuser could have made threats to her or her children, she could be facing poverty if she left, she may have been out of the workforce for years and lack skills and experience necessary to obtain employment, and she may be a rural woman with few resources. She may have reached out to police or clergy in the past and found them not to be helpful. She may be focused on surviving day to day instead of focusing on escape. She may feel ashamed of what she has endured, or guilty for leaving her partner. Whatever the specific reasons, there is no universal answer for why women stay in abusive relationships, it may well be for multiple reasons and it is much more complicated than 'just leaving' (Grovert, 2008).

In Sikkim, most of the women are economically empowered and any of these reasons do not seem valid enough for them to stay in an abusive relationship. Some women who were interviewed and had faced some kind of violence at some point of time in their life said that patriarchy has a strong hold in the society, though women have the right in decision-making yet, they were beaten up by their husbands. The husbands generally beat up their wife under the influence of alcohol or for her sexual infidelities or her neglect of household duties. (*This information has been collected from police diaries*)

The main reasons, which emerged from the study conducted by SPACE, for domestic violence were – excessive traditional and superstitious beliefs, illicit and immoral practices like bigamy and adultery, alcoholism, political polarization within the family, ideological conflict and religious chauvinism. Most of the women who had suffered from domestic violence felt that the apathetic attitude of the public and especially the neighbourhood of a family were the reasons why such crimes are increasing in the society. They felt that people are very self-centred and caught in their own world of self promotion and women, because they are generally lacking in courage and experience a sense of shame in revealing the family affair in public, therefore suffer in silence. Many of the cases are not reported and it is only the serious ones that find mention in police diaries. Sikkim being a very close knit and a small society, affinity plays a very important role and most of the cases are handled in the presence of *panchayats* or by the intervention of a third party or to some extent by the family courts.

Dowry

Dowry is a transfer of property from the bride's family to that of the bridegroom, at the time of marriage (Negi, 1997: 14). According to the present practice, dowry usually subsumes material gifts and cash paid to the bridegroom and his kin. This practice continues even after marriage (Paul, 1986). In Sikkim, there are no cases of dowry deaths, because the marriage here is solemnized by the bride-price system. In the bride-price form of marriage, the parents or guardians of the bride receive, as a compensation, an amount of money from the parents or guardians of the groom for the transfer of the labour and services of the bride from the parents household to her in-law's household. Some ethnographers (Tambiah, 1973; Schlegel and Eloul, 1988) used the term 'bride wealth' for bride price. However, for Schlegel and Eloul's (1988) bride wealth carries the same meaning as given for bride price marriage. Payments are linked with a number of issues: most importantly, status and the economic contribution of the brides to the groom's family (Lindenbaum, 1981); nature of residence and the inheritance system (Spiro, 1975; Yalman, 1967); shortages of potential brides and bridge grooms (Caldwell et al., 1983); and tendencies towards egalitarianism or stratification in a given society (Goody, 1973). In Sikkim, the bride price is given to value the girl and is linked with the status and economic position of the grooms' family. Therefore, in Sikkim, because of the prevalence of this system there are no reported cases of dowry deaths so far.

Eve-Teasing and Rape

Eve-teasing is an act of terror that violates a woman's body, space and self-respect. It is one of the many ways through which a woman is systematically made to feel inferior, weak and afraid. Whether it is an obscene word whispered into a woman's ear; offensive remarks on her appearance; an intrusive way of touching any part of a woman's body; a gesture which is perceived and intended to be vulgar: all these acts represent a violation of a woman's person, her bodily integrity. Eve-teasing denies a woman's fundamental right to move freely and carry herself with dignity, solely on the basis of her sex (*Hindu*, 2 August 1998).

Table 2
Eve Teasing/Molestation

Year	*Eve Teasing/(Molestation)*
2007	11
2008	19
2009	6
2010	12
2011	19
Total	67

Source: Crime Branch of Sikkim.

According to Table 2, in Sikkim the number of eve-teasing has increased over the years but there is no consistent pattern that can be observed. Some acts of eve-teasing mentioned by girl students who were interviewed are: indecent remarks, singing obscene songs, hitting, touching or pinching in crowded places.

Rape is a type of *sexual assault* usually involving *sexual intercourse*, which is initiated by one or more persons against another person without that person's *consent*. The act may be carried out by physical force, *coercion*, abuse of authority or with a person who is incapable of valid consent, such as a person who is unconscious or incapacitated. The term is most often defined in *criminal law*. Many of them go unreported because the nature of the crime is such that the victims and their families find it hard to report such incidences. According to sociologists, the reasons for this sudden increase in the number of rapes can be due to a complex mix of migration, shrinking spaces in cities and the high visibility of women outside their homes. A major reason behind such impulses and excesses is the lack of importance shown towards such issues like gender respect in the education curriculum (Nagpal and Luthra, 2012).

In the rest of the country, where a woman is raped every 30 minutes (*Shreya Dhoundial*), Sikkim still remains a very safe place for women. In Sikkim, there are no custodial rapes and very few gang rapes have been reported, as we can see from Figure 1, but rapes are taking place in society.[2]

Some of the women interviewed felt that earlier there was no nightlife in Sikkim, there were no clubs, discos or late-night parties but with the spread of the current neo-cultural trends and with all the

Figure 1

Reported Rape Cases in Sikkim

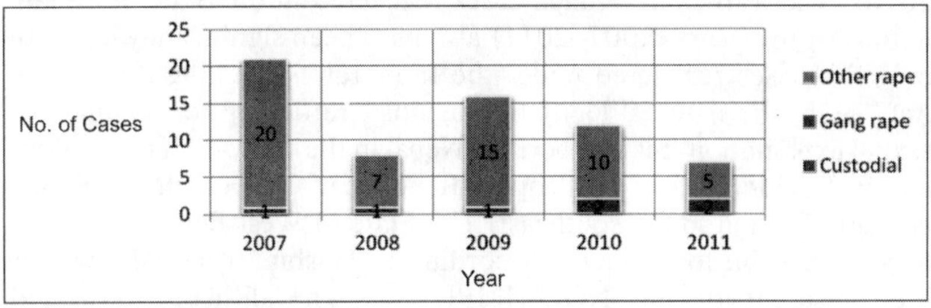

Source: Crime branch of Sikkim.

trappings of modernism, this problem has come to Sikkim. According to them, the figure of rape cases in rest of the country are higher than Sikkim because in these places the basic respect towards women is missing and this number will keep rising if we do not tackle the root cause of the problem. This problem can be solved by inculcating gender respect and creating awareness among people.

Human Trafficking

Human trafficking is a continuously evolving transnational criminal activity. In India, the driving trends of the human trafficking include both push and pull factors leading to demand and supply of human beings and commodification of human beings (Nair, 2007). The United Nations Protocol to Prevent, Suppress, and Punish trafficking among persons, especially women and children (adopted in November 2000) defines trafficking as:

> The recruitment, transportation, transfer, harbouring or receipt of persons by means of threat or use of force or other forms of coercion, of abduction, of fraud, of deception, of the abuse of power or of a position of vulnerability or a giving or receiving of payments or benefits to achieve the consent of a person having control over another person, for the purpose of exploitation. Exploitation shall include, at a minimum, the exploitation of the prostitution of others or other forms of sexual exploitation, forced labour or service, slavery or practices similar to slavery, servitude or the removal of organs.

In India, human trafficking is generally equated with commercial sexual exploitation. The country does not have any systematic record of the number of persons trafficked. Both the victims and their families do not come forward to report incidents because of the stigma attached to it. Therefore, the figures available are mostly from the rescue operations that are carried out from time to time (Sharma and Choudhury, 2010). The trafficking-related cases registered in the State of Sikkim in the last five years (2007–2011) also have been significantly low with only five cases registered under the Immoral Trafficking Prohibition Act, 1956, the national legislation against trafficking for commercial sexual exploitation. Sikkim borders Nepal in the west, the Tibet Autonomous Region/TAR of the People's Republic of China in the north and east and Bhutan in the southeast. The State of West Bengal (Siliguri) borders Sikkim to its south. According to Hashina Kharbhih, who is the president of the NGO IMPULSE: The difficult terrain of north-east has restricted the illegal migration from TAR, however Sikkim shares a porous border with Nepal and since the population of Sikkim also has close matrimonial ties with Nepal, this problem is coming to the State.

According to Figure 2, the highest number of cases of abduction and immoral trafficking were reported in 2007. The crime branch of Sikkim Police is the nodal branch to handle the human rights violations and various organized crimes. Under the Ministry of Home Affairs, the crime branch established its first Anti Human Trafficking Unit (AHTU) in the State at Police Headquarters on 18 May 2012. The AHTU were conceptualized as comprehensive Task Force units, involving law enforcement officials, other government department officials and NGOs. Such units are set up to address human trafficking in a holistic and integrated manner, simultaneously attending to prevention, protection and prosecution.

Figure 2

Human Trafficking Data of Sikkim

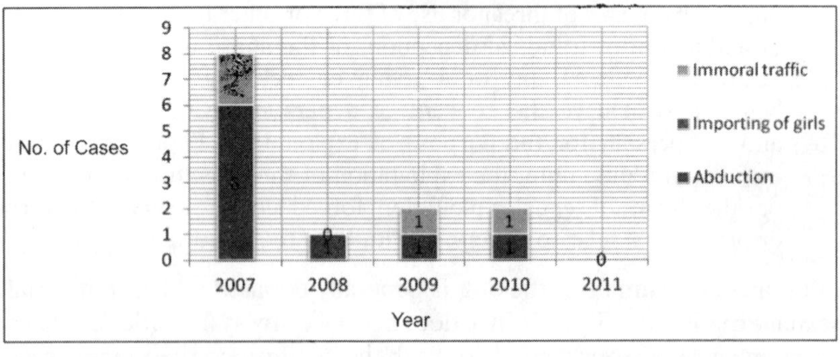

Source: Crime Branch of Sikkim.

The AHTU model has established certain fundamentals in the anti-human trafficking response systems. These include: (1) Best response to human trafficking has to be integrated, holistic and multi-dimensional. (2) All the stakeholders have to work in synergy. (3) There is a need for role clarity and role conformity. (4) Roles of the various stakeholders are not complementary, but are supplementary. Yet there is a process by which the roles are integrated, one leading to the other and may be cyclical at times. (5) The victim remains central in this response system and, therefore, all responses are oriented towards the 'best interest of the victim'. Good and bad response is decided based on this benchmark. (6) Quantitative and qualitative indicators are available for measuring the output and the impact. This helps in evaluation and also in corrective action, whenever required. (7) It enhances help-seeking role of NGOs, public and victims. (8) It enhances help-rendering role of police. (9) It provides for checks and balances and keeps the law enforcement agencies involved in proper action. (10) It facilitates expeditious action and justice delivery. (11) It enhances public trust in police. (12) It facilitates community policing. (13) The model provides a great tool for appreciating the good work done by the responders. The award/reward system will enhance accountability of the responders; improve their morale and output.

Some of the role of the AHTU (Nair, 2011) includes attention in dealing with offences of human trafficking and providing a multidisciplinary approach and a joint response by all stakeholders. It helps to bring about inter-departmental collaboration among the police and all other government agencies and departments, such as women and child labour, health, etc. It conducts rescue operations with the assistance of NGOs whenever they receive information about trafficking activities either from police sources, or NGOs or civil society. It ensures 'best interest of the victim/survivor' and prevents 'secondary victimization/re-victimization' of the victim as well as ensuring a gender sensitive and child rights sensitive approach in dealing with trafficked victims.

This agency functions at the grassroots unit for collection and development of an exhaustive database on all law enforcement aspects of the crime, including information on traffickers and trafficking gangs, which they convey to the District and State Crime Records Bureau for further transmission to the National Crime Records Bureau. Thus, AHTUs facilitate availability of comprehensive national level data on the criminal activity.

Conclusion

This paper highlights some of the crimes committed against the women in Sikkim. From the above discussion, it is apparent that the growing ubiquity of gender specific violence like domestic violence, eve-teasing, rape and trafficking are heaped upon women in Sikkim also. But as mentioned earlier, the crimes committed against them are comparatively less percentage-wise when compared with the rest of India. Even in a society like Sikkim, where women are treated relatively better, the family socializes its members to accept hierarchical relations expressed in unequal division of labour and power over the allocation of resources. The community provides the mechanisms for perpetuating male control over women's sexuality, mobility and labour and these very factors perpetrate violence against them.

Despite the ubiquity of violence against women, both within the home and in the public sphere, the celebration of individual experience has led to the emergence of alternative discourses where the 'truth' and validity of established structures, norms and roles are called into questions. However, research is needed to identify the factors, resources and support by which women can cope up with this violent situation. The state has to work towards changing realities and also restructure gender relations. Media that includes television, radio and newspapers can also play a positive role in creating awareness about the pitfalls of violence against women.

Notes

1. For more definitions of violence against women, refer Sheela Saravanan, *Violence against Women in India: A Literature Review*, Institute of Social Studies Trust (ISST), March 2000.
2. Official police data deals with crime rather than the phenomenon of violence. The reason for this is that the police data is based on complaints and cases that are registered which depend upon the willingness of the victim to report the crime and also the police receptivity to act against these crimes.

References

Adriana. 1996. *Domestic Violence against Women in Albania*, UNICEF.

APWLD (Asian Pacific Forum on Women, Law and Development). 1990. *My Rights, Who Controls?*, Kuala Lampur, Malaysia.

Bhattacharya, A. 1994. 'The Bhutia-Lepcha Women in Sikkim: Tradition and Response to Change', in P.M. Lama (ed.), *Sikkim: Society, Polity, Economy, Environment*, New Delhi: Indus Publishing Company.

Bogards, M. 1988. 'Feminist Perspective on Wife Abuse: An Introduction', in K. Yllo and M. Bogards (eds), *Feminist Perspectives on Wife Abuse*, Newbury Park, CA: Sage Publications, pp. 11–25.

Caldwell, J.C., P.H. Reddy and P. Caldwell. 1983. 'The Causes of Marriage Change in South India', *Population Studies*, 37 (3), pp. 343–61.

Chen, R. 1992. 'Martial Violence in Taiwan: Characteristics and Risk Factors', *Journal of Sociology*, 21, pp. 123–60.

Coomaraswamy, R. 1995. *Report of the Special Rapporteur on Violence against Women: Its Causes and Consequences*, Human Rights Commission.

Diyali, Chandrakala. 2009. *A Situational Analysis of Women and Girls in Sikkim*, New Delhi: National Commission for Women.

Geetha, V. 2002. *Gender Theorizing Feminism*, Calcutta: Stree.

Gelles, R.J. and M.A. Straus. 1979. *Physical Violence in American Families: Risk Factors and Adaptations to Violence in 8,145 Families*, New Brunswick, NJ: Transaction.

Gomez, M.L. 1996. 'Prospective Teachers' Perspectives on Teaching "Other People's" Children', in K. Zeichner, S. Melnick and M.L. Gomez (eds), *Current Reform in Preservice Teacher Education*, New York: Teachers College Press, pp. 109–32.

Goody, J. 1973. 'Bride-Wealth and Dowry in Africa and Eurasia', in J. Goody and S.J. Tambiah (eds), *Bridewealth and Dowry*, Cambridge: Cambridge University Press, pp. 1–58.

Grovert, Amanda J. 2008. *Domestic Violence against Women: A Literature Review*, Master's thesis, Pacific University.

Hoff, Lee Ann. 1990. *Battered Women as Survivors*, London: Routledge.

Karlekar, M. 1995. 'Case Studies of Women's Empowerment in India', *Asian Journal of Women's Studies*, 1 (1).

——. 2003. 'Domestic Violence', in Veena Das (ed.), *The Oxford Indian Companion to Sociology and Social Anthropology*, New Delhi: Oxford University Press.

Kottak, Conrad P. 1994. *Anthropology: The Exploration of Human Diversity*, New York: McGraw-Hill.

Lindenbaum, S. 1981. 'Implications for Women of Changing Marriage Transactions in Bangladesh', *Studies in Family Planning*, 12 (11), pp. 394–401.

Nagpal, Jitendra and Parikshit Luthra. 2012. 'Rape: The Fastest Growing Crime in India', *CNN-IBN*, Tuesday, 26 June.

Nair P.M. 2007. Trafficking women and children for sexual exploitation: handbook for law enforcement agencies in India, New Delhi: UNIFEM and UNODC.

Nair, P.M. 2001. *Human Trafficking: Dimensions, Challenges and Responses,* New Delhi: Konark Publishers.

Negi, Elizabeth F. 1997. *Death by 'Social Causes': Perceptions of and Responses to Female Infanticide in Tamil Nadu,* M.S. Swaminathan Research Foundation, Monograph No. 5.

Paul, M. 1986. *Dowry and Position of Women in India: A Study of Delhi Metropolis,* New Delhi: Inter-India Publications.

Sarkar, T. 1999. *Words to Win: Amar Jiban, a Modern Autobiography,* New Delhi: Kali for Women.

Schlegel, A., and Eloul. R. 1988. 'Marriage Transactions: Labor, Property, Status'. *American Anthropologist.* 90 (1988): 291–309.

Schuler, S. et al., 1996. 'Credit Programmes, Patriarchy and Men's Violence against Women in Rural Bangladesh', *Social Science and Medicine,* 43 (12).

Sharma, M. and Choudhury, J.I. 2010. 'Understanding Human Trafficking: *IGNOU study material*', New Delhi: IGNOU, School of Law, BLE031.

Shreya Dhoundial on 4 May 2008, IBN Live.

Spiro, M.E. 1975. 'Marriage Payments: A Paradigm from the Burmese Perspective', *Journal of Anthropological Research,* 31 (2), pp. 89–115.

Strauss, M.A. Gelles, R.J. and Steinmetz, S. 1980. *Behind closed doors: Violence in the American Family,* Garden City, N.Y.: Anchor Press/Doubleday.

Tambiah, S.J. 1973. 'Dowry and Bride-Wealth and the Property Rights of Women in South Asia', in J. Goody and S.J. Tambiah (eds), *Bridewealth and Dowry,* Cambridge: Cambridge University Press, pp. 59–169.

Thapan, M. 1997. 'Feminity and its Discontents: Women's Body in Intimate Relationships', in *Embodiment: Essays on Gender and Identity,* New Delhi: Oxford University Press.

Walby, S. 2002. 'Towards a Theory of Patriarchy', in *The Polity Reader in Gender Studies,* UK: Blackwell Publishers.

Yalman, N. 1967. *Under the Bo Tree,* Berkeley: University of California Press.

9

Sexual Harassment of Women at Workplace

Legal Control and Judicial Response

PREETI MISRA

Sexual harassment in the form of eve-teasing, molestation, sexual assault and rape is a wrong against the honour, dignity and self respect of a woman. It hurts her immensely and throws her in the background. She loses confidence in life and her career is put at stake. There is a strong need for combating this fast-growing problem. In a country like India, where women are worshipped at par with the Gods, this kind of behaviour against women is unjust, unfair and hippocratic. Sexual harassment at the workplace is a universal problem. Even though the occurrence of sexual harassment at workplace is widespread in India and elsewhere, this is the first time it has been recognized as an infringement of the fundamental rights of a woman, under Article 19 (1) (g) of the Constitution of India 'to practice any profession or to carry out any occupation, trade or business'. Articles 14, 15 and 21 of the Indian Constitution also provide safeguards to women against all forms of discrimination. In recent times, the problem of sexual harassment at the workplace has assumed serious proportions.

Unlike the women of ancient times, the present-day woman is almost at par with the men folk, expects that dignity and status must be given and struggles to establish her position as a separate entity in the society. However, she fails to get the respect she is entitled to as a human being. Sexual harassment of women at the workplace is a fast-growing problem in India. The number of cases filed for sexual harassment has risen but women employees are still reluctant to report the matter to the authority concerned. Indeed, a woman suffers it silently and avoids lodging report because she believes that her complaint would disadvantage her in connection with her employment. About half of working women have suffered some kind of sexual harassment at workplace. Mental and physical harassment and gender discrimination have been the most dominant forms of problems relating to sexual harassment.

Meaning of Sexual Harassment

In less graver sense sexual harassment in India is also termed as 'eve-teasing' and is described as: unwelcome sexual gesture or behaviour whether directly or indirectly as sexually coloured remarks; physical contact and advances; showing pornography; a demand or request for sexual favours; any other unwelcome physical, verbal/non-verbal conduct being sexual in nature. The critical factor is the unwelcomeness of the behaviour, thereby making the impact of such actions on the recipient more relevant rather than intent of the perpetrator. According to India's Constitution, sexual harassment infringes the Fundamental Right of a woman to gender equality under Article 14 of the Constitution of India and her right to life and live with dignity under Article 21 of the Constitution. Sexual harassment can occur in a variety of circumstances. Often, but not always, the harasser is in a position of power or authority over the victim (due to differences in age, or social, political, educational or employment relationships). Forms of harassment relationships include:

- The harasser can be anyone, such as a client, a co-worker, a teacher or professor, a student, a friend or a stranger.
- The victim does not have to be the person directly harassed but can be anyone who finds the behaviour offensive and is affected by it.
- While adverse effects on the victim are common, this does not have to be the case for the behaviour to be unlawful.
- The victim can be of any gender.
- The harasser does not have to be of the opposite sex.
- The harasser may be completely unaware that his or her behaviour is offensive or constitutes sexual harassment or may be completely unaware that his or her actions could be unlawful.[1]

One of the difficulties in understanding sexual harassment is that it involves a range of behaviour and is often difficult for the recipient to describe to themselves and to others, exactly what they are experiencing. Moreover, behaviour and motives vary between individual harassers.

For the first time sexual harassment had been explicitly-legally defined in India in *Vishaka v. State of Rajasthan and Others,*[2] as an unwelcome sexual gesture or behaviour whether directly or indirectly as

1. Sexually coloured remarks
2. Physical contact and advances
3. Showing pornography
4. A demand or request for sexual favours
5. Any other unwelcome physical, verbal/non-verbal conduct being sexual in nature.

It was in this landmark case that the sexual harassment was identified as a separate illegal behaviour. The critical factor in sexual harassment is the unwelcomeness of the behaviour. Thereby making the impact of such actions on the recipient more relevant rather than intent of the perpetrator – which is to be considered.

According to the General Recommendation of 1979, The Convention on Elimination of All Forms of Discrimination Against Women, (CEDAW) sexual harassment of women include: 'such unwelcome sexually determined behaviour as physical contact and advances, sexually coloured remarks, showing pornography and sexual demands, whether by words or actions. Such conduct can be humiliating and may constitute a health and safety problem; it is discriminatory when the woman has reasonable ground to believe that her objection would disadvantage her in connection with her employment, including recruitment or promotion, or when it creates a hostile working environment.' While such conduct can be harassment of women by men, many laws around the world which prohibit sexual harassment recognize that both men and women may be harassers or victims of sexual harassment. However, most claims of sexual harassment are made by women.[3]

Equal Employment Opportunity Commission (EEOC) Definition

In 1980, the Equal Employment Opportunity Commission (in 1984 it was expanded to include educational institutions) defined sexual harassment as:

Unwelcome sexual advances, requests for sexual favours, or other verbal or physical conduct of a sexual nature when:

1. Submission to such conduct was made, either explicitly or implicitly, a term or condition of an individual's employment,

2. Submission to or rejection of such conduct by an individual was used as the basis for employment decisions affecting such individual, or
3. Such conduct has the purpose or effect of unreasonably interfering with an individual's work performance or creating an intimidating, hostile, or offensive working environment.

Type 1 and 2 are called 'quid pro quo' (Latin for 'this for that' or 'something for something'). They are essentially 'sexual bribery' or promising of benefits and 'sexual coercion'.

Type 3, known as 'hostile work environment,' is by far the most common form. This form is less clear cut and is more subjective.

Quid Pro Quo Sexual Harassment

Quid pro quo means 'this for that'. In the workplace, this occurs when a job benefit is directly tied to an employee submitting to unwelcome sexual advances. For example, a supervisor promises an employee a raise if he or she will go out on a date with him or her, or tells an employee he or she will be fired if he or she doesn't sleep with him or her. Quid pro quo harassment also occurs when an employee makes an evaluative decision or provides or withholds professional opportunities based on another employee's submission to verbal, nonverbal or physical conduct of a sexual nature. Quid pro quo harassment is equally unlawful whether the victim resists and suffers the threatened harm or submits and thus avoids the threatened harm.

Hostile Environment Sexual Harassment

This occurs when an employee is subjected to comments of a sexual nature, unwelcome physical contact, or offensive sexual materials as a regular part of the work environment. For the most part, a single isolated incident will not be enough to prove hostile environment harassment unless it involves extremely outrageous and egregious conduct. The courts will try to decide whether the conduct is both 'serious' and 'frequent'. Supervisors, managers, co-workers and even customers can be responsible for creating a hostile environment.

The line between 'quid pro quo' and 'hostile environment' harassment is not always clear and the two forms of harassment often occur together. For example, an employee's job conditions are affected when a sexually hostile work environment results in a constructive discharge. At the same time, a supervisor who makes sexual advances towards a subordinate employee may communicate an implicit threat to retaliate against her if she does not comply.

'Hostile environment' harassment may acquire characteristics of 'quid pro quo' harassment if the offending supervisor abuses his authority over employment decisions to force the victim to endure or participate in the sexual conduct. Sexual harassment may culminate in a retaliatory discharge if a victim tells the harasser or her employer she will no longer submit to the harassment, and is then fired in retaliation for this protest.

Sexualized Environments (Environmental Harassment)

Sexualized environments are environments where obscenities, sexual joking, sexually explicit graffiti, viewing Internet pornography, sexually degrading posters and objects, etc. are common. None of these behaviours or objects may necessarily be directed at anyone in particular or intended as harassment. However, they can create an offensive environment, and one that is consistent with 'hostile environment sexual harassment'.

Retaliation and Backlash

Retaliation and backlash against a victim are very common, particularly a complainant. Victims who speak out against sexual harassment are often labelled troublemakers who are on their own power trips, or who are looking for attention. Similar to cases of rape or sexual assault, the victim often becomes the accused, with their appearance, private life, and character likely to fall under intrusive scrutiny and attack. They risk hostility and isolation from colleagues, supervisors, teachers, fellow students and even friends. They may become the targets of mobbing or relational aggression.

Retaliation occurs when an employee suffers a negative action after he or she has made a report of sexual harassment, file a grievance, assist someone else with a complaint, or participate in discrimination prevention activities. Negative actions can include being fired, demotion, suspension, denial of promotion, poor evaluation, unfavourable job re-assignment – any adverse employment decision or treatment that would be likely to dissuade a 'reasonable worker' from making or supporting a charge of discrimination. Moreover, a professor or employer accused of sexual harassment or who is a colleague of a perpetrator, can use their power to see that a victim is never hired again or never accepted in another school. Retaliation can even involve further sexual harassment, and also stalking and cyber stalking of the victim.

Existing Legal Provisions against Sexual Harassment in India

In a country which considers a female baby being born in the family as a bane to its economic position, harassment of women anywhere is not a surprising phenomenon. Owing to her 'incapacity' to fight out openly, she has been taken for granted in all the situations she faces. Law plays a very mild role in changing the position or the status of women. A number of legislations have been laid down with a fond hope of preventing the harassment of women in general and in workplaces, specifically.

The Indian Penal Code, 1860

In the IPC, there is not any specific chapter on 'offences against women' and, further, in India, there is not any criminal enactment which specifically defines the term 'sexual harassment'. The Honourable Apex Court of India ruled that the present civil and penal laws of India are not adequate to protect the women against sexual harassment at workplace. In Vishaka Case the Honourable court in guideline no. 3, observed that 'where such conduct amounts to a specific offence under the IPC or under any other law, the employer shall initiate appropriate action in accordance with law by making a complaint with the appropriate authority'.

Although there is no specific law against sexual harassment at workplace in India but many provisions in other legislations protect against sexual harassment at workplace, such as *Section 354, IPC,* deals with 'assault or criminal force to a woman with the intent to outrage her modesty' and *Section 509, IPC,* deals with 'word, gesture or act intended to insult the modesty of a woman'.

Some forms of sexual harassment constitute criminal acts and can be prosecuted as such rape, outraging the modesty of women, obscenity, etc. Sections 354 and 509 of the IPC cover the conduct or behaviour which is included in definition of sexual harassment in Vishaka. The above definition is not an exhaustive one and it is inclusive in nature. It does not eliminate the possibility of other serious acts or conducts of sexual harassment being covered under offences that are already defined in the IPC which deal with sexual harassment are as such:

Section 354. Assault or criminal force to woman with intent to outrage her modesty: Whoever assaults or uses criminal force to any woman, intending to outrage or knowing it to be likely that he will there by outrage her modesty, shall be punished with imprisonment of either description for a term which may extend to two years or with fine or with both.

Section 354 deals with the assault or criminal force to a woman, committed with the intent to outrage her modesty. Under Section 354 an offence is committed when:

1. There is assault or criminal use of force on a woman and
2. Assault or use of criminal force is either with the intention to outrage the modesty of a woman or
3. The person, who uses assault or criminal force, must know that he will thereby outrage the modesty of woman.

The offence under this section is cognizable, bailable, compoundable with the permission of the court before which any prosecution of the said offence is pending and triable by any Magistrate. The Supreme Court held that in order to constitute the offence under Section 354, the reaction of the woman concerned is not the test of the offence.

Section 509. Word, gesture or act intended to insult the modesty of a woman: Whoever, intending to insult the modesty of any woman, utters any word, makes any sound or gesture or exhibits any object, intending that such word or sound shall be heard or that such gesture or object shall be seen, by such woman or intrudes upon the privacy of such woman, shall be punished with simple imprisonment for a term which may extend to one year or with fine or with both.

This section deals with words, gestures or acts aimed at insulting the modesty of women. The essentials of the section are:

1. Where the offender utters a word, makes any sound or gesture or exhibits any object.
2. With the intent that it be heard or seen, intrudes upon the privacy of such woman commits the offence. To prove offence under Section 509, it is clear that the intention must be to insult the modesty of some particular woman or women, and not only any class or section of women. As Justice Sarkar said 'intention and knowledge.'

In *Sau. Anuradha R. Kshirsagar and others v. State of Maharashtra and others*[4] the Bombay High Court Single Bench, consisting Justice M.S. Ratnaparkhi, delivered judgment regarding an incident of misbehaviour with lady teachers at the workplace. As per the case, a meeting of teachers including lady teachers was convened on a particular date and time. The accused, himself a teacher and a union worker, was standing outside the door of the hall. The accused wanted the lady teachers sitting inside the hall to come outside the hall so that the meeting could not continue, but when the lady teachers did not leave the room, he uttered the words as catch them with their hair, kick them on the waist, pull them out, etc. The complainant charged the accused of insulting the modesty of women teachers under Section 509 of the IPC and the accused was sentenced to simple imprisonment for two months and fine of ₹ 200 or in case of default simple imprisonment for one month.

In appeal, the Additional Sessions Judge came to the conclusion that the word further uttered by the accused do not make out an offence under Section 509, IPC. Allowing the appeal, he quashed the order of conviction and sentence passed by the Magistrate. The Hon'ble High Court ruled that the utterances of the accused have nothing to do with the modesty of women. These are the common offences vis-à-vis a female or a male. The High Court found him guilty under Section 506 of the IPC.

The term modesty is not defined in the IPC. Only Section 10 says that woman denotes a female human being of any age. The term 'modesty' is the disposition common to both Sections 354 and 509 of the IPC. The question, what is modesty, arose before a three-Judge Bench of the Supreme Court in *State of Punjab v. Major Singh.*[5] According to the majority view, the act of outraging the modesty of a woman was not limited by the age of the victim and whether the victim knew or was conscious about the offensive act being committed on her. According to Justice Bachawat, essence of a woman's modesty is her sex. The modesty of an adult female is writ large on her body. Young or old, intelligent or imbecile, awake or sleeping, the woman possesses modesty capable of being outraged. Whoever uses criminal force with intent to outrage her modesty commits an offence punishable under Section 354. The culpable intention of the accused is the crux of the matter. The reaction of the woman is very relevant, but its absence is not always decisive, as, for example, when the accused with a corrupt mind stealthily touches the flesh of a sleeping woman. She may be an idiot, she may be under the spell of anaesthesia, she may be sleeping, she may be unable to appreciate the significance of the act; nevertheless, the offender is punishable under the section. Justice A.K. Sarkar observed that the test of outraging of modesty must, therefore, be whether a reasonable man will think that the act of the offender was intended to or was known to be likely to outrage the modesty of the woman. In considering the question, he must imagine a woman to be a reasonable woman and keep in view all the circumstances concerning her, such as her status and way of life and the known notion of modesty of such of woman.

In *Rupan Deol Bajaj v. KPS Gill,*[6] the Supreme Court held that the unlimited test for ascertaining whether modesty has been outraged is that the action of the offender could be perceived as one which is capable of shocking the sense of decency of a women. When the above test is applied in the present case, keeping in view the total facts situation, it can but be held that the alleged act of Mr Gill in slapping Mrs Bajaj on her posterior amounted to 'outrage of the modesty' for it was not only an affront to the normal sense of feminine decency but also an affront to the dignity of the lady – 'sexual overtones' or not withstanding.

In *Sau. Anuradha R. Kshirsagar and others v. State of Maharashtra and others*[7] the court said that modesty of a woman is intimately connected with the feminity, including her sex. Catching the hair of woman, kicking on her waist, pulling her out or giving threats has nothing to do with the feminity and, consequently, it has nothing to do with the modesty of a woman.

Under Section 350 of the IPC, 'a person is said to use criminal force when he uses force on another person either to commit an offence or knowing that it will cause injury, fear or annoyance to another person.' For instance:

1. While passing by in a work place, if a male colleague lifts or drags or moves clothes worn by a woman (e.g. dupatta, saree, scarf, shawl, etc.) knowing that he is, thereby, likely to frighten, injure or annoy her, he has used criminal force.
2. If a woman is moving in a rickshaw or car and something is thrown upon her, or the movement of the vehicle is obstructed, it shall also amount to use of criminal force.
3. In the event of sexual harassment, criminal force is used if anything the woman is wearing or has in her possession, is moved or its state is altered or modified to intimidate or annoy her.
4. Leaving an intimidating/annoying message on the computer she works at, on the wall of her office or on the official documents she deals with or forwarding any intimidating or annoying message to her mobile phone shall also amount to use of criminal force. Unnecessarily inspecting her private or official documents or compelling her to give explanations unnecessarily coupled with overt or covert demands for sexual favours will fall in the range of the section.

Law Commission of India in its 172nd Report[8] on 'Review of Rape Laws 2000' recommended to insert Section 376E to cover a wide variety of offences including sexual harassment at work place and sexual perversions. Sub-section (1) of this new section covers touching, directly or indirectly, with a part of the body or with an object, any part of the body of another person (not being the spouse of such person), with sexual intent and without the consent of such other person. In case the other person is below sixteen years of age, we have recommended higher punishment. Sub-section (2) is an extension or elaboration of the offence mentioned in Sub-section (1), while Sub-section (3) deals with a case where such offence is committed on a young person – young person being defined by the Explanation to mean a person below the age of sixteen years. If the offence of unlawful sexual contact is committed on a young person by a person with whom such young person is in a relationship of dependency, the punishment is rigorous imprisonment which may extend to seven years or with fine or with both and in case the offender happens to be the father, grandfather or brother, a still higher punishment is provided for. In the case of a young person, consent is treated as irrelevant. Under Section 376E-Unlawful Sexual Contact (1) Whoever, with sexual intent, touches, directly or indirectly, with a part of the body or with an object, any part of the body of another person, not being the spouse of such person, without the consent of such other person, shall be punished with simple imprisonment for a term which may extend to two years or with fine or with both. (2) Whoever, with sexual intent, invites, counsels or incites a young person to touch, directly or indirectly, with a part of the body or with an object, the body of any person, including the body of the person who so invites, counsels or incites or touches, with sexual intent, directly or indirectly, with a part of the body or with an object any part of the body of a young person, shall be punished with imprisonment of either description which may extend to three years and shall also be liable to fine. (3) Whoever, being in a position of trust or authority towards a young person or is a person with whom the young person is in a relationship of dependency, touches, directly or indirectly, with sexual intent, with a part of the body or with an object, any part of the body of such young person, shall be punished with imprisonment of either description which may extend to seven years and shall also be liable to fine. Explanation: 'Young person' in this Sub-section and Sub-section (2) means a person below the age of sixteen years.'

Industrial Disputes Act

Rule 5 Schedule 5: Cases can be (and have been) argued on the basis of unfair labour practices listed in this schedule. Such cases can be filed if an employee suffers unfair dismissal or denial of employment benefits as a consequence of the rejection of sexual advances. However, this would only be applicable in quid pro quo cases.

Shehnaz Mudbhatkal v. Saudi Arabian Airlines: Shehnaz was subjected to sexual harassment by her boss in 1985, and dismissed when she complained to higher authorities. Her case was won in 1996 when the Bombay labour court judged it to have been a case of unfair dismissal under the Industrial Disputes Act. It ordered her re-instatement with full back payment, perks and promotions.

Civil suit: This can be filed for damages under tort laws. That is, the basis for filing the case would be mental anguish, physical harassment, loss of income and employment caused by sexual harassment.

The Indecent Representation of Women (Prohibition) Act (1987)

Although it is not known to have been used in cases of sexual harassment, the provisions of this act have the potential to be used in two ways. First, if an individual harasses another with books, photographs, paintings, films, pamphlets, packages, etc. containing 'indecent representation of women'; they are liable for a minimum sentence of two years. Second, a 'hostile working environment' type of argument can be made under this act. Section 7 (Offences by Companies) holds companies where there has been 'indecent representation of women' (such as the display of pornography) on the premises, guilty of offenses under this act (cognizable, bailable offense; with a minimum sentence of two years).

Sexual Harassment of Woman at Workplace and Judicial Response

In India, there is a notable gap between the *de jure* and *de facto* situation of women. Flavia Agnes, a noted lawyer and woman activist, says, '*the power balance is not fair, with the senior harassing you, and even the colleagues do not often lend active support. Women prefer to change jobs for the environment may get hostile*'. A recent case is that of Alka Pande (name changed), ex-director of KPMG, one of the country's leading consultancy firms. She had filed a complaint with the National Commission for Women (NCW) for sexual harassment against two of the firm's senior partners. She has also alleged that once she drew the firm's attention to their misconduct, she was denied, 'avenues of promotion, and her clients were taken away from her'. Alka's case isn't isolated. Sexual harassment at workplace is commonplace.

In *Rupan Deol Bajaj Vs. K.P.S. Gill,*[9] a senior IAS officer, Rupan Bajaj was slapped on the posterior by the then Chief of Police, Punjab, K.P.S. Gill, at a dinner party in July 1988. Rupan Bajaj filed a suit against him, despite the public opinion that she was blowing it out of proportion, along with the attempts by all the senior officials of the state to suppress the matter. The Supreme Court in January, 1998, fined K.P.S. Gill ₹ 2.5 lakh in lieu of three months rigorous imprisonment under Sections 294 and 509 of the Indian Penal Code.

In *N. Radhabai Vs. D. Ramchandran,*[10] when Radhabai, Secretary to D. Ramchandran, the then social minister for state, protested against his abuse of girls in the welfare institutions, he attempted to molest her, which was followed by her dismissal. The Supreme Court in 1995 passed the judgment in her favour, with back pay and perks from the date of dismissal.

In *Vishaka Vs. State of Rajasthan and others,*[11] the judgment was delivered by J.S. Verma, the Chief Justice, on behalf of Sujata Manohar and B.N. Kirpal, JJ., on a writ petition filed by 'Vishaka', a non-governmental organization working for gender equality by way of PIL seeking enforcement of fundamental rights of working women under Article 21 of the Constitution. The immediate cause for filing the petition was the alleged brutal gang rape of a social worker of Rajasthan. The Supreme Court, in absence of any enacted law (which still remains absent – save the Supreme Court guidelines as stated hereunder), to provide for effective enforcement of basic human rights of gender equality and guarantee against sexual harassment, laid down the following guidelines:

1. All the employers in charge of work place whether in the public or the private sector, should take appropriate steps to prevent sexual harassment without prejudice to the generality of his obligation, he should take the following steps:
   (i) Express prohibition of sexual harassment which includes physical contact and advances, a demand or request for sexual favours, sexually coloured remarks, showing pornographic or any other unwelcome physical, verbal/non-verbal conduct of sexual nature should be noticed, published and circulated in appropriate ways.
   (ii) The rules and regulations of government and public sector bodies relating to conduct and discipline should include rules prohibiting sexual harassment and provide for appropriate penalties in such rules against the offender.

(iii) As regards private employers, steps should be taken to include the aforesaid prohibitions in the Standing Orders under the Industrial Employment (Standing Orders) Act, 1946.

(iv) Appropriate work conditions should be provided in respect of work leisure, health, hygiene – to further ensure that there is no hostile environment towards women and no woman should have reasonable grounds to believe that she is disadvantaged in connection with her employment.

2. Where such conduct amounts to specific offences under the Indian Penal Code or any other law, the employer shall initiate appropriate action in accordance with the law, by making a complaint with the appropriate authority.
3. Victims of sexual harassment should have the option to seek transfer of the perpetrator or their own transfer.

As stated by the Supreme Court, these guidelines are applicable to:

1. The employer or other responsible persons or other institutions to prevent sexual harassment and to provide procedures for the resolution of complaints;
2. Women who either draw a regular salary, receive an honorarium, or work in a voluntary capacity in government, private or organized sector come under the purview of these guidelines.

Preventive steps:

1. Express prohibition of sexual harassment should be notified and circulated.
2. Inclusion of prohibition of sexual harassment in the rules and regulations of government and public sector.
3. Inclusion of prohibition of sexual harassment in the standing orders under the Industrial Employment (Standing Orders) Act, 1946 by the private employers.
4. Provision should be made for appropriate work conditions for women.

Procedure pertaining to filing of complaints:

1. Employers must provide a Complaints Committee which is to be headed by a woman and of which half members should be women.
2. Complaints Committee should also include an NGO or other organization, which is familiar with sexual harassment.
3. Complaints procedure should be time bound.
4. Confidentiality of the complaints procedure has to be maintained.
5. Complainant or witnesses should not be victimized or discriminated against while dealing with complaints.

6. The Committee should make an annual report to the concerned government department and also inform of the action (if any) taken so far by them.

Miscellaneous provisions:

1. Guidelines should be prominently notified to create awareness as regards the rights of the female employees.
2. The employers should assist the persons affected, in cases of sexual harassment by outsiders or third parties.
3. Sexual harassment should be discussed at workers' meetings, employer-employee meetings and at other appropriate forums.
4. Both Central and State governments are required to adopt measures, including legislations to ensure that private employers also observe these guidelines.

The Court emphasized that the guidelines and norms being laid down by it had to be duly observed at all workplaces or other institutions until a legislation is enacted for this purpose and that these should be treated as law under Article 141 of the Constitution. These guidelines are in accordance with the recommendations and conventions of various international organizations like the ILO and the European Communities Commission.

Apparel Export Promotion Council v. A.K. Chopra[12] is the first case in which the Supreme Court applied the law laid down in Vishaka's case and upheld the dismissal of a superior officer of the Delhi-based Apparel Export Promotion Council who was found guilty of sexual harassment of a subordinate female employee at the place of work on the ground that it violated her fundamental right guaranteed by Article 21 of the Constitution.

The Supreme Court has held in Apparel Export Promotion Council v. A.K. Chopra, that in any case involving charge of sexual harassment or attempt to sexually molest, the courts are required to examine the broader probabilities of the case and not get swayed by insignificant discrepancies or narrow technicalities or the dictionary meaning of the expression 'molestation'. The Court also held that the statement of the victim must be appreciated in the background of the entire case.

In both cases, the Supreme Court observed, that *'In cases involving Human Rights, the Courts must be alive to the International Conventions and Instruments as far as possible to give effect to the principles contained therein – such as the Convention on the Eradication of All forms of Discrimination Against Women, 1979 (CEDAW) and the Beijing Declaration directing all state parties to take appropriate measures to prevent such discrimination.'*

These guidelines and judgments have identified sexual harassment as a question of power exerted by the perpetrator on the victim. Therefore, sexual harassment, in addition to being a violation of the right to safe working conditions, is also a violation of the right to bodily integrity of the woman.

In *U.S. Verma, Principal and Delhi Public School Society vs. National Commission for Women and Ors.,*[13] two teachers, Jayashree Kannan and Shayista Raza, and a former receptionist Shirni Kaul accused the principal of Delhi Public School, Faridabad, U.S. Verma, of vindictiveness because they spurned his sexual advances. The teachers resigned, accusing U.S. Verma of spreading canards against them and scuttling their job prospects.

In *Dr Salma Khatoon vs. Secretary, Government of India, Department of Ayush and Ors.*[14] the guidelines placed in Vishakha's Case were referred again.

Recent Development in Legal Scenario

3 September 2012 became a red letter day when Lok Sabha passed the *Sexual Harassment of Women at Workplace (Prevention, Prohibition and Redressal) Bill, 2010*, without any discussion. The Bill introduced by women and child development minister Krishna Tirath and approved by the Union Cabinet in 2010, covers women workers in the unorganized sector that employs less than 10 people where service rules are not applied. This includes domestic helps also.[15] The case of *Vishakha v. State of Rajasthan* led to the formulation of the *Protection of Women against Sexual Harassment at Workplace Bill, 2010* to ensure a safe environment for women at work places, both in public and private sectors whether organized or unorganized.[16] This measure will help in achieving gender empowerment and equality.

The Bill provides for some stern measures to curb the menace of sexual harassment of women as the proposed Bill, if enacted, will ensure that women are protected against sexual harassment at all the work places, be it in public or private. This will contribute to realization of their right to gender equality, life and liberty and equality in working conditions everywhere. The sense of security at the workplace will improve women's participation in work, resulting in their economic empowerment and inclusive growth.

Salient features of the Bill are as follows:

- The Bill proposes a definition of sexual harassment, which is as laid down by the Hon'ble Supreme Court in Vishaka v. State of Rajasthan (1997).

- The Bill defines sexual harassment as any act of verbal or gestural sexual advances, sexually explicit or derogatory remarks or statements, unwelcome sexually determined behaviour such as avoidable physical contact and advances, touching, patting, whistling, pinching, staring, sexually slanting and obscene jokes, suggestive remarks, compromising invitation, use of pornographic material, demand for sexual favours, threats, innuendoes, physical assault and molestation. Additionally, it recognizes the promise or threat to a woman's employment prospects or creation of hostile work environment as 'sexual harassment' at workplace and expressly seeks to prohibit such acts.
- Staring and simple comments on the physical appearance of female colleagues can land a man behind bars for as many as five years and with a fine of ₹ 20,000.
- The Bill provides protection not only to women who are employed but also to any woman who enters the workplace as a client, customer, apprentice, and daily wage worker or in ad-hoc capacity. Students, research scholars in colleges/university and patients in hospitals have also been covered. Further, the Bill seeks to cover workplaces in the unorganized sectors.
- The Bill provides for an effective complaints and redressal mechanism. Under the proposed Bill, every employer is required to constitute an Internal Complaints Committee. Since a large number of the establishments (41.2 million out of 41.83 million as per Economic Census, 2005) in our country have less than 10 workers for whom it may not be feasible to set up an Internal Complaints Committee (ICC), the Bill provides for setting up of Local Complaints Committee (LCC) to be constituted by the designated District Officer at the district or sub-district levels, depending upon the need. This twin mechanism would ensure that women in any workplace, irrespective of its size or nature, have access to a redressal mechanism. The LCCs will inquire into the complaints of sexual harassment and recommend action to the employer or District Officer.
- Employers who fail to comply with the provisions of the proposed Bill will be punishable with a fine which may extend to ₹ 50,000.
- Since there is a possibility that during the pendency of the enquiry the woman may be subject to threat and aggression, she has been given the option to seek interim relief in the form of transfer either of her own or the respondent or seek leave from work.

- The Complaint Committees are required to complete the inquiry within 90 days and a period of 60 days has been given to the employer/District Officer for implementation of the recommendations of the Committee.
- The Bill provides for safeguards in case of false or malicious complaint of sexual harassment. However, mere inability to substantiate the complaint or provide adequate proof would not make the complainant liable for punishment.

The passing of Bill has received criticisms also, it is apprehended that landlords who employ more than 10 agricultural workers would be outside the ambit of the law. It is also alleged that the Bill does not cover women in the armed forces. Lawyer-activist Vrinda Grover said, 'I hope the Bill does not have provisions for penalizing the complainant for false complaints. This is the most under-reported crime. Such provision will deter a woman to come forward and complain.'[17]

Implementation of the Bill will be the responsibility of the Central Government in case of its own undertakings/establishments and of the State governments in respect of every workplace established, owned, controlled or wholly or substantially financed by it as well as of private sector establishments falling within their territory. Besides, the State and Central governments will oversee implementation as the proposed Bill casts a duty on the employers to include a report on the number of cases filed and disposed of in their Annual Report. Organizations which do not prepare Annual Reports would forward this information to the District Officer.

Through this implementation mechanism, every employer has the primary duty to implement the provisions of law within his/her establishment while the State and Central governments have been made responsible for overseeing and ensuring overall implementation of the law. The governments will also be responsible for maintaining data on the implementation of the Law. In this manner, the Bill will create an elaborate system of reporting and checks and balances, which will result in effective implementation of the Law.

Conclusion

India is rapidly advancing towards its developmental goals and more and more women are joining the workforce. It is the duty of the state to provide for the well-being and respect of its citizens to prevent frustration, low self-esteem, insecurity and emotional disturbance, which, in turn, could affect business efficacy, leading to loss of production and loss of reputation for the organization or the employer.

In fact, the recognition of the right to protection against sexual harassment is an intrinsic component of the protection of women's human rights. It is also a step towards providing women independence, equality of opportunity and the right to work with dignity. For any sexual harassment law to be successful in India, it is important to be aware of the difficulties confronting our society and ways to overcome them. We all know that India is a patriarchal society and most cases of sexual harassment remain unreported. Women are reluctant to complain and prefer silence due to lack of sensitivity on the part of Indian society. There is a need to gender-sensitize our society so that the victim does not feel guilty and is encouraged to report any form of harassment. The victim's privacy must be protected. The police and the judiciary, in particular, also need to be gender-sensitized. There should be speedy redressal and an increase in the conviction rate. Women themselves should be made aware of their right to a safe and harassment-free work environment.

In any civilized society, it is the fundamental right of people to be able to lead their lives with dignity, free from mental or physical torture. To ensure this, transgressors must pay for their unsolicited sexual advances. To effectively prevent Sexual Harassment of Women we need both a top-down initiative by the state and employers and civil society initiatives from citizens' groups, women's organizations and trade unions.

In the words of Swami Vivekananda, 'Country and Nation which do not respect women have never become great nor will ever be in future.' It should be borne in mind by the Indian employers that workplaces are an integral part of the country and it becomes the duty of every employer to make sure that the women employees are in a comfortable and cordial atmosphere in the workplace to ensure peaceful and progressive functioning. With the passing of this Sexual Harassment of Women at Workplace (Prevention, Prohibition and Redressal) Act, 2013, it is hoped that there will certainly be a decrease in the number of cases of sexual harassment as this will prove itself to be a strong weapon in the hands of women to prevent sexual harassment and combat it.

Notes

1. R. Heyman, *Why Didn't You Say That in the First Place?*, San Francisco: Jossey-Bass Publishers, 1994.

2. AIR 1997 SC 3011.
3. US Equal Employment Opportunity Commission Statistics.
4. 1991 Cri. L.J. 410.
5. AIR 1967 SC 63.
6. (1995) 6SCC194.
7. Supra note 5.
8. http://www.lawcommissionofindia.nic.in
9. 1998 SC.
10. 1995 SC.
11. AIR 1997 SC 3011.
12. AIR 1999 SC 625.
13. 163 (2009) DLT557.
14. MANU/DE/1468/2010.
15. http://articles.timesofindia.indiatimes.com/2012–09–04/india
16. *The Hindustan Times*, LKO Edition, Monday, 21 June 2010, p. 8.
17. http://articles.timesofindia.indiatimes.com/2012–09–04/india

10

Globalization, Migration and Trafficking of Women in Odisha

SUBASH RANJAN NAYAK

Globalization is synonymous to the phenomenon of acceleration. From last 17 years, rapid changes have been taking place in terms of social developments and in the political and economic sector. Acceleration is seen in vast technological changes, media revolution, global economic integration and massive changes in production systems and labour markets. All these rapid increases in transnational flow of capital, trade and technology have marked its effects on migration as well. Global economic restructuring has led not only to disruption in less developed or developing economies, it has also been a factor in unemployment, wage decline or job insecurity in dominant market economies.[1] Nowadays it is noticeable that migration has been impacted by globalization of technology especially communication technology. Telephone and fax have replaced what used to be snail-pace letter communication. Relation between immigrant communities abroad and home communities have been facilitated by these new possibilities. The globalization of mass communication, including TV, film, video and music has reinforced dreams of easy life abroad. This lifestyle reaches even to peasants in remote villages and due to all these things migration becomes very attractive and promising to them.

Earlier studies in migration have ignored the role of gender. The presence of women was usually attached to family reunification, hence dependent upon husband. After globalization, trends however show that women are migrating independently. New migratory flows are no longer male-dominated. There is growing demand for female labour and new social needs have created a demand for services in which only immigrant women are prepared to work. There exists a division of labour – structured activities in a society are gendered. Not only do men and women undertake different tasks, but women are responsible for activities in the domestic sphere. These different tasks are the basis for the social construction of gender in which women are excluded from some activities, confined to others, dependent on males, docile, subservient and assigned secondary status in the labour market.[2] They often take up the menial and low-paid occupations, with particularly difficult working conditions. Generally it is found that women migrants are working in sweet shops, as domestic servants, as entertainers, thereby exposing them to sexual exploitation. Women migrants face degradation due to stereotypes that devalue women and women's work. Women migrants are vulnerable to gender-related violence like rape, sexual harassment and physical abuse. One of the other serious global problems no doubt is trafficking. This paper is an attempt to give a clear picture of the super-cyclone of 1999, which upturned the lives of many villagers and proved to be a happy hunting ground for the middle men or *dalals*/pimps to carry on trafficking. The traffickers pursue the gullible and helpless parents to give away their daughters on the assurance of finding suitable grooms. After trafficking them from their parents' house, these helpless girls were tortured both physically and psychologically in an inhuman manner. Hence, trafficking of women is a major incident now-a-days through which the suffering of women has increased manifold.

However, trafficking is perhaps most complicated by its link to migration. Various researches show that most of the women who are trafficked have a strong desire to migrate and are, thereby, abused in the process. Women desire to migrate often because there is abuse in the community or because of dire poverty. To counter trafficking by preventing women's migration is to lock them into domestic system of oppression. Measures taken to prevent women from migrating such as requiring permission of male members of the family or government sanction actually compound the problem.

The growth of economies and transnational criminal networks in states are negative effects of globalization, arising from expanding economic, political and social transnational linkage that are increasingly beyond local and state control. An important component of globalization is the transnational linkages created by migration. Increased migration also serves as a cover for traffickers in transporting women to destinations in the sex industry. Privatization and liberalization of markets have created wider and more open marketplaces throughout the world. Another important component of globalization is computer communication of international crime, which decreases the probability of detection and apprehensions. This technological aspect of globalization enables the money gained through illegal activities, like trafficking in women, to be transferred and laundered.

Trafficking, the selling of women and adolescent girls for monetary profit, most often leading to bonded prostitution, has been a burning issue in India. It is very difficult to explain with reliable data that trafficking of women and children takes place along the path of undocumented migration. Data collection is notoriously difficult. Owing to the clandestine nature of women and child trafficking, it is very difficult to count the number of women and children victimized by the practice. Moreover, even in places where prostitution is openly practiced, the participation of women and adolescent girls in the industry are often concealed making it difficult to count women and adolescent girl sex workers. Many women and adolescent girls in the commercial sex industry lie about their age to authorities and use fake identity cards. The purposes of trafficking not only include prostitution, debt bondage, and domestic labour, but also the 'trafficking of children as slave labourers, child soldiers, camel jockeys and sex slaves'.

Trafficking of humans involves moving men, women, and children from one place to another placing them in conditions of forced labour. The practice includes forced sex work, domestic servitude, unsafe agricultural labour, sweet shop labour, construction or restaurant work and several violations of human rights occur within countries and across borders, region and continents.

'Trafficking in persons' includes recruitment, transportation, transfer, harboring or the holding of persons by mean of threats or use of force or other forms of coercion, abduction, fraud, deception, the abuse of power or a position of vulnerability or of the giving or receiving of payments or benefits to achieve the content of a person having control over another person for the purpose of exploitation.

Definition

The word 'trafficking' does not have a single, universal definition, resulting in different numbers of women being counted for each different definition of the term used. In writing and analysing, 'trafficking is any practice that involves moving people within and across local or national borders for the purpose of sexual exploitation'.

Trafficking may be the result of force, coercion, manipulation, deception, abuse of authority, initial consent, family pressure, past and present family and community violence, economic deprivation or other conditions of inequality for women and children (Hughes, 2000).

The United Nations Protocol on Trafficking in Persons, adopted in November 2000, defines trafficking as: 'the recruitment, transportation, transfer, harboring or receipt of persons, by means of the threat or use of force or other forms of coercion, of abduction, of fraud, or deception, of the abuse of power or of a position of vulnerability or of the giving or receiving of payments or benefits to achieve the consent of a person having control over another person, for the purpose of exploitation. Exploitation shall include, at a minimum, the exploitation of the prostitution of others or other forms of sexual exploitation, forced labour or services, slavery or practices similar to slavery, servitude or the removal of organs'.

Facilitating Factors of Trafficking

The dramatic growth in migration and trafficking flows has resulted from a combination of push, pull and facilitating factors. Push factors include uneven economic growth and the breakdown of economic systems, environmental degradation, natural disasters, and increasing levels of family violence. Gender inequality and discrimination in many countries means burden of poverty and the impact of violence disproportionately on women, causing a growing migration of women from poor countries and other areas. Many of these women are particularly vulnerable and end up being trafficked.

At the same time, economic growth, relative prosperity and peace in industrialized and newly industrializing countries act as 'pull' factors. Growing economies create increased demand for imported labour as citizens increasingly refuse to take low-paying jobs. Young women are in particular demand because they are regarded as more compliant and less likely to rebel against substandard working conditions. Some are pulled into migration by the prospect of marriage and a better life abroad. Growth in the industrialized economies has been accompanied by a quantum leap in low-cost transportation and communication technologies, which facilitates all aspects of migration and trafficking.

Changes in both the supply of and demand for female labour, partly due to changes in gender roles in industrialized and developing countries, have also increased the proportion of women and children in migration streams and therefore of women and adolescent girls being trafficked. On the supply side, would-be migrants may be pushed to leave their areas of origin by poverty or lack of economic opportunity. Globalization has had both winners and losers, slashing economic opportunities in rural areas and in poor countries that are not competitive in the global marketplace. Women are often most affected by loss of employment, whether directly or indirectly when male family members lose their jobs, increasing the pressure on them to emigrate in search of work.

Major changes in fashion and media trends are also one of major causes of trafficking. Women exposed to this type of culture think 'maximum profit in minimum loss' and such women make little effort to lead luxurious life.

The demand for trafficked labour has also increased. Too often this has been seen solely as a demand for prostitution and other forms of sexual exploitation. However, globalization has also created a growing demand for cheap, low-skilled labour in both developed and developing countries in agriculture, food processing, construction, domestic service, labour-intensive manufacturing, home health care, sex work and the service sector in general.

Theoretical Orientation

Prostitution, sale and purchase of girls, the trafficking and transhipment, sexual slavery and other related issues have been found to have existed at all times and virtually at all places. References have been made in the local literatures about such issues and history has also testified many such records. It is difficult to make any claims about the magnitude of this issue especially when it comes to the commodification of girls and their transhipment for the purpose of sexual exploitation. It is only now that we have some staggering figures that have been made available to us by several government, non-profit agencies and the media (Mallik, 2004). However, any attempt at situating the issue within the sociological context must consider some of the existing theories. These theories are Feminist, Marxist, and Functional.

Feminists believes that gender is the organized pattern of social relations between women and men, not only in face-to-face interactions and within the family but also in the major institutions of society, such as social classes, the hierarchies of large scale organizations and other occupational structure. The social reproduction of gender in individuals sustains the gendered social structure. It is argued that in most society women and men are not only perceived as different but are also differently evaluated and these supposed differences in characteristics and capabilities justify power differences. Its opponents argue that in all societies, the belief that women and men are inherently different provides the moral justification for allocating certain kinds of work to women and men and for relegating the rearing of children to women. Religion, language, education and culture teach and reinforce the society's values for women and men. The result is gendered moral order. This gendered moral order is sustained by 'gender identity' and 'gender differentiations'. Gender identity refers to the way in which people view themselves along feminine/masculine lines. Gender role differentiations, however, is fairly universal across societies. Men and women are assigned different behaviours, tasks, rights, obligations, privileges and resources (ibid.). Besides gender, patriarchy has often been used as an essential category of analysis through which the nature of girl/women's oppression, both theoretical and social, has been mirrored.

Marx and Engels in their work 'Capital: A critique of political economy' referred to some abstract recognition of the humiliation of women in modern society in some of the early works. They specifically mention the suffering of proletarian women with the disintegration of the proletarian families and with the problem of prostitution (Sinha, 1987). According to Marxist theory, one can explain the issue in terms of exploitation of proletariat by the bourgeoisie, feudal mindset of the economically well off sections and commodification of the 'other' sex as part of the globalization of market forces. Thus, the demand side is domain of the 'haves' (the bourgeoisie) and supply side of the 'have nots' (the proletariat). And it is this tilted relation of power in favour of the bourgeoisie that propels, sustains and governs this illicit trade in girl child and women trafficking. Besides the bourgeoisie, proletariat polarity that has been employed here, alienation of a large section of society is argued to be the primary force (Mallik, 2004). Marx stressed that the capitalist economic system, rather than industrialization as such, is the primary source of alienation. It is a system, he argued, of maximization of profit rather than the satisfaction of real human needs. Trapped within the system, both capitalists and workers are alienated from there true selves. Members of both groups are preoccupied with self-interest in a system, which sets man against man in a struggle for survival.

Functional theory emerged in the 19th century as a result of an analogy: society is like a biological organism, and hence its part can be analysed in terms of their functions for maintaining the body social.[3] Prominent among the theories that are said to exist within the discourse of functionalism are those of Anomie and Deviance. For sociologist *anomie* is most frequently associated with Emile Durkheim.

Durkheim (1984) used the French word *anomie*, meaning 'without norms', to describe the disruption that societies experienced in the shift from an agrarian, village economy to one based on industry. It has been referred to as a state of society and not of individuals, although individuals were affected by these forces. By this, Durkheim didn't mean to imply literal normlessness but rather a state of relative normative disorder. Robert K. Merton's use of 'anomie' is very similar to that described by Durkheim. Merton (1949) used the concept of anomie to describe how social structure produced individual deviance. According to him, when there existed within a society a disjuncture between the legitimate goals that members of a society are to aspire to and the legitimate way of achieving these goals, then that society was in a state of *anomie*. For Durkheim and Merton, frustrated aspirations were important cause of norm violation and deviance (Mallik, 2004). It would be simplistic to argue that girl child and women trafficking is abetted or is resultant primarily of *anomie* or deviance or both, it would also be extremely naïve to conclude that there is no *anomie* or deviance in the Indian society and that it has no role to play in fuelling and sustaining the issue under present concern. In fact, if one looks at the places of origin and destinations of girl child trafficking, a state of relative anomie and subsequent deviance can easily be cited.

It can be claimed henceforth that no single approach can be employed to understand the problem of trafficking. Yet all three approaches are having appropriate standpoints to approximate the problem. Gender identity and patriarchy (Feminist), alienation and capital mindset (Marxist), *anomie* and deviance (Functionalists), all have a role to play in creating fertile grounds for trafficking problem. They also assist in sustaining and further promoting trafficking business.

Trafficking in Odisha after Super Cyclone (October 1999)

Odisha is one of the most resource-rich states in the country. The state is endowed with vast natural resources, minerals, marine, agricultural and forest wealth. Still, today Odisha is considered as the poorest state of India with 47.08 per cent (Orissa Human Development report, 2004) living below the line of poverty. There is also wide regional variations existing as obstacles towards the development of Odisha. Odisha is one of the less developed states in India and poverty in Odisha perpetuates due to prevalence of frequent floods, cyclones and droughts etc. People living below poverty line in the state are further impoverished due to the adverse ecological situation. Furthermore, women are always at the receiving end. The electronic and print media reveals that many girls and women are trafficked every year from coastal, border and tribal areas of Odisha. The super cyclone of October 1999 had a tremendous impact on the growth of trafficking of women in Odisha. The worst affected districts have been Balasore, Bhadrak, Jagatsinghpur, Kendrapara and Khurda. Thousands of Odisha's mariginalized women and adolescent girls became widowed, homeless and helpless. Many have been pushed into forced marriage and prostitution. Women became vulnerable to trafficking by the traffickers or by local pimps. After being trafficked, they are forced into domestic labour, begging, industrial labour, etc. but are largely used for prostitution. Besides poverty and illiteracy, natural disasters and their wake, unemployment, an adverse impact of the electronic media and consumerism are some of the other factors responsible for the increase in trafficking of women in Odisha.

The state of Odisha's involvement in this trade, growing in scale and complexity, was highlighted after the super-cyclone in 1999. An earlier study by the Tata Institute of Social Sciences (TISS), Mumbai, in 1999, estimated that Odisha had 1,15,333 commercial sex workers. But there is no consensus either on the number of women involved in the sex industry or on the number who are trafficked within and beyond the boundaries of Odisha. A study by the Institute for Socio-Economic Development (ISED), an NGO in Odisha, says 80 per cent of the victim families are landless and 70 per cent of those trafficked are illiterate. Dowry-related problems lead more and more poor girls into getting duped by false promises to marry; 49 per cent of the women victims were deserted by men after being sexually used. Families refuse to take them back for fear of social approbation and spoiling the marriage prospects of younger sisters (Jena, 2003).

Investigating trafficking reports after the 1999 super-cyclone, the Odisha State Commission for Women found that in five coastal districts, each had its own established marketing destinations, determined by road and rail connections. Today, 21 of the 30 districts in Odisha have been sucked into the illicit current. The sourcing districts now include the coastal districts of Bhadrak, Jagatsinghpur, Cuttack and Jajpur as well as tribal-dominated border districts of Koraput, Rayagada, Nuapada and Mayurbhanj.

After the super-cyclone it was found that quite a large number of girls are going out for seeking job outside. Many girls were also going out for sake of marriage. Earlier, most of the girls were migrating for employment. But later on following the super cyclone the migration of girls rapidly increased. It was found that most of the migrant girls were coming back to the village in a miserable condition. Some of the girls came back with a child whose father was not known. These girls could not reestablish contact with their so-called husbands and in-laws. Some of the girls who left the village for jobs, returned with child whose father was also not known. Quite many girls didn't return over the years at all. Sometimes it was seen that when the family members wanted to invite their daughters for attending the family functions, they did not get their address and whereabouts. The family members going in search of their daughters were coming back home with a broken heart, due to their failure to get into touch with the girl. Still the people of that area were not aware about the problems involved. Some people were coming from outside to their village for vending purposes. They used to select a poor family to settle down in the village. Then gradually they tried to get closer to the family members. After building a familiar relationship with them, they used to propose the marriage of their daughter with persons. Then they could take the girl with them and sell her away afterwards. After the super cyclone, trafficking by this way has been taking place in this area.[4]

Needless to mention, poverty and illiteracy are main barriers for women to get into the mainstream. Despite 33 per cent reservation for women in the Panchayati system, they are still unsafe and dependent on others. Thus, the position of a woman at present is as vulnerable as it was in the past. As per the State Commission's Report, on an average about 30 girls were being trafficked from this area every month. A number of cases of false marriage were informed to the office each month. Taking advantage of the vulnerability of the women, some people having vested interests were doing all sorts of nefarious activities with them. It is not only the case of this area. Such types of incidents are happening throughout the State. The report gives instances of Balasore, Nayagarh, Baripada and some other parts of the State. Why such incidents are taking place all over the State? It is because the poor parents are not able to maintain their large family. Generally, they want to dispose off the burden of their daughters, so as to be free from the financial hassles.

As per the Crime Branch Police, Government of Orissa, these are overall reported cases of trafficking of women. Accurate figures on cases of trafficking of women are hard to get, since some of these cases remain unreported. Some researchers are of the opinion that the numbers of unregistered cases are very high, more than that of registered cases. Women in Odisha are victim of increasing violence but many cases remain unreported due to the social stigma associated with it.

Table 1

Reported Cases of Immoral Trafficking of Women in Odisha

Year	*No. of Cases*
1990	11
1991	09
1992	12
1993	08
1994	13
1995	24
1996	16
1997	11
1998	11
1999	26
2000	18

Source: Human Right Protection Cell; and Crime Branch of Police, Government of Odisha.

Possible Planned Interventions

The trafficking of women in Odisha, therefore, seems to be a journey from marginalization to stigmatization and ostracism via exploitation and torture. After having all this discussion, it clearly shows that the possibility of re-trafficking of women is always there. Therefore, this paper in its conclusion would like to provide certain suggestions in order to combat trafficking. Some of them are:

- Trafficking problem is directly linked to poverty. It is not possible for any government or NGO to improve the economic condition of disadvantaged families overnight. With active cooperation from state government, NGOs and central government, however, some strategies can be framed for identification of families living below poverty line and they can be offered alternative earning options as per their aptitude. Women should be imparted proper training in different skills, so that they can earn their livelihood.
- Trafficking among women is associated with illiteracy. If government as well as non-government organizations provide proper infrastructure, adequate number of qualified teachers and

proper teaching quality, as well as sufficient amount of teaching materials to these poor family children and attract them to attend school rather than drop-out, with their children also attending school, then they will become aware about the problem and it will reduce the risk of trafficking.

- Another viable option is to involve the local Panchayats. They can maintain a register on girls going out to work and also keep tabs on the families, since many willingly sell their daughters. We can involve Anganwadi workers as they have easy access to families at the grassroots.
- Police personnel and judicial people must be sensitized to make the police stations and court environment friendly towards the victims of trafficking. This will help them to take up the cases more sympathetically.
- Awareness can be generated through various slogans, pamphlets and wall writings, etc. and public information sharing through various local workshops, conferences, popular media, street play and debate and public rallies should be organized to sensitize and educate the mass about the problem of trafficking.
- The problem of trafficking does not end with the return of the survivors. There should, therefore, be proper rehabilitation and integration programmes for those who return to their homeland.

Conclusion

In Odisha, the state being the poorest in the country, the status of women continues to remain backward. Due to low economic status, women in Odisha are also victims of increasing violence but many cases remain unreported due to social stigma associated with it. It is clear from the above discussion that due to super-cyclone, the women and girls become more vulnerable to trafficking as they have lost their houses, parents and relatives. With nobody to take care of them, the traffickers easily lure them in name of providing support. Traffickers keep close contact with the local middle men and give handsome amounts to them to continue the chain of trafficking. Traffickers assure the helpless women and girls to find suitable jobs and grooms. After taking them from their parental house they supply them to different brothels. After reaching there, the women and girls have no way out. Many cases remain unreported due to political interference, shyness of the victims and social stigmas associated with such incidents in our society. To sum up, we can say the means of trafficking among women and girls is increasing at an alarming rate in the state, more so in the wake of natural calamities. The issue of trafficking cannot be understood in isolation since it involves variety of other socio-economic evils. For addressing the issue, host of related ones like underdevelopment, poverty, patriarchy, gender, corruption, delayed/lack of justice, poor law enforcement, commodification/misrepresentation of women, etc will have to be addressed simultaneously.

Notes

1. M. Hamilton and N. Chinchilla, 'Global Economic Restructuring and International Migration', *International Migration*, 34 (2), 1996.
2. Anny Misa Hefti, 'Globalisation and Migration', European Solidarity Conference on the Philippines Responding to Globalization, 19–21 September 1997, http://www.philsol.nl/solcon/Anny-Misa.htm.
3. *Encyclopedia of Sociology*, Vol. II, New York: Macmillan, 1992.
4. Report of the Seminar on 'Trafficking of Women and Children in Orissa', held at Block Headquarters of Mahakalapada in Kendrapara District in 2003.

References

Census of India 2001. Provisional Population Total, Paper-I, Director of Census Operations, Orissa.

Coomaraswamy, Radhika. 2005. 'Human Security and Gender Violence', *Economic and Political Weekly*, XL (44 and 45), 29 October, p. 4730.

Deb, Sibanath. 2005. 'Child Trafficking in South Asia: Dimensions, Roots, Facts and Interventions', *Social Change*, 35 (2).

Durkheim, Emile. 1984. *Division of Labour in Society*, Translated by W.D. Halls, London: Macmillan.

Dutta, Pranati. 2005. 'Nepali Female Migration and Trafficking', *Journal of Social Science*, 11 (1), pp. 49–56.

Hamilton, M. and N. Chinchilla. 1996. 'Global Economic Restructuring and International Migration', *International Migration*, 34 (2).

Hefti, Anny Misa. 1997. 'Globalisation and Migration', European Solidarity Conference on the Philippines Responding to Globalization, 19–21 September, http://www.philsol.nl/solcon/Anny-Misa.htm

Hqyzr, Noleen. 2002. 'Combating Trafficking in Women and Children: A Gender and Human Rights Framework', paper discussed in Honolulu,

Hawaii in United Nations Development Fund for Women (UNIFEM) programme.

Hughes, Donna M. 2000. 'The "Natasha" Trade: The Transnational Shadow Market of Trafficking', *Journal of International Affairs*, Spring, 53 (2), pp. 625–51.

Human Development Report 2004. Government of Orissa.

Jena, Manipadma. 2003. 'Trafficking in Overdriven', Seminar organized by Women Feature Service.

Mallik, Vaishaki. 2004. 'Girl Child Trafficking: A Study of Institutional Responses in India', M. Phil. Dissertation (Unpublished), Jawaharlal Nehru University, New Delhi.

Marx, Karl. 1906. *Capital: A Critique of Political Economy*, Edited by Frederick Engels, New York: Modern Library.

Mishra, R. and L. Mohapatra. 2005. 'Trafficking of Women in Orissa in the Post-cyclone Period: A Study', *Women's Link*, 11 (5), pp. 11–14.

Mobakoug, Ifeyinwa Annastasia. 2004. 'Exploring the Forms of Child Abuse in Nigeria: Efforts at Seeking Appropriate Preventive Strategies', *Journal of Social Science*, 8 (1), pp. 22–27.

Patnaik, P.P. 2005. 'The Invisible Minority: An Analysis of Trafficking of Women in Orissa', *Women's Link*, 11 (5), pp. 29–32.

Report of the Seminar on 'Trafficking of Women and Children in Orissa', held at Block Headquarters of Mahakalapada Block in Kendrapara District in 2003.

Sinha, Salini. 1987. 'Patriarchy and State', M.A. Dissertation (Unpublished), University of Delhi, Delhi.

11

Stigmatization and Victimization of Single Women in Indian Scenario

BARNALI MAITY

> Woman is the comparison of man, gifted with equal mental capacities. She has the right to participate in the minutest details of the activities of man and she has the same right of freedom and liberty as he.
>
> — Mahatama Gandhi

A disparity in the social role of women is manifested culturally in the Indian society. The position and status of women in the society vary according to its ritual practices. Certain customs and institutions impose limitations, which all women face in receiving actual rights and privileges. Now the question is that how these customs, institutions, functions and their impact upon women vary. Across the cultural diversity, a woman's life is strongly influenced by her father and husband – as reflected in the practice of patrilocal residence, patriarchal descent and by inheritance systems and family relations. Such patriarchal practices are further reinforced by the legal system. Marriage has an overwhelming importance in a woman's life. The event of marriage determines almost all her life options and subsequent livelihood. Traditionally, single persons received shelter from the extended family. But now breakdown of this type of family hampers their dignified survival due to lack of family support. Remaining single is more acceptable for men than it is for women. Being single for women is still concerned as living with some disadvantages.

In some societies, widows, divorced or abandoned women may be subject to social exclusion, isolation and harassment, making it very difficult for them to maintain a livelihood for themselves or their children. Women heads of households with young children may face great time constraints and may have to limit their work hours. Even though female-headed households are a relatively small proportion of households, evidence shows that in the last 20 years, their share in the total is increasing in most regions of the world (Buvinic and Gupta, 1997).

Single women with self-headship face so many hurdles. Female-headed households are encompassed with feminization of poverty. In the last 10–15 years, pronouncements about women-headed households being the 'poorest of the poor' have proliferated in writings on gender not only in developing regions, but at a global scale (Buvinic and Gupta, 1993).

In Indian scenario, the existence of single womanhood has not yet been accepted as a common phenomenon. As a result, it has emerged as another prominent face of gender injustice. The predominantly patriarchal order has not yet succeeded in assigning an individual status to single women and thereby, have confined them to an oppressive environment. This article has tried to show various factors that lead to remain single and to identify the various problems viz economic, social, psychological and physical faced by single women.

After 62 years of Independence, women continue to suffer indignities and are subjected to humiliation and ill treatment of society and this is especially true for the existence of single women. In Indian society, where a women's existence is only that of an appendage to a man, whether she is a daughter, a wife or a mother, any deviation from this pattern is considered as unclean, evil or diseased and is seen with suspicion. While women are constantly being victimized and exploited by society, single women are victims of double exploitation – one as women and secondly as single. They, lacking the protection of a man and sometimes of a family, are vulnerable to economic exploitation, social victimization, psychological depression and social harassment.

The majority of single women undergo psychological trauma because of being single. This problem manifests itself in loneliness, insecurity and consequent depression or desertion. Such negative emotions and continuous suppression of feelings affect their overall physical and mental make up which makes themselves to withdraw from society. But it is the attitude and the reactions of the society which has been responsible for their unique behaviour. If society continues to reject them, it will be reinforcing their loneliness and its allied insecurities thus affecting their potential to contribute to the development of society (Krishnakumari, 1987).

Legal protection through progressive development and strengthening of national laws and emancipation against women through policy measures, such as the national policy for Empowerment of Women adopted in 2001, as a follow-up action to the commitments made by India during the Fourth World Conference on Women held in Beijing during September, 1995 has following objectives:

1. Creating an environment through positive economic and social policies for full development of women to enable them to realize their full potential.
2. Women should have equal basis with men in all spheres: political, economical, social, cultural and civil.
3. Equal access to participation and decision-making of women in social, political and economical issues.
4. Equal access for women to health care, quality of education at all levels, career and vocational guidance, employment, equal remuneration, occupational health and safety, social security and public offence, etc.
5. Strengthening legal systems aimed at elimination of all forms of discrimination against women.
6. Changing social attitude and community practices by active participation and involvement of both men and women.
7. Mainstreaming a gender perspective in the development process.
8. Elimination of discrimination and all forms of violence against women and the girl child.
9. Building and strengthening partnership with civil society, particularly women.

It has been a vital part of India's efforts to combat practices contrary to the human rights of women and to change social attitudes on which discriminatory practices have been based. In the policy, it is declared that all types of discriminations faced by women must be eliminated from the society.

The year 2001 was celebrated as 'Women's Empowerment Year' in our country. It focussed on creating an environment through positive economic and social policies for full development of women to enable them to realize their full potential, to create wide spread awareness of the integral linkages between development and women's empowerment, to highlight the interdependence of the progress and gender equality, to achieve the desired goals and affirmative action through forward looking national and state governments propounded policies and radical strategies. This type of national effort is very much important and welcomed in respect of women's position of dishonour, disrespect, and oppression in the society. In Indian scenario, for majority of women, singlehood is not a choice but has become the reality of their lives. They are bound to remain single due to their own circumstances as for maintaining of family burden, for husband's death, for lack of compatibility with the partner.

Who are Single

In this article, single women are those women who live without any male protection and security. These women are mainly (1) unmarried women who have reached at a marriageable age but are yet not married, (2) widows, (3) divorced, and separated women. These single women, in the absence of male protection and security, are resented by society and therefore, lack social status.

Status of Women in Earlier Period

The position of women in Indian society has been a controversial subject, as it reflects contradictory and paradoxical nature of our society. While on the one hand, a woman has been called *devi* or goddess, the abode of gods, the perfect guide or guru of her children; on the other hand, she has been criticized for the weakness of her character, for her unpredictable and impulsive nature and has ever been denied the basic right of existence as a human being (Goswami, 2007: 1).

In the Vedic period (i.e. the period between from 2,500 BC to 1,000 BC when the four Vedas – *Rig Veda, Sam Veda, Yajur Veda* and *Atharva Veda* – were compiled, women were active participants in different spheres of societal activities) (Pinkham, 1941: 1). In this period, women used to be well educated, well-cultivated and were refined in their manners and etiquettes and enjoyed all the rights in social, economic and political and religious domains, as were enjoyed by their male counterparts. Some of the hymns of the *Rig Veda* have been attributed to female *rishies* (Altekar, 1973: 10).

But, in the epic period, the *Ramayana* and *Mahabharata* had played key roles in determining the ideologies and practices towards women. This civilization was accompanied by social discriminations towards women. The degradation of women started since 300 BC. The patriarchal joint family system, structure of property ownership, early marriage, self-immolation of widows (*sati*) or state of permanent widowhood, all became obstacles in the development of women.

The period from 200 AD to 1000 AD was again a period of deterioration for the position and status of women, as Manusmriti writes, who flourished at this period, imposed new restrictions upon the body, soul and the very existence of women of the day. Manu, for example, believed and insisted that women should never be allowed a free and independent status. In her childhood, she should remain under the control of her father, in her youth, she should remain under the control of her husband and in her old age, she should remain under the control of her sons (*Manusmriti*, 2000: 167). 'A woman, who leads an independent life without any control, can bring ill fame to the family' was the belief of Manu.

The period from 1000 AD to 1900 AD was one of the rapid decline in woman's position and completed the process of woman's subordination. Many new practices emerged in the Indian society, which further degraded the status of women. Practices like polygamy, *sati, jauhar*, child and unequal marriage (even those of child-widows), the ill-treatment of the widows, single women and the negations imposed upon them completed the circle of their exploitation and made them fully subservient and dependent on their male counterparts (Goswami, 2007: 30).

Since the late 19th century and early 20th century of the Common Era, several reformers fought against these aspects of the system that have resulted in the oppression of females. To them, women should labour under no dissatisfaction, not suffered by men, and because of their efforts, independent India has adopted several rules and regulations to protect the rights of women and establish equality of status. In the pre-independence era, social reformers took an active initiation against social injustice of women. Women's active participation in freedom movement provided them the platform to come out of the four walls of their homes.

When India got Independence, the Constitution of India was formed and it provides Fundamental Rights to the citizens. Article14 stated that the State shall not deny to any person equality before the law or the equal protection of the laws within the territory of India. Article 15 (1) stated that the State shall not discriminate against any citizen on grounds only of religion, race, caste, sex and place of birth or any of them. Article 16 (1) stated that there shall be equality of opportunity for all citizens in matters relating to employment or appointment to any office under State. The Constitution of India brought drastic changes in the lives of women, at least is in pen and paper.

Sufferings of Single Women

The Hindu caste system structures Indian society in a complex hierarchy that can be socially oppressive for the majority of women. In different Census, the actual data regarding single women are not registered. For the want of actual data, there is no fixed principle on planning for single women. In our country, widow allowance and old age allowance have been introduced recently. But the amounts of these allowances have been insignificant. Besides, in accepting these allowances, long-term bureaucratic processes hamper them in many ways. Some imposters exploit them. Many bluffers harass them to take this type advantage. In this context, we see that social position of single women is in despair in spite of state's cooperative mentality. According to government report, the female-headed households are approximately 15 to 16 per cent (Duttagupta, 2001).

The evil custom of child marriage restricted opportunities for mental and physical development of the girls and also accounted for high incidence of child widows. The 1973–94 National Opinion Research Center (NORC) General Social Survey shows that the chances of women being widowed are three times that of men (56% to 18%) (Joseph, 2007). The widows do not go through the purificatory rites and were prevented from participating in social and religious rituals. Widows are treated by society as an insufferable appendage. Widows have a very low status in society. Society prescribes a set of norms, which have to be strictly adhered to by these women, failing which they are ostracized. They are considered inauspicious, the consequent shunning of their presence and the altogether unhealthy treatment that is doled out to them, makes them stay away from the functions. Ill-treatment and indifferent treatment and the difference of opinions with married sons and their spouses seemed to be the major problem confronting these women. Often the mother in-laws do not want them to stay in the house due to loss of privacy. Their cordiality and interference makes discomfort for in-laws' life. The constant friction in the family and the unhappy home environment causes them to feel 'unwanted'. There are about 33 million widows in India, representing 8 per cent of the female population. Anthropological studies have also highlighted the fact that many widows suffer from social marginalization and psychological hardship, in addition to being particularly vulnerable to poverty (Dreze and Sen, 2004).

Divorced women are ill-treated, harassed and regarded as aggressive women. They are shunned and regarded as aggressive, permissive and social outcastes for deviating from the customs and traditions of the society. Therefore, it is extremely difficult from them to lead a satisfactory social life. Neighbours are always afraid of them. Even married women avoid them. They are treated as loose character or unable to manage household or husband. No restriction is imposed on their participation by custom, but they prefer to avoid the unnecessary social exposure and the related embarrassment of their marital break-up. In the Indian scenario, there is a cultural, religious and social stigma associated with divorced women. Community disapproval is stronger for divorced women than it is for divorced men.

Even unmarried women who might have chosen a career instead of a home life, preferred independence and freedom to chains of bondage in marriage are rebuked and considered as social deviants. Their professional success is often seen with suspicion and their moral behaviour is the focus of almost all discussion. The modern family gives independence to a woman, she is no longer able to cope with the stress and strains of marriage in view of the dual role, which she has to play both as a mother and housewife and that of a working woman. When they are denied this respect at home, which they expect in the family, the suppressed personality of these women revolts and the seeds of conflict are planted. Traditionally, parents who could not provide a suitable groom for their daughters were ostracized and looked down upon.

Westernization has brought social changes through widespread education and employment opportunities in the mental make up of its populace. Women have begun to think of their liberty and freedom. Yet, being single is still a taboo. In view of the taboo and stigma attached to singlehood and the negative attitude of the society towards single women and their consequent alienation, they find it difficult to find living accommodation as the landlords prefer married women.

Single Indian women experience a multitude of problems in the social arena. Moreover, they hesitate to make friends with men (either single or married) because the friendliness might be misinterpreted. They have to be careful about that. In fact, a large proportion of single women face problems with sexual harassment, in the workplace and on the social scene. It is, therefore, not surprising that a majority of Indian single women experiences problems with loneliness and insecurity.

Women continue to suffer indignities and are treated like second-class citizens and subjected to humiliation and ill treatment to society and this is especially true for single women. Without any male support, single women play the dual role of both men and women and in the process face huge problems. Socially they are boycotted and victimized, psychologically they are subjected to innumerable mental tensions, sexually they are totally vulnerable and added to this if they are economically dependent they find themselves doubly abused and exploited. Being single is treated as taboo. They are neglected, humiliated, harassed and accordingly doled out the lowest status in the society. They are condemned for defying the conventions of the society.

The exploitation does not end in the family but is extended outside, i.e. at the workplace and society. Being single, they become vulnerable and are victimized. If separated and divorced, they are looked on with suspicion and on the other hand as morally loose women. Widows are sympathized with for their misfortune. Sometimes, they are lured and victimized. Exploited by men at workplace and deprived of a respectable position in society, they are not spared by their fellow women colleagues who are subjected to unhealthy discussion on their personal lives so that it upsets their mental balance. Insecurity outside the household is today greatest obstacles in the path of these women. In addition, the atrocities outside the house, scolding within the house are non-endurable for their dignified survival. Therefore, these women are bound to survive with inferiority in the house and society.

Conclusion

In India, initiatives to address the situation of women were already under way when the fourth world conference was held. The National Commission for Women had been set up by an act of Parliament in 1990, to safeguard the rights and legal entitlements of women. The national policy for empowerment emphasized the formation of collectivities to stand against violation of human rights. For the single women, firstly, fellow feelings from women and the own community is needed. Then formation of civil society or social capital to gain proper rights and privileges should be initiated.

In such a pitiable plight, legislation provides an orientation to set things right in their life. It helps them to face new challenges and to take up new roles, to enter new commitments and to enjoy new experiences. Nevertheless, the existence of personal laws according to religion or culture should be eradicated. In addition, they have to be aware of changing social milieu that encourages and supports them to overcome the traditional stigma concerning singlehood and welcomes a tomorrow, which treats them as responsible, dignified and creditworthy citizens. They can start over, succeed and beat the odds.

The single women are not free to live their life. Continuous threatening by the social and cultural norms determines their day-to-day life-style. They have to be surviving with strict social rules, which determine their nature of work. Society determines how they should survive and their boundary of interactions. Social rejection, disadvantages and non-cooperation suppresses their full potentiality. If society continues to reject them, it will be reinforcing their loneliness and its allied insecurities, thus affecting their potential to contribute to the development of society. To develop society, women have to participate with their full potentiality in the development process. According to Human Development Report, UNDP, 1996 – 'Investing in women's capabilities and empowering them is the surest way to contribute growth and overall development'. Therefore, for these women, society should provide support services on prior basis, on which they may give their services to the nation with full potentialities.

None of the problems exists in isolation. They are interlinked and one perpetuates the other. There should be a conscious mobilization of awareness of all sections of society, starting from the family as a unit to overcome certain misconceptions and practices connected with single women in the society and treating them with human dignity and understanding. Society is characterized as human and single women should live with humanity. Women have to achieve own rights and dignity with the help of lawful measures. They have to be aware of their own self. In addition, government needs to mobilize these type of women to participate in the development process with creation of employment opportunities among them through different development programmes initiated to live with proper rights of freedom and liberty.

References

Altekar, A.S. 1973. *Position of Women in Hindu Civilization*, Delhi: Motilal Banarsidass, p. 10.

Buvinic, Mayra and Geeta Rao Gupta. 1997. 'Female-Headed Households and Female-Maintained Families: Are They Worth Targeting to Reduce Poverty in Developing Countries?', *Economic Development and Cultural Change*, 45 (2).

——. 1993. 'Responding to Insecurity in the 1990s: Targeting Woman-Headed Households and Woman-Maintained Families in Developing Countries', paper presented at the International Workshop on 'Insecurity in the 1990s: Gender and Social Policy in an

International Perspective', London School of Economics and European Association of Development Institute, London, 5–6 April.

Dreze, Jean and Amartya Sen. 2004. 'Gender Inequality and Women's Agency', in Manoranjan Mohanty (ed.), *Caste, Class, Gender*, New Delhi: Sage Publications.

Duttagupta, Bela. 2001. 'Ekak Naree: Artha Samajik Abasthan', in Pabitra Sarkar (ed.), Bharater Samaj Bharater Naree, West Bengal: Paschimbanga Rajya Pustak Parishad.

Goswami, Sambodh. 2007. *Female Infanticide and Child Marriage*, Jaipur: Rawat Publications, pp. 1–30.

Joseph, B. Ramola. 2007. 'Widowhood and the Law in India', in Kamal K. Misra and Janet Huber Lowry (eds), *Recent Studies on Indian Women*, Jaipur: Rawat Publications.

Krishnakumari, N.S. 1987. *Status of Single Women in India*, New Delhi: Uppal Publishing House.

Manusmriti. 2000. First Edition, Delhi: Manoj Pocket Books, p. 167.

Pinkham, M.W. 1941. *Women in the Sacred Scriptures of Hinduism*, New York: Columbia University Press, p. 1.

12

Why Deprivation Matters for Girls and Women from Pre-natal to Geriatric Stage?

PRASAMITA MOHANTY

Genetically, girls and women are born with more diseases than men, structurally boys are longer and stronger, and functionally girls are soft, tender and beautiful than boys. Both genders vary significantly in bio-physiological characteristics and abilities, but are complementary and supplementary to each other in many ways. What makes girls to be devalued before males? A male child is born in a similar manner as a female child to the same parents. What makes girl to be of less worth to parents and in-laws? Unlike other progressive nations where both parents are equally responsible for rearing children, Indian society has inherited the mother-centred child rearing practices. It means both boy and girl are grown for equal amount of time during infancy and childhood by the mother. How does a woman discriminate girl child? Why do parents prefer to have a boy child rather than a girl? Researchers currently explored that social and ethical crimes against women and girls are the major fear factors for parents to have and rear girl children in India. After all, recent incidents of gang rape are sufficient to justify the terror that parents having girl children feel.

Despite the fact that the source of growth, development, maturation and learning is the same, it is ironical that males pick up tendencies to dominate females and females find themselves inferior to males. Is this difference attributed to within home factors? Or, is it attributed to socio-cultural factors? Is this because of the low impact of ethical norms in Indian society? It needs to be resolved in the first century of this new millennium; otherwise gender exclusion will be more cancerous for social stratification process. It may further aggravate Indian economy because of delimiting about half of population to reach at zone of proximal development.

Contributing substantially toward the prosperity of families (in parental and in-laws) since childhood till death, each girl is socially useful and constructive, economically productive and above all an effective human resource. Girls learn informally many things from within the family and from the neighbourhood and such informal functional knowledge help them to grow within society and nation at large. 'Nor negligible in terms of number, nor less in capabilities, women continue to survive with their identity parallel to the patriarchic social structure prevailing in the societies across nations for ages. History could never explain; scientific insights and technological inventions could never prove; humanities could never discover; researchers and practioners could never establish that girls are less potential than the boys'. Scholars having keen interest on the issue of gender equality have widely examined and explored through interdisciplinary and trans-disciplinary approaches and found that gender equality is critical and central to the national development. 'Gender parity is the affordable social intervention that could yield much more returns to the society; thereby the need has been felt for bridging the gaps between boys and girls' (ibid.). Girls contribute much more than boys not only at school stage but also in the entire ladder of education. Girls' social and professional roles are symmetrical and progressive across all ages, though they are accorded low socio-metric status. Girls are supportive to their mothers at young age while at the later stage they shoulder the responsibilities of family, neighbourhood and society. Bringing girls at par with the boys could fuel the economies of the developing countries to extremes. Ironically, gender disparities exist and are significantly prevalent in many countries in Asia and Pacific and Africa. Besides poverty, gender disparity is the most powerful and independent factor that holds nations back from attaining inclusive growth and development.

Sufferings from Pre-natal to Geriatric Stage

It is beyond imagination that girls are within a vicious circle of sufferings across all stages of human development – pre-natal, post-natal, babyhood, childhood, adolescence, adulthood and old age.

During the pre-natal stage, female foeticide has become the most prominent social problem in India. Gender determination and sex selection is the sole cause of dipping sex ratio in India. The girls have not vanished overnight. 'Decades of sex determination tests and female foeticide that has acquired genocide proportions are finally catching up with states in India', says UNICEF. The traditional method of getting rid of the unwanted girl child was female infanticide, where the female baby was done away with after birth in various ways – either by poisoning the baby or letting her choke on husk or simply by crushing her skull under a *charpoy*. With the advancement of medical technology, sophisticated techniques can now be used or rather misused, to get rid of her before birth. Through ultrasound scans and amniocentesis, the sex of the foetus can be determined during the pregnancy of the woman and then the foetus is aborted if found to be female. Despite enactment of Pre-Natal Diagnostic Techniques (Regulation and Prevention of Misuse) Act–1994 (came into force on 01.01.1996); female foeticide continues to be great threat in India, though states vary significantly from one another. According to the Census of India, the sex ratio in the 0–6 age group in India went from 104 males per 100 females in 1981, to 109.4 in 2011. Such trend of drop in the sex ratio indicates that modern society fails to comprehend female foeticide as an illegitimate social ill practice.

From post-natal through childhood stage, girls invite displeasure and unhappiness among parents, family members, relatives and friends. Across various localities in India, celebrating birth ceremony of girl children is a never-seen event, while people either educated or otherwise enjoy celebrating the birth ceremony of boys in a royal manner irrespective of localities. The prevailing irrational attitude of parents and family members fuels well the process of discriminating girl child from the very day she steps out of mother's womb. A study (conducted by the CSR) recently published in the *Times of India,* reveal that parents feel growing girls is relatively difficult from safety and security perspective. Since babyhood through childhood, girl child is under a continuous physical threat from society, either in the form of physical abuse within family or on streets, or in the form of early sex abuses within and outside of family. Using case study/history approach to discuss a social problem of sexual abuse during early childhood stage, an author (elsewhere) revealed the prevalence of sexual abuse among girls and boys during childhood in India. Within schools, colleges and universities, girl and women face a number of threats from teachers, administrators and fellow students. In the job sector, they are not away from various forms of atrocities. Gender parity, a major social issue, is more prevalent in institutions of higher learning. Governance continues to be in the hands of masculine thinkers than feminine starting from public administration, business administration, and administration in educational institutions at large. 'Woman who is protected in her adolescence by the father, in her youth by her husband, and in her old age by her son, deserves no freedom at any time', reveals *Manusmriti*. Thousands of years after the *Manusmriti* prescribed a very restrictive code of conduct for women; Indian society is compelled to inherit certain psychological negative elements in the form of atrocities against women – taking into cognizance the recent decadal record crimes reported before the eyes of law. Delhi Gang Rape 2012, Rajasthan; Minor Girl Rape 2013; and Khap Panchayats across decades are some of the recent cases that have attracted attention of many thinkers. While debating upon dresses and costumes of girls and women, Indian society has its own norms. If parents of any girl or husband of any woman allow them to wear the way they like, then questioning dress or clothes of girls and women may prove to be illogical, provided the fiancé of girls, or husband of lady, brother or father should have abilities to protect them physically. Social and political participation of women is restricted in families and many of the parents (rather parents of all per se) don't encourage girls to participate socially and politically. We hardly notice equal participation of girls/women in universities. Quite a few girls (generic estimation of 10% of total student) are leaders or youth leaders of India. Notwithstanding these achievements, 65 years after Independence, the condition of women in general is deteriorating (*Hindustan Times*, 2012). Today, a woman is not safe if she is not in the company of her father, husband or son. This ironically justifies the *Manusmriti*.

According to statistics of crimes in India in 2011 (National Crime Record Bureau), within every two minutes one crime is committed against women in our country and one molestation takes place every 12 minutes, while a rape takes place in every 22 minutes on one woman. Every 61 minutes, one dowry death and a sexual harassment case is reported. One child is either kidnapped/nabbed/abducted in every 15 minutes. One murder is reported to be in practice in every 16 minutes. Almost 5, 00,000 girls are killed annually before they are born. About 1,000 (mostly girls) are victims of honour killing per annum. Based on Human Development Index (HDI), India finds its ranking at 134 in the list of 187 countries in the world.

Pre-natal through Babyhood

Female Foeticide

Abortion is prevalent in rural and urban areas. A total of half a million unborn girls are aborted in India annually, a joint study by researchers of India and Canada reported. According to 2011 Census, the country has an average sex ratio of 940 females to 1,000 males. Kerala has the highest sex ratio at 1,084 while Haryana has the lowest at 877. The union territory of Daman and Diu has a sex ratio of 618. Things don't look set to get better. According to the GOI's Ministry of Health and Family Welfare, there will be 931 females per thousand males in 2016 and 930 in 2021. The idea that the sex ratio is more skewed among the uneducated or rural population isn't entirely true. In 1901, it stood at 979. More than a century later in 2011, it has fallen to 947. In urban areas, it was 910 in 1901; it now stands at 926 in 2011. In real terms, India lags behind in implementing laws at grassroots level though it has enacted quite significant acts and statutes. It is estimated by the UN that 50 million girls are missing in India due to foeticide, a few hundred cases are registered under the PNDT Act.

Infanticide

Infanticide has been practised throughout human history in societies where boy children are valued, economically and socially, above girls. Advances in technology permit the modern horror of selectively aborting female foetuses. Medical testing for sex selection, although officially outlawed, has become a booming business in China, India and the Republic of Korea. Coined the definition on infanticide given by Stedman's *Medical Dictionary* (2000) which stated that 'it is defined as the killing of an infant, where an infant is defined as a child under the age of 1 year'. And Oystein explained that this definition does not just cover the act of terminating the life of an infant, but also passively allowing an infant to die without intervening when this would mean saving the infant's life. Bergman, Beckwith, and Ray (1969) argued that infanticide must be differentiated from Sudden Infant Death Syndrome (SIDS). The SIDS is 'the sudden death of any infant or young child which is unexpected by history and in whom a through necropsy fails to demonstrate an adequate cause of death'.

Tandon and Sharma (2006) reported that most of the women reveal that they killed their babies under pressure from their husbands. Many a time the husbands would beat up their wives and force them to kill the female child because she is an economic burden. Such situations occur more so among poverty stricken families. Srivastava (2001) states that 'the spectre of domestic violence chokes their voices and silences their opposition to attitudes and practices derogatory to their dignity. This social reality does not allow women to protest against any suggestion or coercion to get the female child aborted. It is unthinkable that any woman would readily agree to be a party to the crime. They do so under male pressure, coercion and domination. Thus, willingly or unwillingly they become party to the crime for they have no control even over their bodies.' In the case of infanticide, things are trickier as these cases are often reported as still-births or not reported at all. Indian Penal Code is the guiding law, but many girls die within a few weeks from their birth. While urban is not that safe for people to practice due to strict vigilance, rural India brings huge number of real episodes of girl infanticide. Tandon and Sharma (2006) concluded in their article that 'it is, therefore, essential that these sociocultural factors be tackled by changing the thought process through awareness generation, mass appeal and social action. In addition to this all concerned, i.e. the religious and social leaders, voluntary organizations, women's groups, socially responsible media, the doctors, the Medical Council/Association (by enforcing medical ethics and penalties on deviant doctors) and the law enforcement personnel should work in a coordinated way'. Karlekar (1995) reported that 'of the 1,250 families covered by the study, 740 had only one girl child and 249 agreed directly that they had done away with the unwanted girl child. More than 213 of the families had more than one child whereas half of the respondents had only one daughter.'

The Hindu (on 9 October 2012) published an article titled 'India loses 3 million girls in infanticide.' It further noted: 'According to the report, female child population in the age group of 0–6 years was 78.83 million in 2001 which declined to 75.84 million in 2011. The population of girl child was 15.88 per cent of the total female population of 496.5 million in 2001, which declined to 12.9 per cent of total number of 586.47 million women in 2011. Similarly the male children population has also declined from 85.01 million in 2001 to 82.95 per cent in 2011. During the period, 1991–2011, the child sex ratio declined from 945 to 914, whereas the overall sex ratio showed an improvement from 927 to 940.' A statistical appraisal on Children in India 2012, revealed that 'As per Census 2011, the State/UTs with alarmingly low (<900) child sex ratio are, Haryana (830), Punjab (846), Jammu & Kashmir (859), Delhi (866), Chandigarh (867), Rajasthan (883), Maharashtra (883), Uttrakhand (886), Gujarat

(886), Uttar Pradesh (899). The State/UTs which are having better (> =950) child sex ratio are Mizoram, (971), Meghalaya (970), A & N Islands (966), Puducherry (965), Chhattisgarh (964), Arunachal Pradesh (960), Kerala (959), Assam (957), Tripura (953), West Bengal (950).'

Malnutrition

Malnutrition during babyhood is a major impediment of holistic development of children during early years. Since nutrition is central and critical to physical, mental, social, motor, moral and aesthetic development at all stages, babyhood through childhood account for more than three quartile of cognitive development continuum by the age of eight years of every normal child. All such developments are interrelated to significant extent and grossly affected by malnutrition. Girls are more likely to be malnourished than boys in India.

India is one among the many countries where child malnutrition is severe and also malnutrition is a major underlying cause of child mortality in India. The problem has caught the attention of policy makers and researchers for several decades. Various studies and surveys have been conducted to find out the root causes of child malnutrition. All these studies, including the three National Family Health Surveys (NFHS), reveal that malnutrition is not the result of a single cause; the problem is multifaceted, the causes acting singly or in combination with other complex factors like poverty, purchasing power, health care, ignorance on nutrition and health education, female illiteracy, social convention, etc.

Higher is the percentage of underweight female children (< 5 years) than male children, whereas females are in a slightly better position compared to male children (< 5 years) while considering stunting and wasting. The NFHS 3 (2005–06) results also indicate that malnutrition is more prevalent among children in the higher birth order category. The rural India is witnessing more malnutrition among children < 5 years as higher percentage of stunted, wasted and underweight children were reported from rural areas. High malnutrition of all types prevails in the group of illiterate mothers and mothers with less than five years of education. Malnutrition among children is the highest for underweight mothers. The percentage of underweight children in the lowest wealth index category (56.6%) is nearly three times higher than that in the highest wealth index category (19.7%). The states with more than 50 per cent children, under five years of age, underweight are Madhya Pradesh (60%), Jharkhand (56.5%) and

Bihar (55.9%). District Level Household Survey (DLHS –3 2007–08) shows only 40.5 per cent children are fortunate to be breastfed within one hour of child birth. Among male and female children (6–59 months), the percentage of children with any anaemia was reported as 69 per cent and 69.9 per cent, respectively, severe anaemia was reported for 3.2 per cent male children and 2.7 per cent female children. Anaemia was more prevalent in rural areas (71.5%), than in urban areas (63%). For 81.9 per cent severely anaemic mothers, their children were anaemic, whereas 61.5 per cent mothers without anaemia reported anaemia among children. Percentage of children with severe anaemia among severe anaemia mothers was nearly seven times higher than that among mothers not anaemic. About 76.4 per cent of children (6–59 months) in the lowest wealth index are suffering from anaemia whereas 56.2 per cent children of the highest wealth index are suffering from anaemia. Anaemia prevalence among children (6–59 months) is more than 70 per cent in Bihar, Madhya Pradesh, Uttar Pradesh, Haryana, Chhattisgarh, Andhra Pradesh, Karnataka and Jharkhand. Anaemia prevalence among children of (6–59 months) is less than 50 per cent in Goa, Manipur, Mizoram, and Kerala. For the remaining states, the anaemia prevalence is in the range of 50 per cent to 70 per cent. National Nutrition Policy was introduced in 1993 to combat the problem of under-nutrition. It aims to address this problem by utilizing direct (short term) and indirect (long term) interventions in the area of food production and distribution, health and family welfare, education, rural and urban development, woman and child development, etc.

According to Sample Registration System (2010), the male-female gap in under 5 mortality rate (U5MR) was more in rural areas than in urban areas. In 2010, among bigger states, U5MR varies from lowest in Kerala (15), followed by 27 in Tamil Nadu to alarmingly high level in Assam (83), followed by Madhya Pradesh (82), Uttar Pradesh (79), Odisha (78) while other states figure in between. All the bigger states have higher U5MR for female than male. The Ministry of Statistics and Programme Implementation (2012) reported that early childhood, that is the first six years, constitutes the most crucial period in life, when the foundations are laid for cognitive, social and emotional language, physical/motor development and cumulative lifelong learning. The young child under 3 years is most vulnerable to the vicious cycles of malnutrition, disease/infection and resultant disability all of which influence the present condition of a child at micro level and the future human resource development of the nation at the macro level. The assessment of the ground reality as reflected by the statistics on nutritional status of children becomes very significant in this context. The consequences of child malnutrition for child morbidity and mortality are enormous and there is an adverse impact of malnutrition on productivity so that a failure to combat child malnutrition reduces potential economic growth at the macro level. At the micro level, malnutrition both protein energy malnutrition and micronutrient deficiencies directly affects children's physical and cognitive growth and increases susceptibility to infection and diseases.

As a major human resource, girls encounter many social, emotional and physiological traumas before they enter the joyful world of childhood years. Why girls matter? It is only because womanhood gets reared by the babyhood and childhood. Growth and development are cumulative and progressive by nature and so is maturation and learning. Better environment during these critical years of life leaves lasting impressions on girls to become useful and productive resources for the nation. Infant mortality, foeticide, infanticide, and malnutrition are found to be primitive social problems and can be compared to animal world. Girls are nurtured not like humans but rather animals.

Early Childhood through Late Childhood

Though years of life after birth are more meaningful and important as compared to during young adult and adulthood, there is to have a consensus or general standardized agreement on what constitutes early years. How many years are to be given top priority? – The answer to this has always been a search for scholars. A Victorian Government Initiative (2010) revealed: 'People use the term "the early years" in slightly different ways. To some it means the years from birth to eight years; to others it means the years before school; while others focus mainly on the first three years of life. All these periods are critical in every child's life. The important thing is that we provide real opportunities for children to learn, develop and have fun during those years, regardless of what term we use.' While environment provided by home and school are quite important for all children, an intra-gender study on high and low achieving rural scheduled caste rural primary school girls revealed an interesting finding. It was found that academic achievement of rural scheduled caste primary school girls is not influenced by home and school environment. Since there are no significant differences in mean scores of home and school environment, it means both high and low achieving rural scheduled caste girls are drawn from similar home and school environment. Environment is narrowly defined in rural context. It is not the infrastructure, or any ICT equipment only, more critical aspect of the environment is activities that are carried out in home and schools. Healthy interactions and instructions could sufficiently promote each child during these years. What are some of these important areas of learning? 'Health and physical well-being are the basis for all learning and development. Such areas include eating habits, attitudes towards exercise and self-care routines built from the child's earliest experiences. One of the most important things children learn in early years is about themselves – that is they develop a picture of themselves that affects the ways they approach any situation, task, or relationship with another person. An important part of that self concept is the picture they have of themselves as learners'. The experiences drawn by the author (Mohanty, P.) from the Child to Child – Project Motivation in Delhi (1994), Curriculum Analysis of Nutrition Health Education and Environmental Sanitation Component at Primary Stage (1996), Balika Shiksha Shivir (1997) in Bikaner, Rural SC Primary School Girls in Rural Haryana (1999, 2005), Adolescent Girls in Tigri Slum in Delhi (1995), Girl Children of Scavengers in Lucknow (2010), Scholarship and Educational Status of Children, including girls in Ambedkar Villages (2012), display more of a deprivation among girls of under privileged communities. Girls are found to be in jeopardy – born as girl in rural context in the lap of class and caste based society.

Child Labour

With especially girls, the moment they start walking and running, parents start sharing many domestic tasks and put them into local indigenous vocations, either at tea stalls or near the road side restaurants, or in any local shops. In villages, girl children of low socio-economic status are employed in domestic jobs and serve families of higher economic status. Girls are very often used by their mothers to carry food and water to the fields for their fathers. Child labour prompts girls to pick up many social evils since they come in contact with a wide range of community members with wide variety of age groups. International Labour Office, Geneva (2009), reiterated through a publication titled 'Give Girls a Chance: Tackling Child Labour, a Key to the Future' that 'the majority of girls who work are in agriculture, with large numbers also working in services and small scale manufacturing. The report looks at the nature of girls' work in a number of sectors and gives examples of the problems confronting girls. It also considers what can be done to tackle various types of child labour and notes that urgent action is required to remove girls from the worst forms of child labour. It also points to the need for strategies that prevent girls entering the workforce at an early age and for stronger enforcement of laws against child labour.' Save the Children (India) cites on its web portal that 'India is home to more than 12.6 million children who are forced to work in order to survive. These children are working as domestic help, on streets, in factories and farmlands silently suffering abuse. Save the Children works to end exploitative child labour.' The NSSO Survey 2009–10 puts the number of working children at 49.84 lakh and 19.25 per cent were female. However, UNICEF's data of 2004–05 had put the number of working children at a much higher figure of 60 million.

Child labour, as a practice, is not only against the violation of child rights rather it is the illegitimate social practice that exclude children, including girls from the other subsequent rights in life. Child labour appears early in societies and empower the children with employment. The earning (economic) helps children to live with delimited needs and aspirations. Though they have imaginations and abilities to go beyond and work much more beyond than what they do as child labourers, yet lack of facilities (educational and recreational) coupled with social and emotional deprivation at home and neighbourhood drag children away from developmental pattern. Those who survive by the grace of Almighty tend to lead a deprived life across all stages of their development. This brings a challenge before the law to curb such practice because the law can never provide funds rather it can detect the ill or bad practices. But remedial and corrective measures are taken by the local and national government with the help of social welfare department.

Child Marriage

Child marriage has kinship with child labour. India has inherited child marriage practices from the medieval period. Though political turmoil during pre-British period was the root cause of child marriage practices in India, yet social, economic, and cultural factors continue to be the major factors alike other countries of the world. When the female partners become ill or inactive due to reasonable grounds, males of the family seek for the house hold services from girl who gets married to the son of that family. Therefore, child marriage has kinship with child labour because the main motive of such child marriage is not the sexual exploitation alone rather exploitation in terms of physical labour and emotions. UNICEF (2011) cited in an Information Sheet:

'Child marriage is social concern and a violation of children's rights – whether it happens to a girl or a boy – as it denies the basic rights to health, nutrition, education, freedom from violence, abuse and exploitation and deprives the child of his/her childhood.' It further reported that nearly half (43%) of women aged 20 to 24 are married before the age of 18. A decline trend is noticed in incidence of child marriage in nearly all states (from 54% in 1992–3 to 43% in 2007–8). UNICEF (2010) reported that 47 per cent of girls are married by 18 years of age, and 18 per cent are married by 15 years of age. For every women aged below 18 getting married in urban areas, they are doing the same in rural areas. Jammu & Kashmir has seen the largest dip in under aged brides at 83 per cent. Kerala is the only state that has seen a 50 per cent increase in girls getting married by the age of 18. Child marriage affects 48 per cent women in rural areas and 29 per cent in urban regions. In 2006, the Government of India replaced the Child Marriage Restraint Act, 1929 with the prohibition of Child Marriage Act, violation of which is punishable with rigorous imprisonment. Despite the Delhi High Court declaring the child marriage a violation of human rights, the practice is still rampant. The states with the highest incidence of child marriage in the country are Bihar, Rajasthan, Jharkhand, Uttar Pradesh, West Bengal, Madhya Pradesh, Andhra Pradesh and Karnataka. Some of the factors (reported by the UNICEF, 2011) that form basis or grounds for child marriage in India include, unmarried girls are considered a liability to family honour; child marriage is a way to ensure chastity and virginity of the bride; dowry perpetuates child marriage as it encourages parents to marry off their girls early to avoid an increase in the dowry amount (more educated girls usually require a higher dowry). Girls are considered an economic burden for their family of origin and a *paraya dhan* or property that belongs to the marital family.

Education

One of the prime reasons of deprivation among girls is the level of education. Parents are seldom keen to invest more on education of girls mainly because of two important reasons. One of them relates to the social and cultural biasness towards education of boys and secondly, a girl child sooner or later will be a member of the marital family. 'Investing in girls' education is not considered worthy as girls will be moving to the groom's household and will be employed in household chores. On the other hand, the limited education and livelihood options for girls lead to marriage being one of the few options for girls' future' (UNICEF, 2011). Malnutrition at babyhood and child hood, social and cultural biasness, negative attitude of parents and community, male-dominated educational set-up, male-dominated classrooms and gender-biased pedagogy make each girl child to suffer from negligible to significant extent than a boy. Regular participation of girls in educational programme is adversely affected due to their involvement in household chores and often taking care of younger siblings. There is 20–40 per cent shortfall of attendance for girls in Rajasthan, Bihar, Utter Pradesh, Gujarat, Andhra Pradesh, Jammu & Kashmir and Odisha. The shortfall in female schooling is 5–10 per cent in Assam, Punjab, Gujarat, Maharashtra, Karnataka and Tamil Nadu. The Right to Education was enacted in 2010 that ensured all children in the age group of 6–14 years free and compulsory education. But by the age of 6 years, before they could avail the constitutionally enacted education, many girls disappear and remain away from educational networking; either they are being abused or married or being trafficked.

Child Trafficking

Since children are soft, tender and easily convinced, people take advantage of this age and start doing lucrative business especially with girls. Reported that India's trafficking patterns indicate that 90 per cent of trafficking in persons (TIP) is domestic (i.e. intrastate or inter-state trafficking), with only 10 per cent taking place across international borders. In addition to being a source for trafficking, India is also a destination and transit country. Factors such as economic development and vulnerability to natural disasters highly impact TIP patterns from region to region. Issues like poverty increase individual's vulnerabilities to the manipulations of traffickers and social norms (e.g. sexism towards women and girls) allow communities and families to subject their loved ones to the scourge of trafficking, sometimes voluntarily. Trafficking creates long-lasting social, economic and health impacts. India's legal framework is severely flawed. Instead of protecting victims and prosecuting offenders, more often than not, victims are prosecuted and offenders are protected. There are two million child commercial sex workers between 5–15 years of age. They form 40 per cent of the total population of commercial sex workers in India. Five lakh children are forced into this trade every year. Section five of the Immoral Traffic Prevention Act of Prevention of Immoral Trafficking Act of 1986 states that procuring or inducing a child into prostitution will be met with a minimum seven years prison sentence which can be extended to a life term. The Juvenile Justice (Care and Protection of Children) Act 2000, intends to help the large number of children in need of care and protection but many fall victim to abuse at state too. Minor continues to be forced into begging, prostitution, pornography, the organ trade and sex tourism. It is often difficult to distinguish between the cause and purpose of trafficking. Cultural and religious sanction is the cause of trafficking for religious prostitution. Marriage becomes cause or purpose for trafficking young girls for labour or prostitution. People also traffic children, especially girls, by making adoption a plea.

Late Childhood through Late Adolescents

Sexual Violence

Violence against girls and women is universal and causes of such aggression by males have never been explained well. Saravanan (2000) cited that physical, sexual and psychological violence occurs within the general community, including rape, sexual abuse, sexual harassment and intimidation at work, in educational institutions and elsewhere, trafficking in women and forced prostitution. Physical, sexual and psychological violence is perpetrated or condoned by the state, wherever it occurs. Opined that unlike many other countries, laws in India don't distinguish child sexual abuse from rape. Indeed, the laws against child abuse are only in their developing stage. Reported that the most common type of violence that women experience worldwide is Intimate Partner Violence (IPV). The WHO multi-country study observed that lifetime prevalence of physical or sexual violence from an intimate partner was reported by 15–17 per cent of women from 15 cities in ten countries. Women who reported being abused at least once in their lifetime were also more likely to experience a range of poor physical and mental health outcomes than those who had never been abused. Sexual, psychological and emotional violence inflicted by an intimate partner is also widespread. It is estimated that at least one in three women are subjected to some type of IPV over their lifetime. One out of two children in schools have faced sexual abuse according to 'Study on Child Abuse India 2007' conducted by the Ministry of Women and Child Development.

Atrocities Against Girls at Home, Neighbourhood, Schools

Lack of freedom for girls is the single most variable that influences other vital variables that accounted for the highest level of actualization. Families that are educated or semi educated or illiterate (who produce first generation learners), whether they are located in urban, semi-urban or cosmopolitans, all families by and large restrict girls to significant extent than boys. These restrictions are imposed on girls by mothers and on boys by fathers. Such restrictions are not the brainchild of mothers rather these are governed and informed by the masculine thoughts. These are considered to be certain form of atrocities against our own girl children that marginalize them in terms of self-respect, personality pattern, and learning abilities. Physical abuses are equally critical as the sexual violence. Since they are perceived by society as emotional, society takes the advantages of girls as weaker and abuse physically.

Psychological Deprivation among Adolescent Girls

Adolescent is the stage where children transform significantly than any other stages in the entire stage of human development. Physiological changes coupled with psychological factors play significant role in each of the adolescents including girls. Reported that the prevalence and onset of abuse in adolescent girls with behaviour disorders. Conduct disorder and major depression were more prevalent in abused girls, and internalized symptoms and truancy were much higher in the dual abuse group. Results from interviewing 49 girls with behaviour disorders and their parents indicated a poorer psychiatric prognosis in victims of dual abuse. Middle adolescence, from age 14 to 17 years, is marked by an increasing intensity of separation from parents, with the emergence of more conflict with parents, who become devalued in the teenager's perception. This is a period of heightened narcissism, a feeling of grandiosity and a sense of invulnerability that is facilitated by a pervasive use of denial. The teenager at this stage angers parents, who often complain of his or her selfishness and arrogance. Parents feel exploited and unloved and experience a heightened anxiety as they learn of their teenagers' risk-taking behaviours. The adolescent experience of loss of the parents intensifies and cognitive capacities increase as abstract thinking becomes a new tool available for coping with psychological distress. Teenagers who have grown up in environments that encourage and facilitate expression of thought (oral or written) as an alternative to action may resort to keeping journals in which they record their sometimes confusing, conflicting and fluctuating feeling states. Where such a psychologically healthy outlet (referred to as sublimation) is not available to a youngster, impulsive action may be the outcome of a state of feeling distressed.

Stansfeld et al. (2004) concluded that high rates of depressive symptoms in non-UK White girls may be related to recent migration. Low rates of psychological distress in Bangladeshi pupils in this sample relative to White pupils, despite socio-economic disadvantage, could be associated with cultural protective factors that require further investigation. While substantiating the finding of the study on educational aspirations of adolescent girls, Kaur (2011) reported that home environment was also found to be correlated with the educational aspirations of the adolescents. These results are in line with the findings of who found that personal factors like home environment had a strong, direct influence on educational aspirations. Emphasized about family background differences as a factor for adolescents' achievement, aspirations and their educational attainment. Though found substantial expansion in the educational aspirations of the adolescent students, but their families' environment and background had played no role. Emphasized on creating conducive home environment conditions for a student's high educational achievements and aspirations. Further, the results of the study as reported by showed that there was a negative correlation between family environment and educational aspirations. On the contrary, revealed that home environment and educational aspirations have no significant relationship with each other in a sample of school students.

Sanitation

According to a 2010 survey by AC Nielsen became Nielsen in 2010, nearly 90 per cent women in India use ashes, newspaper, dried leaves, even husk sand during their periods due to unaffordability of sanitary napkins (SNs). Menstrual hygiene is lowest in eastern India with 83 per cent women saying their families can't afford SNs. Due to inadequate protection during menstruation, adolescent girls miss five days of school every month, 23 per cent drop out of school after they start menstruating and over 70 per cent of the women have some kind of Reproductive Tract Infection (RTI) in their lifetime increasing the risk of contracting associated cancers.

Young Adults through Pre-geriatric Stage

Domestic Violence

Domestic violence has turned into a severe epidemic across the globe and has taken away the lives of a lot of women and might persist to do so, if not prevented. Though it is difficult to end it completely but awareness is among the top priorities for breaching the cycle of domestic violence. According to the United Nations (1996), domestic violence is defined as 'violence that occurs within the private sphere, generally between individuals who are related through intimacy, blood, or law'. The United Nations Declaration on the Elimination of Violence against Women (1993) defines violence against women as 'any act of gender-based violence that results in, or is likely to result in, physical, sexual or psychological harm or suffering to women, including threats of such acts, coercion or arbitrary deprivation of liberty, whether occurring in public or in private life.' Violence in the domestic sphere is usually perpetrated by males who are, or who have been, in positions of trust and intimacy and power – husbands, boyfriends, fathers, fathers-in-law, stepfathers, brothers, uncles, sons, or other relatives. Domestic violence is, in most cases, violence perpetrated by men against women. Women can also be violent, but their actions account for a small percentage of domestic violence. Violence against women is present in every country, cutting across boundaries of culture, class, education, income, ethnicity and age. Even though most societies proscribe violence against women, the reality is that violations against women's human rights are often sanctioned under the garb of cultural practices and norms, or through misinterpretation of religious tenets. Domestic violence occurs when a family member, partner or ex-partner attempts to physically or psychologically dominate or harm the other. Domestic violence includes all actions/behaviour of family members which causes either physical injury or emotional trauma, or both to a woman. The available statistics indicated that in India 1.5 lakh crimes against women were registered annually, out of which, nearly 50,000 were related to domestic violence only. Around two-third of married women in India were victims of domestic violence and one incident of violence translates into women losing seven working days in the country, a United Nations report reveal. As many as 70 per cent of married women in India between the age of 15 to 49 years are victims of beating, rape or coerced sex, the United Nation Population Fund report said. The rate of domestic violence is much higher in Egypt (94%) and Zambia (91%) followed by Pakistan (91%), Russia (75%), Japan (59%), Bangladesh (50%) and India (45%). Domestic violence in India came into sharp focus in 1980s when there was a widespread coverage by the mass media of the growing incidence of torture of brides, dowry deaths and protests against such heinous incidents. Domestic violence has a debilitating effect on women's physical as well as psychological health.

Honour Killing

It is estimated that 1,000 honour killings take place per year across India, against the global figure of about 5,000 across the world. (India figures according to 2010 independent study by lawyers Anil Malhotra and Ranjit Malhotra of Malhotra & Malhotra Associates, Chandigarh. Global figures according to UNHRC, 2010).

Dowry

Although legislations against dowry system are in place – the first one becoming a law in 1961 and another stringent one against dowry deaths formulated in 1986, the practice continues largely because Indian society internalizes a patriarchal culture, which is becoming increasingly consumerist.

Sexual Harassment at Work

According to an all India study by NGO Sakshi, 80 per cent women confirmed that sexual harassment existed in their work place. The Supreme Court defines sexual harassment as any unwelcome gesture, behaviour, words or advances that are sexual in nature.

Divorce

Indian divorce laws are skewed against women because most of them do not enjoy high economic status. Even in the case of claiming maintenance, men can feign loss of wealth. Tracing property in India is tough and women seldom have the means to do so. Men often buy property in the name of their relatives and plead poverty in divorce courts.

Pre-geriatric to Post-geriatric Stage

Socio-psychological Deprivation

The stage is characterized by decreasing physical contact with male partners by the females. Emotional detachment is also noticed that create a gap in the marital relationship between the inmates. This brings substantial amount of socio-psychological deprivation among women than men. Such deprivation is more commonly found among urban non-working but educated females. It is only because the urban environment is not conducive for socialization because of its structure. In rural areas, the concept of neighbourhood helps women to share emotional feelings. In this stage, family members seek maximum economic support and lack of adequate funds for the welfare of children and family is found to be one of the main reasons because of which both males and females face significant level of deprivation. Since male members get sufficient avenues for ventilation of their frustration and depression, females fail to adjust with such social turmoil.

Widowhood

Women in their old age become subject to more subjugation as they are discriminated against for share in property by inheritance or otherwise. Widows, who are left with no socio-economic standing of their own after their husband's death, are abandoned by their families in the religious town of Vrindavan. A Supreme Court appointed panel has highlighted their pathetic condition.

Conclusion

Towards the later days in life, women exert more physically, mentally, emotionally than men. The old stage of women is supported less whereas they have been a support to all throughout their lives. In real terms, in each stage women suffer substantially and lead a cursed life. A very few women are fortunate to have comfort at each stage, but they also enjoy relatively less than males. How to overcome such practices relating to gender inequalities or gender disparities? The only solution to such a massive social problem is to practice the best equally for both boys and girls within each and every family – after all, it is said that 'charity begins at home.'

References

All India Educational Surveys: II to VI, National Council of Educational Research and Training, New Delhi.

Annual Administrative Report, Directorate of Primary Education, 1991–92 to 1998–99, Government of India.

Annual Report 2011. Ministry of Health and Family Welfare, Government of India.

Bergman, A.B., J.B. Beckwith and J.B. Ray. 1969. 'Sudden Infant Death Syndrome', proceedings of the 2nd International Conference on Causes of Sudden Death in Infants, University of Washington Press, Seattle and London.

Biswas, A. and S.P. Agrawal. 1994. *Development of Education in India*, New Delhi: Concept Publishing Company.

Chen. 1994. Based on a 1991–92 Survey of 562 Ever-widowed Women in 14 Indian Villages (Two Each in North Arcot Ambedkar District, Tamil Nadu State, South India).

Chunkath, Sheela Rani and Venkatesh Athreya. 1996. Have Reported on Direct Evidence from Sample Household Surveys on PHC Done by Directorate of Public Health.

Educational Statistics, Directorate of Primary Education, 1991–92 to 1998–99, Government of India.

Five-Year Plans: III to VIII, General Administration Department, Government of India.

Karlekar, M. 1995. 'The Girl Child in India: Does She have Any Rights?', *Canadian Woman Studies*, March.

Kaur, Jagpreet. 2011. 'Effect of Gender and Home Environment on Educational Aspirations of Indian Adolescents', *Journal of Social and Psychological Sciences*.

Ministry of Statistics and Programme Implementation. 2012. 'Children in India 2012: A Statistical Appraisal', Social Statistics Division, Central Statistics Office, Government of India.

Ministry of Women and Child Development. 1997. 'Study on Child Abuse in India', Government of India.

Prakash, Satya. 2012. 'Enough is Enough', *Hindustan Times*, p. 10.

Sabu George, Rajaratnam Abel and B.D. Miller. 1986. Carried Out Their Research on Pregnant Women in 12 Villages of K.V. Kuppam Block, North Arcot Ambedkar District, Tamil Nadu State, South India.

Saravanan, Sheela. 2000. *Violence against Women in India: A Literature Review*, Institute of Social Studies Trust (ISST), March.

Srivastava, S.P. 2001. 'The Perils of Pre-Birth Murder: A Sociological Analysis of Female Foeticide', *Journal of Social Welfare*, 47 (10), January, pp. 7–12.

Stansfeld, S.A. 2004. 'Ethnicity, Social Deprivation and Psychological Distress in Adolescents: School-based Epidemiological Study in East London', *British Journal of Psychiatry*, 185, pp. 233–38.

Statistical Data on National Crime Record Bureau. 2011. Government of India.

Statistical Data on United Nations Human Development Report 2011. USA.

Tandon, Sneh Lata and Renu Sharma. 2006. 'Female Foeticide and Infanticide in India: An Analysis of Crimes against Girl Children', *International Journal of Criminal Justice Sciences*, 1 (1).

UNICEF Annual Report 2004–05.

United Nation Human Rights Commission 2010.

UNICEF Annual Report, 2011.

Part III

Liberalization and Women Entrepreneurship

13

Liberalization and Transformation of Womens' Work in India

SWAPNA S. PRABHU AND NIRANJAN MOHAPATRA

> 'There are multiple images of a woman's work: cooking on a *chulha*, transplanting in the field, carrying a child on her back, teaching in a school, overburdened at home ... . And yet, the question is often asked: what is women's work?'. Throughout history, women have aimed for a status and recognition in the society like Marie Curie in science, Mary Wollstonecraft in writing, and Simone de Beauvoir in philosophical debates. (Gandhi and Shah, 1993: 160)

The onset of globalization and liberalization accompanied by a revolution in the IT sector has provided women with new opportunities to create a platform to diffuse their ideas. However, on the other hand, liberalization has also transformed women's work in India in several ways. Economic reforms are one of the factors that have changed the entire scenario of social and cultural environment within the country, especially for the women. Liberalization and the adoption of the New Economic Policy (NEP) by the Indian government in 1991, calls for an assessment of the role and impact of globalization, structural adjustment and deregulation of the economy on the employment of women in small scale sectors. The present paper seeks to examine the role of liberalization in transforming the nature of women's work in India with a special reference to women in rural India employed especially in the unorganized sector. The paper also places the woman worker, in particular the poor woman worker, at the centre of analysis since it is her hard work and enterprise which creates half of the wealth of the nation and whose labour leads to national growth.

The globalization and liberalization of the world's economy and the intensifying interdependence among nations present challenges and opportunities for sustained economic growth and development, as well as risks and uncertainties for the future of the world economy. Development, within the framework of economic reforms, is often equated to growth rates which are highlighted as the only solution to all problems – be it poverty, unemployment or inequalities based on gender, class and caste. The Fourth World Conference on Women, which met at the Beijing International Conference Centre in September 1995, reported that the most commonly found economic phenomenon in the post-Second World War has been that in countries with economies in transition or in those that have undergone fundamental political, economic and social transformations, the new conditions have often led to a reduction in women's income or to women being deprived of income. The Indian case truly substantiates this point.

New economic policies and the structural adjustment programmes, introduced in many countries, have provided greater impetus to the process of Globalization. In India, these policies had been informally working since the beginning of 1980s and the new industrial policy of 1991 gave a further push to these policies of privatization, liberalization and marketization of the economy and globalization. The process of liberalization was started by removing the controls which hindered investment in the private sector. Free flow of foreign investment was encouraged. The multinationals were allowed to invest in all areas by acquiring up to 51 per cent equity stake without any government permission, but in high-tech areas even 100 per cent foreign concerns were allowed (Kaur, 1999: 119). At the same time, there has been rapid privatization of government owned companies, of state or community held resources, of hitherto reserved areas like banking and insurance. At the same time, there has been deregulation of labour protection leading to massive growth of contract labour and sub contracting (Jhabvala and Sinha, 2002: 2037).

Economic reforms are often projected as a panacea for economic progression and economic invigoration which, according to the advocates of globalization, will lead to reduction in poverty levels, squalor and regression. These global reforms, though are discernible options, can itself be lopsided, increasing the trauma of the poor and thus bring down the status of women if the communities in the developed world are not empowered on the effects of such reforms. The direction of globalization, as one observes, is quite skeptical to what changes the globalization can do to ameliorate poverty or in altering the status of children and women in the developing world (Gupta, 2009: 108). However, on the other hand, it can be rightly pointed out that a woman needs security, a decent life, a share in the prosperity of the nation and she dreams of a good life for her children. In a way, the change in economy has brought about a visibility for the woman worker which did not exist before. The term 'feminization of labour' is now widely used and women are becoming more visible in many areas of work which were traditionally barred to them.

Further, ideological change with an increasing trend towards consumerism, violence, individualism and sexual promiscuity is likely to have dangerous consequences for the society and especially for women. Increasing violence, both outside and domestic, also has disastrous consequences. Increasing trend of crimes against women, especially the sex related crimes, points towards a further deteriorating situation. According to the information provided by the crime records bureau of the Home Ministry in the year 1994–95, a woman is raped every 47 minutes, another is kidnapped or abducted every 44 minutes, while a third is subjected to cruelty by her husband or relatives. Nearly 17 dowry deaths are reported every day. All these instances are directly linked to the rise of a culture of consumerism in the country. Increasing consumerism, which is intentionally promoted in the market-oriented economic policy, further devalues the house hold role of women (Kaur, 1999: 127–128).

Globalization and Employment

Major discussions of connections between globalization and economic security have focused on questions of employment. Champions and critics of globalization alike, agree that unemployment constitutes a major challenge for the 21st century. According to UN estimates, the world labour pool of 2.8 billion people in the early 1990s included about 800 million unemployed (120 million of them officially registered as such) and over 700 million underemployed. Globalization has often undermined job security in the context of structural adjustment programmes. Most of these policy packages agreed by governments with multilateral financial institutions have prescribed a significant contraction of the civil service. Likewise, privatization and liberalization policies at the heart of neoliberal structural adjustment have often brought job losses when local trade and industry are exposed to global competition. Proponents of conventional structural adjustment programmes have argued that rejuvenated market forces will correct these problems with expanded employment opportunities in the medium and long term. However, little evidence has as yet emerged in the South and the East to substantiate this claim (Scholte, 2005: 296–297).

Liberalization, in India, has meant the opening of trade by reduction of import duties and removal of quantitative restrictions. It has also meant entering the WTO regime. At the same time there has been loosening of the licensing systems, especially on the private sector of firms, as well as lifting of reservations for many products. There has also been rapid privatization of government owned companies, of state or community held resources, of hitherto reserved areas like banking and insurance. At the same time there has been deregulation of labour protection leading to massive growth of contract labour and subcontracting (Jhabvala and Sinha, 2002: 2037).

Impact of Liberalization on Women's Employment

There has been a trend towards feminization of the labour force in the 1980s in India, as the spread of low wage employment is usually associated with women taking up such jobs under compelling circumstances. There are indications that Structural Adjustment Policy (SAP) is likely to shrink women's employment opportunities in the organized sector where already minor portions (2%) of working women are employed. New opportunities are likely to be in a small segment of export industries, which provide low paid, irregular, part-time and temporary contract jobs in which women are likely to be employed as they are seen as the docile and cheap labour force (Kaur, 1999: 124). At the same time, the government is withdrawing itself from the responsibility of interfering between the management and the workers, the role which it has been playing till now. In the absence of government protection and interference, workers will be left to the mercy of the owners and exploitation of women will further increase.

The Indian government, in its latest move in September 2012, to help in the recovery process of the economy, has allowed 51 per cent FDI in multi-brand retail and 49 per cent in aviation. To reduce the fuel subsidy burden, the government has also raised the diesel price by ₹ 5/litre and put a cap on use of cooking gas. Will these moves help economy gather pace and have a positive impact on investment flows is a question that remains to be answered. However, it can be clearly seen that the government's decision will have a long-term effect on the business of small-time traders and grocery shopkeepers who deal in cereals, clothes, cosmetics, hardware and other such products. This, in turn, will affect the women working in such sectors quite adversely.

As Nivedita Menon rightly points out, the 'demise of the nation-state' in the era of globalization is a myth. The nation-state is at once being reconstituted in all oppressive aspects simultaneously with its retreat from development and welfare responsibilities. Whether it is the US, India, or Bosnia, or Rwanda, the discourse of xenophobic and jingoistic nationalism is in full swing and the nation-state's repressive face is very much in evidence towards the dissident and/or marginalized voices within it. She again points out that the delegitimation of the state's authority only pertains to whatever positive effects (from a democratic point of view) were generated in anti-imperialist struggles, simultaneously with the reinforcement of every negative and repressive quality we associate with the state (Menon, 2004: 103).

Liberalization has in some sectors caused loss of employment without creation of new employment. This happens when an Indian product is displaced by import from the market. For instance, in the food processing sector, as the multinational companies with huge investments and state-of-the-art technology are entering the domestic market, they are visibly pushing out the small and unorganized units out of the market. In the country's manufacturing sector (both organized and unorganized sectors) food-processing is the fourth largest employer of women. It is estimated that nearly 3.10 lakh women workers (0.35% of the total women workforce) are employed in this sector, mostly in the unorganized segment of the industry and this is in addition to the 2.92 lakh (0.37%) deployed in grain mill sector. Due to lack of finances and lack of access to latest technologies and modern quality control facilities, these units are not able to meet the required high quality standards for the production of new range of attractive consumers' products for a rapidly changing market. As a result of this there has been a decline in the average number of women workers per manufacturing unit since 1981; from a figure of 21.7 to 14.8 in 1992. Evidently, as the food processing industry is becoming highly modernized, women workers who work at the lowest rungs of the ladder have been far more adversely affected than their male counterparts (Jhabvala and Sinha, 2002: 2038–39).

Besides the above mentioned trends, the growth-oriented policies of the government have also taken away whatever control women had over traditional occupations and also deprived them of upcoming better avenues of employment. At the same time, these policies have affected a shift in agriculture from food crops to cash crops with its high capital inputs like power, water, chemicals and fertilizers and have prevented women from their role in the means of production. In the near future, there will be further possibility of extreme food scarcity and cutbacks on women's labour. The ruthless exploitation of resources has led to increasing inequalities between regions, between men and women, increased feminization of poverty and ecological degradation (Ramanamma, 1999: 111).

Further, the onset of liberalization also resulted in the marketization of the economy. The dominance of the market processes leads to commoditization of all aspects of everyday life and work and undervalues everything which is not directly calculable in those terms. This tendency is likely to affect women as the role played by women in their household is not given any recognition. Any work being conducted by women inside the home is considered non-work. A women is considered as working only when she goes out to earn money. With the increased magnetization, the value of non-marketed works is likely to decline, thus further devaluing the household role of women (Kaur, 1999: 124).

There are also indirect effects of globalization, where global, cultural and social norms begin to effect employment in India. An example is the anti-tobacco campaign, which is beginning to cause a reduction in the work available to the bidi workers. Another indirect effect of liberalization has been the growth of concern about the environment. As part of this concern, employment and environment are often counter posed to each other and in recent years, environmental issues have taken precedence over employment, where industries have been shut down causing large scale job losses. In Delhi, for instance, nearly one lakh workers lost their jobs with the closing of small and home based industries (Jhabvala and Sinha, 2002: 2038).

Besides the above mentioned implications, it is also to be remembered that New Economic Policy (NEP) in operation since 1991, involved devaluation, deregulation and deflation. These measures, directly or indirectly, affect the volume and quality of employment that will be generated in the future. While deflation will reduce the fiscal deficit, devaluation and deregulation are expected to make allocation of resources more efficient than in the past by correcting the distortions in factor prices (Deshpande and Deshpande, 1992: 2250).

Deflation, by itself, will increase unemployment among women in two ways. Firstly, some women will be laid off as a part of the cut back in production and employment. Secondly, as men lose jobs, their wives and children will be forced to enter the labour force to keep the pots boiling. Further, if deflation is accompanied by reduction in subsidies on essential consumption, the fall in real income will increase the pressure on women to work for market.

Women as Economic Beings

If violence was the rallying issue for women's organizations, the marginalization and impoverishment of the majority of women within the transforming economy became the entry point for academics into the women's movement. The Committee on the Status of Women in India (CSWI), in its initial analysis was based more on inferences, the cries of thousands of poor women across the country voiced before the committee and demographic evidence of a secular trend of decline in women's value in the economy and society as a whole. However, the Women's Studies Programme of the Indian Council of Social Science Research (ICSSR) helped to start off a research process heavily biased in favour of 'invisible women', i.e. poor working women in rural and urban areas. This focus not only fed new information to the movement but transformed many of the academics into active participants in the women's movement, where they exerted a definite influence in the choice of priorities and line of advocacy for dialogues with policy-makers. A third factor was the emergence of some large organizations of poor women in some of the informal sectors in the country. The dynamism in struggle demonstrated by these groups became a major focus in the search for alternative strategies of development with organized groups of women form the grassroots as primary agents of change. The ICSSR's Advisory Committee on Women's Studies highlighted in one of its memorandums, the problems of increasing devaluation of women in the economy and society and recommended special strategies for employment, health and education. It also recommended that the family/household approach in programme thrusts be replaced by 'explicit mention of women as a target group' since the 'invisibility' of women to planners and administrators was rooted in the 'tendency to view women only through the screen of families and households and not as individuals in their own right'. This further reinforced the perspectives of women's economic role as 'marginal and supplemental' (All India Women's Conference 1980). The demands put forward during the All India Conference on Women held in 1980 included a special approach which earmarked resources and separate monitoring arrangements in each of the sectoral programme thrusts such as inclusion of child care centres within the Minimum Needs Programme and the demand for joint 'pattas' (land titles) for women and men already voiced by the poor peasant women (Agnihotri and Mazumdar, 1995: 1874).

Today, Indian women feel that the structural adjustment programmes and the package of economic reforms threaten not only earlier gains, but also the stated national goals by successive governments. While the women's movement was critiquing the development model, SAP has now removed the few regulatory and compensatory aspects of India's mixed economy, leaving 'global market forces' as the sole players in the field. These processes especially those with inconvenient historical memories, bear significant resemblance to what happened to the Indian economy and to women's role in the economy in particular, during the colonial period (ibid.: 1876).

The Gender Dimension

In most countries of the world, women very often form a disadvantaged section vis-à-vis men and India is no exception in this regard. If the country's economy has to fight an unequal battle with the developed countries in the international market, its society is doubly burdened by the inequities suffered by women, enhanced by the effects of this unfavourable competition. It is true that a section of Indian women belonging to the elite and upper middle class has gained by the exposure to the global network. In India, statistics show that unemployment rate for educated women and men has declined considerably throughout the late 1970s to the early 1990s, though it is still very high. It was 22.36 per cent of the total female population in 1993–94 compared to 41.89 per cent in 1977–78 (Ray, 2002: 23).

But what about the majority? A few examples show that since globalization is introducing technological inputs, women are being marginalized in economic activities and men traditionally being offered new scopes of learning and training. Consequently, female workers are joining the informal sector or casual labour force more than ever before. For instance, while new rice technology has given rise to higher use of female labour, the increased work load for women is in operations that are unrecorded and often unpaid, since these fall within the category of home production activities. Whereas, application of commercial inputs (fertilizers and other plant treatment), essential for new (HYV) rice technology, are done exclusively by men. Secondly, since SAP has led to the unemployment of a large number of men and has increased frustration, tension and a fear of job insecurity which has indirectly made evils such as rape an everyday event and escalated dowry dreams. Further, the economy, strained to the utmost under the challenges of globalization, is unable to bear the burden of necessary health care and educational expenses. The weaker sections, especially the women, are denied the physical care they deserve, the best example being the extremely high maternal mortality rate (ibid.)

In addition, the massive increase in gender inequality, the escalation of rampant consumerism accompanied by the explosion of new media that brings all the lavish new lifestyles into open public view, all serve to add to the resentment and frustration of the have-nots. This gulf between aspiration and reality becomes even wider, which in turn creates a strong urge to somehow get at those who are seen as 'responsible'. Of course, the real agents of these processes – the unresponsive state, the large companies and multinational corporations, the foreign investors – are all too large, too distant, and too powerful to be touched. How much easier, then, is to direct one's ire against those who are most accessible – women within and outside the household. The other philosophy that is invoked lies at the heart of the reliance on markets – individualism. The 'competitive spirit' is unleashed and used to make people feel that it is each man or woman for himself or herself and that individuals can succeed in making gains at the expense of others in their own social group. This has two significant effects: it makes each act that of an individual and it reduces the possibility of solidarity among victims and possibilities of collective action (Gupta, 2009: 115).

Further, women are most affected by changes due to mechanization which reduces the employment of the manual workers by displacing it by workers who run the machines. As such, the total number of jobs is reduced drastically. Moreover, women are generally replaced by men, although the income earned may actually increase. For instance, in the agricultural sector men have taken over from women those activities in which technology has substituted machinery for manual labour. All other labour intensive tasks are still left to women. Therefore, the introduction of tractors, harvesters, insecticides, weedicides, hormone accelerators, high yielding variety of seeds and mechanical cotton pickers has meant that tasks traditionally performed by women and on which many women depend for their livelihood have been appropriated. Various micro studies have proved true the above mentioned situation. Some other examples can be cited to ascertain this stand. Weeding in paddy producing areas is a female dominated task. When chemical spraying replaces weeding, the spraying is performed by men. Similarly, the introduction of rice mills has displaced hand pounding done by rural women. Rice mills utilize husking equipment with the consequence that women who use traditional husking mechanisms have lost their means of livelihood. Again, in some sub-sectors in the textile and garment industry, mechanization has displaced women workers (Jhabvala and Sinha, 2002: 2038).

A large number of women workers are employed in the construction industry. According to NSSO Survey (1993–94), 4.17 per cent of all male workers and 1.27 per cent of all female workers were engaged in construction activity. Among women construction workers more than 98 per cent are casual workers, whereas the proportion of casual workers among women workers in all industries together is far less, about 75 per cent. In construction, under the prevailing WTO regime, the essential requirement of global tendering has facilitated the entry of many large companies in the Indian construction scene in a big way. The presence of some of these companies is increasingly visible in the many infrastructure development projects being undertaken under government funding as well as under bilateral/multilateral assistance arrangements. With increased mechanization, there would be massive displacement of labour in nearly all construction operations. Women labour would be completely eliminated from the main operations in which they have been traditionally deployed, such as, soil digging and carrying, concrete mixing and placing and brick carrying. It is estimated that the overall deployment of labour will become 1/50th to 1/5th of the earlier numbers. Certainly, manual labour, especially women workers, would be increasingly eliminated from construction sites (ibid.). In the same manner, there would be an increase in factory production as well as growth in the need for various construction skills such as masons, tile fitters, painters, plumbers, cement finishers, glaziers, electricians, etc. Unfortunately, no woman worker possesses these skills in a practical sense.

The UNDP's Human Development Reports, released since 1990, have repeatedly pointed out that people are the real wealth of a nation. Human progress is not about income expansion and increasing commodity production, but about expanding human capabilities. Development is defined as a process of enlarging people's choice. The Human Development Report of 1995, for instance, draws our attention to the persistence of severe gender disparities in human development. The report points out that women still constitute nearly 70 per cent of the world's poor and two-thirds of the world's illiterates. The report further says that many of women's economic contributions are grossly undervalued or very often not valued at all. It estimates the values of such non-monetized, invisible contribution of women to be around $ 11 trillion or almost 50 per cent more than the officially estimated $ 23 trillion of global outlet.

Opportunities from Trade

Due to economic liberalization trade rules has changed and simultaneously, it exposes the weakness of the domestic producing industry. For instance, a large proportion of women in India are employed in the manufacture of textiles and clothing and this is one area in which developing countries have a comparative advantage and achieve a trade surplus with industrial countries. However, these are the goods against which developed countries have had the highest barriers through the Multi Fibre Arrangement (MFA), which continues to restrain the potential growth of this industry in developing countries (Mehta, 1999: 70).

However, lowering of protection in the West and increased market access to developed countries could be viewed as an opportunity for promoting exports while providing employment opportunities and higher incomes especially for women. Governments, NGOs, bilateral donors and UN agencies could help promote equality, marketing and value addition in export of products that provide intensive employment to women. Expansion of global market share in any sector means additional income and employment. Yet, it is critical that we identify and strengthen employment and income generating opportunities available for women, especially those who will not be able to survive the threat of competition (ibid.).

The Structural Adjustment Policy (SAP) gives an overwhelming importance to trade liberalization. Since export-led growth is regarded as the only viable development strategy, there is bound to be emphasis on export-oriented industries. In order to increase international competition, the industries will focus on cutting costs. The export sector firms often employ women and girl children. However, since there has always been international hue and cry to stop employing child labour, the small scale industries (SSIs) have started employing more and more women. New technologies are being introduced, the unskilled women become casual labour or do 'put-out' work as home-based workers. This leads to insecurity, low wages and also rejection of goods by the multinational companies. Further, women will not get social security benefits because of deregulation of labour legislation. In the urban self-employed sector, in petty trade, rag picking and personal service will increase and the economic remuneration given to them will also be reduced because of too many women trying to earn money through such employment. Thus, competition will undercut their value and they would be adversely affected by the processes of globalization (Ramanamma, 1999: 115).

Marketization of the Economy and Subsequent Decline in State's Intervention

The dominance of the market processes leads to commoditization of all aspects of everyday life and work and undervalues everything which is not directly calculable in those terms. This trend is likely to affect women as the role played by women in their households is not given any recognition since any work being performed by women inside the home is considered non-work. With the increased marketization, the value of non-marketed works is likely to decline, thus further devaluing the household role of women (Kaur, 1999: 124).

Environmental degradation is another significant consequence of privatization of common resources. Experiences across the globe have clearly revealed that in their emphasis to increase exports, indigenous resources are exploited at high rates, leading to very serious repercussions. On the other hand, it would result in common resources of the community like fuel, fodder and food unavailable or scarcely available to the people. And women, especially those whose whole life pattern is integrated with these natural resources, will have to work harder for securing these basic necessities for their families. Inflation is another factor that is likely to have an impact on poor families and more adversely on women. India is experiencing the highest inflation rates in the recent years which have been accompanied by increased unemployment and family incomes of the poor likely to become insufficient. Increasing unemployment, spiralling prices and increasing cuts in government's spending in the social sectors, as a result of SAP, is likely to make the goods and services in the market less accessible to the poor households. As a result, either the distribution of the available goods and services within the household is so changed that the already skewed distribution becomes more skewed to the disadvantage of the women who have to increase the amount of goods and services to be provided at home or to be marketed. This again increases the burden on women. This situation very often compels the women belonging to poor households to seek employment outside irrespective of the low wage rate and adverse working conditions (ibid.: 124–25).

In this context of marketization of the economy, the state's interventionist role is likely to decline. This will have its implications for all categories of people who, by virtue of their already weak position in spheres of knowledge, need some protective legislations and provisions. An open market competition is likely to further deteriorate their conditions. Similarly, a reduction in subsidies of basic amenities such as energy resources, sanitation and water supply and of basic services such as health not only puts a pressure on household income but also increases the burden on women for carrying out daily activities of the households and for providing these goods and services within the household.

The Invisibility of Women's Work

Several feminist critiques have pointed out that the globalization process is not necessarily integrating 'men' and 'women' into a homogeneous entities in the sphere of economy, culture, technology and governance. On the contrary, many of the feminist writers consider that the globalization and neo-liberalization have geared the process of euphemism for ultra imperialism. Indeed, neo-liberalization and globalization have led to severe fragmentations and the emergence of divergent views and identity politics. In that sense, globalization certainly gets ambiguous to be entitled as esoteric, universal and equal (Sarkar and Srivastava, 2011: 115).

Many maintain that women's economic dependence on men impacts their power within the family. With increased participation in income-earning activities, not only will there be more income for the family, but gender inequalities would be considerably reduced. This issue is particularly salient in India because studies show a very low level of female participation in the labour force. This under-reporting or false reporting can be attributed to the frequently held view that women's work is not economically productive. Further, in a report of the National Commission on Self-Employed Women and Women in the Informal Sector, the director of social welfare in one state said, 'there are no women in any unorganized sector in our state.' When the Commission probed and asked, 'Are there any women who go to the forest to collect firewood? Do any of the women in rural areas have cattle?' the director responded with, 'Of course, there are many women performing that type of work.' Working women, as such, are invisible to most of the population (ibid.: 130).

According to Sandhya Venkateswaran, citing Shiva, the Green Revolution, which focused on increasing yields of rice and wheat, entailed a shift in inputs from human to technical. Women's participation, knowledge and inputs were marginalized and their role shifted from being 'primary producers to subsidiary worker'. 'Commercialization and the consequent focus on cash crops has led to a situation where food is lifted straight from the farm to the market. The income accrued is controlled by men. Earlier, most of the produce was brought home and stored and the women exchanged it for other commodities. Such a system, in turn, vested more control with the women' (Sharma, 2009: 131).

The onset of globalization and liberalization of the world economy has clearly shown that massive disparities in income exist between nations. Compounded with a gender bias, this has made the life of most women in the developing world very difficult. As such, the impact of international trade practices on women on account of liberalization needs careful attention.

Conclusion

In backward agrarian economies where alternative avenues have not been developed or emerged with time so as to fruitfully engage labour that has become redundant because of mechanization, the fallout has numerous dimensions which are, in some cases, not even acknowledged by policy framers. There can really be no second opinion to the need of backward agrarian economies like India, in attempting to catch up with the developed world but can it be done by leaving a large majority of the population behind, in fact far behind. India's large unemployed rural population, especially women, surmounts all its other problems, but somehow it does not appear to have secured the requisite priority. In the case of rural women, there has been much talk of political empowerment, but of what benefit is it, if it is not preceded or followed by economic empowerment. Political and social empowerment can only be a natural sequel to economic empowerment of women, this cannot precede it. Hence, it can be rightly maintained that if women in the Indian context begin to earn what they call their own, political empowerment would follow in due course.

In the wake of globalization, employment avenues for women have also changed drastically in the past few years. With employment for women almost becoming a compulsion in the recent past, they would be ready to work for larger hours even for a meagre pay. With large-scale opportunities for women in trans-national corporations, especially in the call centres and BPOs during the late evening and night hours, women will be overburdened with a dual responsibility of managing the domestic vis-à-vis service fronts effectively and efficiently. However, social taboos and other outdated social conventions acting as a burden on the working women have gradually started fading away on account of the constantly rising standard of living and the pressure to make both ends comfortable. In the developing world, the denial of basic needs still remain the main issue as far as the violation of human rights is concerned. Globalization and Liberalization have further rendered large numbers of women unemployed, homeless and devoid of basic economic security. Women's groups in

India are trying to come to grips with this reality and the issues arising out of it. However, the search for gender justice especially with regard to the women workers will remain meaningless unless our immediate attention is focused on the issues of justice between the rich and the poor, between the powerful and the weak and among human beings and nations.

References

Agnihotri, Indu and Vina Mazumdar. 1995. 'Women's Movement in India, 1970s–1990s', *Economic and Political Weekly*, 22 July.

Bose, Jayshree and G. Sushuma. 2008. *Gender Discrimination: Perspectives and Experiences*, Hyderabad: The ICFAI University Press.

Deshpande, Sudha and L.K. Deshpande. 1992. 'New Economic Policy and Female Employment', *Economic and Political Weekly*, 10 October.

Gandhi, Nivedita and Nandita Shah. 1993. *The Issues at Stake: Theories and Practice in the Contemporary Women's Movement in India*, New Delhi: Kali for Women.

Gupta, Juhi. 2009. 'Economic and Social Reforms: Violence and Increasing Insecurities against Women', in Meenu Agrawal and Shobana Nelasco (eds), *Empowerment of Rural Women in India*, New Delhi: Kanishka Publications.

Jhabvala, Renana and Shalini Sinha. 2002. 'Liberalization and the Woman Worker', *Economic and Political Weekly*, 25 May.

Kaur, Malkit. 1999. 'Globalization and Women: Some Likely Consequences', in Raj Mohini Sethi (ed.), *Globalization, Culture and Women's Development*, Jaipur: Rawat Publications.

Mehta, Aasha Kapur. 1999. 'Globalization and Women', in Raj Mohini Sethi (ed.), *Globalization, Culture and Women's Development*, Jaipur: Rawat Publications.

Menon, Nivedita. 2004. 'Refusing Globalization and the Authentic Nation: Feminist Politics in Current Conjuncture', *Economic and Political Weekly*, 3 January.

Ramanamma, A. 1999. 'Globalization, Women and Economic Development', in Raj Mohini Sethi (ed.), *Globalization, Culture and Women's Development*, Jaipur: Rawat Publications,

Ramani, V.V. and Ratnaja Gogula. 2006. *Women in Workforce: Triumphs and Tribulations*, Hyderabad: The ICFAI University Press.

Ray, Bharati. 2002. 'Globalization and Women in India: A Women's Studies Perspective', in Donald Lamberton (ed.), *Managing the Global: Globalization, Employment and Quality of Life*, London: I.B. Tauris.

Sarkar, Sumita and Manjari Srivastava. 2011. *Globalization and Gender*, Jaipur: Rawat Publications.

Scholte, Jan Aart. 2005. *Globalization: A Critical Introduction*, New York: Palgrave Macmillan.

Sharma, Meenakshi. 2009. 'Social Economic Condition of Women in India', in Meenu Agrawal and Shobana Nelasco (eds), *Empowerment of Rural Women in India*, New Delhi: Kanishka Publishers.

Tanwar, Reicha. 1999. 'Women and Falling Incomes: The Impact of Cash Economy in Rural India', in Raj Mohini Sethi (ed.), *Globalization, Culture and Women's Development*, Jaipur: Rawat Publications.

Tyagi, Rupesh and Bhawna. 2009. 'Changing Occupational Pattern of Rural Women', in Meenu Agrawal and Shobana Nelasco (eds), *Empowerment of Rural Women in India*, New Delhi: Kanishka Publications.

Venkateswaran, Sandhya. 1995. *Environment, Development and the Gender Gap*, New Delhi: Sage Publications.

14

Participation of Tribal Women in Social Entrepreneurship

A Case of Santal Tribe of Purulia District in West Bengal

GURUPADA SAREN

In West Bengal, the scheduled tribe population consists of more than 5 per cent, in which more than 51 per cent represents Santal tribe of total population. The productive age groups are involved in migration to the rice bowl areas of Bardhaman and Hooghly from the drought prone areas of *junglemahals* for agricultural labour with the hope of better income and accumulation of resources. At the place of origin, they are deprived of health, education and necessary infrastructure for survival. As a result, they are unable to earn enough to sustain their livelihood; therefore, they migrate elsewhere for searching of jobs. Initially, they have migrated to nearby places – Bardhaman and Hooghly as agricultural labourers; after certain amount of exposure and economic well-being, the Santal women organized themselves to form Self-Help Group (SHG) with the aim of better standard of living. In due course of time, these Santal women gained momentum as SHGs and started an entrepreneurship programme.

Through the regular meeting of SHGs, the women folk have learnt about various social problems as well and they tried to adopt certain strategies to address issues like health, education and basic infrastructure for betterment. These SHGs have been given technical support and capacity building through local NGOs and panchayat. They have initiated various entrepreneurship programmes to better off their economy and sustain their livelihood. This paper argues the way

SHGs have started. This paper examines how the tribal women have been involved in social entrepreneurship to fight against poverty. The study attempts to look into the entrepreneurship process which leads them towards social transformation. It also seeks to investigate and analyse how the Santal women have taken initiative through SHGs to promote various entrepreneurship programmes to get rid of poverty; the steps to be taken to strengthen the process of social transformation at the community level and take initiative towards acceleration and strengthening the strategy to fight against poverty in West Bengal.

Scope of Social Entrepreneurship Development

In recent past, the social entrepreneurship field has been adopted by researchers and policy makers to bring the social problems in the limelight and venture into its practices towards betterment. The women folk have been considered to be an important human resources for upliftment of society which requires them to be economically empowered. There is plenty of scope for entrepreneurship which can be moulded to throw out various social problems exists in the society. In India, there is a scarcity of qualified in industry, who can accelerate the growth of entrepreneurship development programme through out the country for the intensification of Indian economy. The policy makers have recognized the significance of the entrepreneur development in economic prosperity and income generation for the rural mass. The government has also launched various schemes for the budding entrepreneurs in rural areas, with emphasis on women and unemployed youth.

More than 300 million people are living below the poverty line in India. To uplift those people, the government(s) has taken initiative to involve people in various entrepreneurial programmes. For the success of any entrepreneurship development, there is a need to support and encourage efforts in social, political and economical spheres towards the betterment. It has also been trying to promote the entrepreneurship scheme and encourage them to develop a positive mindset which can facilitate at individual level and the government should encourage and venture into capital and infrastructure development.

Social entrepreneurship aims to bring the desired social change in the society. It tries to utilize various principles to organize, create and manage the social venture. The social entrepreneurship broadens its scope in social, cultural, political and economical spheres to curb the social menace. It involves practice of starting new organizations to identify various opportunities. Entrepreneurship is a creative human act involving mobilization of resources for productive uses. It is a process in which an individual pursues opportunities with economic benefit and contributes towards the betterment of respective community. Besides, it also highlights the ingredient of entrepreneurship by sensing opportunities and intervening in various chaos, contradiction and confusion.

Women as Entrepreneurs

The development of women entrepreneurs and their immense contribution to the economy in developing country like India, has a great role. As we know, women are also considered as bread earners in rural India. During the 1990s, women entrepreneurs have grown with the scope of globalization and found their place in India too. But they lack basic education and exposure to the outside world from their restricted four walls. As a result, they are far behind in technology utilization in various social ventures. The government officials and policy makers should try to expand social entrepreneurship talents in the society for expanding economic conditions and the quality of life (Austin et al., 2006).

There is need of development of women folk as better human resources to empower them economically, socially, politically and so on. Through social entrepreneurship various existing social problems can be countered and smoothen the path of rural women towards entry into the field of entrepreneurship can be facilitated. The need and significance of entrepreneurs have been realized by the policy makers, which can gear up various income generation programmes for the rural masses. The government has also launched various schemes for the budding entrepreneurs in rural and tribal areas, with special emphasis on women and unemployed youth.

Rural society has acknowledged the role of women at the family level as how the women play a pivotal role in farm and home system. She contributes towards the physical aspects of farming, management of livestock and allied agricultural activities. With the help of NABARD, the rural women folk have organized themselves under Self Help Groups (SHGs) and have started income generation programmes which helps-meet their ends. They have been provided various skill development training, basic accounts and management of the entrepreneurial programme. This will not only generate income for them but also improve the decision-making capabilities that lead to overall empowerment.

After 73rd and 74th amendments to Constitution Act, 1992, the women folk have participated in the electoral system and govern the

Panchayats. The process of political participation is complex and they face multiple hurdles and find it difficult to participate in the political process. Until and unless specific conditions are addressed, women face multiple impediments to make it mandatory for local governments to include women in the local governance system. One-third of the seats in local bodies, gram or village panchayats, municipalities, city corporations and district bodies, are reserved for women.

It has been experienced that entrepreneurship is the only solution for growing employment among rural women and youth. It can help to generate employment opportunities for a number of people within their own social system. This is the process which facilitates the women in rural areas towards empowerment, as it enables them to add to the family income while taking care of their own home and livestock-centred tasks. Rural women possess rich unused resources to take up as enterprises. Hence, she can efficiently carry out both the production and processing oriented enterprises in rural areas. Entrepreneurship expansion among rural women assists to add to their personal capabilities and involve themselves in various decision-making processes in the family as well as in society all together.

Changing Attitudes of Society Towards Women

In ancient times, the position of women was quite respectable, but the evolution of changes itself degraded the women. The attitudes toward women vary from society to society and the members of the society are responsible for that. It depends on cultural perceptions and gender discrimination towards women. In the age of globalization, there has been a great budge in attitudes towards women globally as society critically examines the position that women should play in society and adopt accordingly. The women have extended their support in social, economical, religious and political spheres at the family as well as society level. They have been well equipped with modern technology in the case of urban settings; though the rural women have been deprived of the upgradation in the field of technological aspects. In India, both in rural and urban areas, the women play a pivotal role in family to sustain core values of family, caring for family and generating the income.

Education being an important vehicle for social empowerment of women, several policies and programmes are being implemented for the development of women through entrepreneurship and affirm their stake and role in the society. The initiative of entrepreneurship by the women folk help them to establish in various positions in the society. The role of women is undergoing a radical social transformation in the modern society. The marriage is the only career for women in India, but the rural women play an important role in developing economy and to participate in all stages of production. They are the invisible contributors to the national economy. After 73rd and 74th amendment to the Constitution Act, the women contribute in economical, social, political and religious spheres and strengthen their involvement in decision-making processes at family as well as community level.

Role of SHGs in Social Transformation

Self Help Groups (SHGs) is well accepted strategies to meet the people's need and desires. It helps the members to plan for development activities as an individual and strengthen the group activities through mutual understanding to resolve their own social problems among the women. It is based on self-reliance, self-production and employment opportunities through mobilizing local resources at the community level. By virtue of taking the membership of the SHGs, the women can understand themselves through various activities and enhance towards new status and roles in the community level. It influence on the individual member and social institutions towards positive mindset in which women affecting in their day to day activities. Thus, it is applicable to the changes in the material aspects of life as well as in the ideas, values and attitudes of the people.

These are voluntary congregation of persons who share their needs and problems that were not addressed by the formal organizations. It is a group of rural poor who have agreed upon to organize themselves into a group for eradication of various social problems in their own community. They agree to save money regularly and discuss about issues or problems which affect their daily life, e.g. alcoholism, poverty, migration, etc. Social transformation is a process of change in social and cultural systems. In fact, these are inherent methodological problems of identification and measurement of change; as a result, the entire society is involved in a process of social change. This change may be so incremental that the members of the society are hardly aware of it. A society is characterized by change; the rate of change, the process of change and the directions of change are realized after meeting the ends.

A society is in the process of unrest due to various factors such as biological, cultural and technological, etc. which determine the rate and directions of social change. The individual SHG members are inspired by joining the group(s), learn various social problems, adopt individual strategy to address these issues at their own level. Through the SHGs activities, an individual member's income starts increasing and it plays a significant role in improving economic status. Regular savings in the group enhance self-confidence of the individuals, as it is a sign of group encouragement at the time of taking loan.

The SHGs help the members to know about political system and how they can be part of it. It provides the awareness on local self governance and their participation can bring some effective results in the spheres of social, economical and political arenas. It enhances the knowledge to decide on local self-governance and how rules can be set up effectively in identifying problems, formulating alternatives and allocating resources for their respective community. As their economic status changes, their confidence also uplifts various other social problems. They are ready to take up the new challenges by using science and technology in the rural areas and human resources development in perfect manner. They are made aware about national policies on rural people in general and rural women in particular.

The SHGs have the power to create a socio-economic revolution at their community level and get rid of their problems and traditional bounds. Self-help groups have smoothened the way to bring social transformation and ensure the participation of rural people. Besides, they also contribute towards social and economic progress of the society; engage them to bring forth the required changes in economic conditions, social status, decision-making and increases women's participation in out door activities.

Skill and Capacity Development of Tribal Women

In the context of tribal women in entrepreneurship, there is an urgent need to develop their skills and the capacity at the village level through SHGs. The community-based SHGs are not well equipped with their vision and prospects. However, the local NGOs and government help them to frame their aspirations. The capacity building activities of SHGs fulfills the needs of the individual members and extends support to the group as a whole. Individual members are given proper training on capacity building which contributes towards empowering the community. Capacity development programmes prepare individual members to adapt to technological upgradation, adapt strategies according to the needs as and when required. They meet the needs of an individual and the community and expand to include other interrelated issues. Capacity building becomes an incremental mode, which has impacts on all aspects of developmental activities.

As far as capacity building of tribal women is concerned, it assists communities to draw on skills and resources which empower members by providing proper training. It also throws light on their participation as stakeholders, assembles local resources and intensifies the links to outside agents. It is a systematic approach that enlightens the understanding of social problems surrounding their community and search for alternatives for the betterment of the community. It is an encouragement of attitudes, behaviour and competencies at the individual level and in partner organizations.

The capacity building ropes in individuals, groups, organizations, institutions and systems to develop themselves and their social and methodological competencies. It enables the stakeholders to identify and prioritize their needs in order to sensitize their life and development tasks. Capacity building generates suitable atmospheres by providing information and opportunities about alternative ways of assisting people to build a different social system that reflects their desires and fulfils their needs. It includes the strengthening of skills, competencies and abilities of people and communities in developing the basic amenities at the community level.

Contribution of Tribal Women in Entrepreneurship

The Santal women play a major role in management of their family through proper management of natural resources, social, economic resources and agricultural development. They take care of every minute detail of crop production, livestock production, etc. Due to lack of literacy they remain backward with traditional values, superstition and many other social and cultural factors which obstruct their ways towards development. Through participation in SHGs, their role in improving their living conditions by fully exploring natural endowments and alternative uses must find an appropriate place in the strategic approach. They have been provided with proper training on skill and capacity development, they are fighting against the poverty and other social constraints at their community level.

As they have started various entrepreneurship programmes, they have been able to develop their self-confidence at the individual level which helps them to participate in various social and political milieus.

Through their involvement in entrepreneurship programme, the Santal women have adopted various modern values in the day-to-day life. Today, the Santal women have stopped to migrate to Bardhaman and Hooghly as they can earn sufficient livelihood at their place of origin. More particularly, they have been exposed to the processes related to modernization and globalization. The effect of such changes can be seen in their changing cultural values, institutions and role perceptions. It is a fact that the diminishing significance of patriarchy in the social life of Santal is evident. In the traditional tribal society, specific role was assigned to men and women for maintenance of their age old tradition, customs, etc. Dependency on forest-based economy also influenced their cultural norms, traditions and values. But as a result of exposure to modern way of life and economy, these tribals have come close to new forms of life, institutions and values that have encouraged social transformation in their society. With involvement in entrepreneurship process, the Santal women have brought various changes in their day-to-day activities, age old customs and traditions. They have been influenced by the people. In this sense, entrepreneurship activities have exposed them to various aspects of modernity.

It is clear that entrepreneurship has several direct and indirect impacts on the traditional culture, tradition and social norms of the Santals. The impact is evident in their day-to-day activities. The processes of entrepreneurship has helped them to learn about new methods of agriculture, cooking style and food habits, language, dress pattern, accustomed to readymade clothes, aware of political mobilizations, imbibe the habit of saving, etc. It also helps the Santal women understand the need of education for their children, get exposure to modern health practices and begin to doubt superstitious practices like witchcraft and sorcery by the priests.

Challenges Ahead

Empowering women particularly tribal women is a big challenge in today's context. Though various entrepreneurship programmes help them to meet their basic needs at the familial level but there are bigger challenges that await them at the community level. They lack basic education which is the main hurdle in the way to prosperity, as an individual and society as a whole. However, various initiatives have been taken to educate them through Sarva Siksha Abhiyan (SSA) by the government and local NGOs to help them.

They also lack proficiency in the mainstream language, i.e. Bengali, which is also very much needed to carry out entrepreneurship activities. They have grown up in Santal community without much exposure to the outside community. Now the traditional leaders and local self governance officials are trying to cope with the situation to educate the Santal women to lead better lives and improve their standard of living at the community level and practice their entrepreneurial initiatives beyond their community. Besides, there is an urgent need to upgrade about various technological development, including mobile phones, uses of calculators, etc.

It is also important to note that the traditional Santal leaders along with local self-governance officials and government support should initiate various programmes which directly benefit the Santal community in basic education and health practices in their day-to-day activities. However, education should be propagated to uplift their community as we all know education is a vehicle of development.

Conclusion

The participation of Santal women in entrepreneurship activities involves various factors which have direct or indirect impact upon them as individual and as a community. SHGs open up plenty of avenues to exchange ideas, values, social norms, etc. with fellow members from their own community. In the long run, entrepreneurship helps them to survive economic hardship, learn new habits and practices and explore new opportunities having much better facilities. On the whole, therefore, entrepreneurship among the Santal women promotes awareness about various social problems, makes them aware about modern education and health practices, improves their rationality regarding superstitious practices, inspires them to do savings and so on. The process of entrepreneurship helps them to meet various challenges at the community level as women and establish their presence in their society as well. It empowers them economically, socially and politically, while preparing them to face various challenges at the community and societal level.

References

Austin, J., R. Gutierrez, E. Ogliastri and R. Reficco (eds). 2006. *Effective Management of Social Enterprises*, Cambridge, MA: David Rockefeller Center Series on Latin American Studies, Harvard University.

Donelson, R.F. 1990. *Group Dynamics*, 2nd Edition, California: Cole Publishing Company.

Jairam, K. 2004. *Sociology and Social Change*, Delhi: Dominant Publishers and Distributors.

Karmakar, K.G. 1999. *Rural Credit and Self Help Groups*, New Delhi: Sage Publications India Pvt. Ltd.

Lawani, B.T. 2004. *Non-Government Organizations in Development*, Jaipur: Rawat Publications.

15

Women, Business and Emancipation

SANGEETA ROY MAITRA

For men and women throughout the developing world, the prospect to start and run a business or get a good job is the surest hope for a way out of poverty. Building the kind of environment in which this hope can thrive requires effort in a broad range of areas, from security and infrastructure to education and health. It also requires good business regulation, suited to the purpose, streamlined and accessible, so that the opportunity to build a business or have a good job is dependent on an individual's initiative and ability.[1] Until the 1800s, most of the world's women enjoyed fewer legal rights than men in areas that have a potential impact on women's economic opportunities. This was true for what are now developed economies as well as those that are still developing. Since then many economies have moved at different speeds towards a more equal legal system for men and women.[2] The last two decades have witnessed a striking evolution in the conception of not only human rights, but of development, as both relate to promoting freedom, well-being and dignity of all people. The recent and ongoing convergence of these two approaches is invigorating the dialogue regarding the field of women in development and reshaping policy and practice promoting women's advancement.[3] Though there has been much progress toward legal parity between women and men throughout the world, important distinctions still exist that may prevent women from improvii g their own and their families' well-being by working or by running a business.[4] This paper focuses on two aspects of – women and business: one is to dwell upon the human right to equal opportunities in exercise of economic rights and the second is to review the recent development of human rights approach to business in light of gender issues. It seeks to explore women's economic roles and opportunities and their aspirations for advancement. It reviews various limitations they face in fulfilling them and considers the relationship between women's rights and capabilities on the one hand and development policy and practice on the other.[5] The object is to take a two-fold account of women vis-à-vis business and human rights. On the one hand, it tries to explore the need and ways of economic independence as the actual basis of women empowerment and on the other, the effect of various human rights policies in business on women taking into account the gender bias perspective.

Women and Business: The Concept

Gender is a concept that refers to the socially constructed roles, functions and responsibilities of women and men. Gender roles vary depending on the cultural context and over time. Gender is, therefore, a socially constructed phenomenon, as opposed to sex, which is generally accepted as a biological given. Gender equality is an important human rights issue because gender differences can be the basis upon which people are discriminated against, i.e. not granted the same rights or ability to enjoy rights.

Adopting a 'gender perspective' or 'integrating gender' into work on business and human rights means that any analysis looks at the way in which a business entity may have a differential, disproportionate or unforeseen impact on women or men, boys or girls, as a result of their different social, cultural or legal roles, rights and responsibilities. First, business activities may create or exacerbate gender inequality. If a community is resettled for the purposes of a large-scale infrastructure project, for example, the corporate entity should consider the impact such resettlement may have on women and men. Women and men often have differentiated familial responsibilities, economic opportunities and child care responsibilities. If in relocating a community, a compensation scheme envisages cash compensation to heads of households for familial held plots of land, this could have different consequences for women and men. For instance, a gender-neutral approach to compensation can exacerbate existing gender inequalities by paying compensation solely to the male head of the household and not to female-headed households, single or widowed women. As such, inequality may arise or existing inequalities may be exacerbated. Attention must also be paid to compensation for loss of livelihood or provision of alternative livelihoods with recognition that women will often be more vulnerable to inequity in this regard. Secondly, world-wide women work disproportionately in the informal employment sector, where they have less secure jobs, worse working conditions and poorer pay. This in turn contributes to women's disproportionate impoverishment globally (the so-called feminization of poverty) – a serious issue of gender inequality in the business and human rights context.[6]

The Role of the United Nations in Shaping the Gender and Business Agenda

The concept of equality is a central pillar of the international human rights regime. Gender mainstreaming is a specific focus of the United Nations, as overwhelming evidence reveals that a gender-neutral approach to policy-making renders invisible important gender issues and marginalizes women's experiences. Gender equality has been recognized as a human right since the establishment of the United Nations. The text of the Universal Declaration of Human Rights, adopted in 1948 by the General Assembly of the United Nations, opens by emphasizing that 'recognition of the inherent dignity and of the equal and inalienable rights of all members of the human family is the foundation of freedom, justice and peace in the world.' Article 1 of the Universal Declaration proclaims all human beings to be 'born free and equal in dignity and rights,' while Articles 2 and 7 lay the groundwork for specific legal protections concerning equality and nondiscrimination. All of the major human rights treaties adopted by the international community since the Universal Declaration have carried through on this fundamental commitment to equality. As such, the principles of equality and nondiscrimination cut across the full panoply of human rights and fundamental freedoms, whatever their nature. Beyond this cross-cutting commitment to equality in general, the international community further elaborated its commitment to gender equality through the Convention on the Elimination of All Forms of Discrimination against Women (CEDAW). The Convention prohibits all forms of gender-based discrimination against women and provides for the full equality of women with respect to all human rights and fundamental freedoms, whether in the public or private sphere. While coverage of the Convention is comprehensive, a substantial portion of the text is devoted specifically to women's economic and social rights.[7] The 1948 Universal Declaration of Human Rights (UDHR) and the 1976 International Covenants on Civil and Political Rights (ICCPR) and Economic, Social and Cultural Rights (ICESCR), all contain clear statements on the right of women to be free from discrimination. Importantly, governments at the 1995 Fourth UN

World Conference on Women in Beijing laid out specific actions set to attain the equality and empowerment standards set by CEDAW in the Beijing Platform for Action.

Efforts focused on improving the private sector impact on human rights have been growing significantly within the UN system over the past decade. This can be seen starting with the creation of the UN Global Compact in 2000. Another key milestone was the 2003 'Norms on the Responsibilities of Transnational Corporations and Other Business Enterprises with Regard to Human Rights' adopted by the Sub-Commission of the then UN Commission on Human Rights. Although the Sub-Commission's work was not carried forwarded by the Commission, it is worthwhile noting that the commentary in the norms document, specifically mentioned women in relation to equal opportunities, conditions of work and environmental protection and impact assessments. It is also worth highlighting that the Women's Environment and Development Organisation (WEDO) produced a short piece entitled 'Engendering the UN Norms for Business'.

The Calvert Women's Principles were developed in June 2004 by the investment firm Calvert in cooperation with the United Nations Development Fund for Women (UNIFEM). They were re-launched as the *Women's Principles* in March 2009 by the UN Global Compact and UNIFEM as part of an event to mark International Women's Day and are now subject to a consultation phase. This voluntary code of conduct is the first of its kind to specifically propose how the private sector should approach gender issues. It originated within an investment firm and therefore, represents a strong call to action to businesses on this subject. The *Women's Principles* are clearly grounded in human rights principles and go beyond the narrow scope of non-discrimination or access to board level positions. The human rights content of note within the principles includes:

- Provisions to stop violence against women in the workplace and to prevent trafficking.
- Steps to ensure the safety of female employees in the workplace.
- Protection from exposure to hazardous or toxic chemicals in the workplace, particularly those that have adverse effects on women's health.
- Provision of gender equitable health services and insurance.
- Refusal to tolerate situations where cultural differences or customs are used to deny the basic human rights of women and girls.
- Ensuring a grievance policy is established for employees concerning their treatment in the workplace.

- Forbidding business-related activities that condone, support, or otherwise participate in trafficking[8].
- Forced labour and the particular risks experienced by female migrant workers.
- The right to privacy – in particular not interfering with reproductive rights, or refraining from it is directly relevant to the performance of the role.
- The right to an adequate standard of living, including adequate food, clothing and housing – this may apply in the context of migrant workers or workers based in Export Processing Zones where the responsibilities of employers may be greater.

Business can have positive and negative impacts on virtually all human rights. For this reason, the United Nations Global Compact – the UN's initiative for businesses that are committed to greater corporate sustainability in the spirit of universal values – calls on businesses everywhere to support and respect internationally proclaimed human rights as its first principle. The Guiding Principles on business and human rights endorsed in June 2011, by the UN Human Rights Council and the UN *Protect-Respect-Remedy Framework,* that they elaborate, are helpful in explaining the differentiated roles that governments, businesses and other actors play with regard to human rights, adding much needed conceptual and operational clarity. Among other things, they reinforce that it is governments' role to protect human rights and business' role to respect human rights. The Guiding Principles are also helping to accelerate efforts by business to make the management shifts required to ensure that human rights are respected.

In March 2010, the UN Global Compact and UN Women launched the Women's Empowerment Principles – Equality Means Business (WEPs). Informed by real-life business practices and input gathered from across the globe, the WEPs provide seven steps for business on how to empower women in the workplace, marketplace and community. They are the result of a collaboration between the United Nations Development Fund for Women (UNIFEM, part of UN Women) and the United Nations Global Compact. Sub-titled Equality Means Business, the principles emphasize the business case for corporate action to promote gender equality and women's empowerment and are informed by real-life business practices and input gathered from across the globe. Rather than being prescriptive or a new initiative to which business is asked to subscribe, the *Women's*

Empowerment Principles seek to point the way to best practice by elaborating the gender dimension of good corporate citizenship, the UN Global Compact, and business' role in sustainable development. As well as being a useful guide for business, it is hoped that principles will inform other stakeholders, including governments, in their engagement with business.[9] The seven key guidelines are:

1. Establish high-level corporate leadership for gender equality;
2. Treat all women and men fairly at work – respect and support human rights and nondiscrimination;
3. Ensure the health, safety and well-being of all women and men workers;
4. Promote education, training and professional development for women;
5. Implement enterprise development, supply chain and marketing practices that empower women;
6. Promote equality through community initiatives and advocacy.
7. Calls on businesses to measure and publicly report on progress towards gender equality.

To date about 466 executives from around the world have signed a CEO Statement of Support to signal their commitment to gender equality and the goals of the Women's Empowerment Principles. Companies that have signed the CEO Statement of Support for the Women's Empowerment Principles, as well as other businesses and stakeholders, will convene to discuss how corporate behaviour and practices are being transformed to align with the WEPs. As in previous years, participants will share their experiences in implementing the WEPs, including best practices, challenges and lessons-learned. The meeting will also provide an opportunity for discussion on key topics and themes, including how gender equality fits into the agendas of corporate sustainability and sustainable development.[10]

The World Bank also carried out a study covering 141 economies of the world to assess the actual economic development of the women. The 2012 Report investigates the claims of the governments in improving business regulation, women entrepreneurs and workers benefit alongside men. It examines those regulations and institutions which differentiate between women and men in ways that affect their incentives or capacity to work, earn an income, own and manage property or set up and run a business. *Women, Business and the Law* focuses on gender differentiations in legal treatment that can affect women's economic opportunities. This focus overlaps to a significant degree with human rights work on gender equality issues, particularly in the area of women's economic and social rights. For the first time, the report includes an annex, providing a better basis for understanding the overlap between human rights for women and women's economic opportunities. It establishes six indicators of gender differences in formal laws and institutions: accessing institutions, using property, getting a job, providing incentives to work, building credit and going to court.[11]

Women's Role in Business and the Gender Specific Problems in the Path of their Empowerment

Women's rights and economic development are highly correlated. Historically, even in countries that are now rich women had few rights before economic development took off.[12] Studies indicate that increasing the number of women in management can increase organizational innovation, cause a fundamental positive change in the boardroom and enhance corporate governance. Further, research demonstrates that organizations with gender-diverse senior management tend to perform better financially. Investors are increasingly demanding gender-specific information from businesses to inform their decision-making, as research suggests that businesses that empower women and encourage gender diversity may outperform those that do not, over the long term. They see that management diversity can be a strong indicator of future financial performance and hence is one of a range of non-financial factors accounted for, as they analyse investment risks and opportunities.[13] A report by McKinsey and Company (2010), 'The Business of Empowering Women', presents a case for why and how the private sector can intensify its engagement in the economic empowerment of women in developing countries and emerging markets. The report draws on insights from interviews with more than 50 leaders and experts in the private and social sectors who focus on women's empowerment, as well as findings from a global survey of nearly 2,300 senior private sector executives, among others. Research by the London Business School Centre for Women in Business found that gender parity in teams leads to more innovation, making a clear business case for diversity. Additional examples supporting the business case for gender equality include two recent studies on gender diversity and corporate performance by McKinsey and Company, conducted in partnership with the Women's Forum for the Economy and Society. Their research demonstrated the link between the presence of women in corporate management teams and companies' organizational and financial performance, suggesting that the companies where women are most strongly represented at board or top-management level are also the companies that perform best. Further, research on female leadership showed that behaviours more often applied by women reinforce a company's organizational performance on several dimensions and will be critical to meet the expected challenges companies will face over the coming years.[14]

Here we can refer to a few government initiatives towards recognition of women's unparallel role in economic development of a country. There are regulations on gender diversity pertaining to any enterprise wishing to contract with the US Government. Australia requires companies to disclose information on the numbers of women in management. In a recent move in India, the Securities and Exchange Board of India (SEBI) has mandated the top 100 listed entities on the Bombay Stock Exchange (BSE) to report on Environmental, Social and Governance performance as a part of their Annual Reports, in line with the principles set out in the 'National Voluntary Guidelines on Social, Environmental and Economic Responsibilities of Business' by the Indian Ministry of Corporate Affairs (MCA). While not specifically requiring gender disclosures, it represents a growing trend towards disclosure requirements on social performance extending to emerging economies. Increasingly, other countries are considering similar kinds of requirements to fast track women's economic empowerment, so pre-emptive action towards disclosure can put a business in the lead.[15]

The 'multiplier effect' of gender equality has been increasingly acknowledged. Studies continue to show that lowering the social, economic and political barriers faced by women and girls extends education, decreases child mortality and vulnerability to HIV and AIDS. Women's greater labour force participation reduces poverty through increased productivity and earnings. Conversely, systematic discrimination against women and girls will make it impossible for many to meet the poverty and other targets of the Millennium Development Goals (MDG). Millennium Development Goal 3 is to promote gender equality and empower women and is one of the eight MDGs drawn from the Millennium Declaration that was adopted by 189 Governments in 2000. The MDGs address the world's main development challenges, and have time-bound and measurable targets accompanied by indicators for monitoring progress, with a timeline for achievement by 2015. Growing concern that the MDGs will not be met is accompanied by growing recognition that achievement of gender equality is critical to achievement of all other MDGs.[16]

But this role of women is often cut short on account of gender discrimination. Gender discrimination is a human rights issue. It cannot be separated but needs to be understood as a cross-cutting theme.

Developing potent strategies to achieve gender equality requires an understanding of the gender-specific dynamics that push women into insecure work. The most basic and acute problems with respect to gender equality are related. The major problems may be summarized as:

- Gender-based discrimination with respect to both hierarchy and type of work remains wide-spread. Women make up the majority of the workforce in the garment, toy, electronics and agricultural sectors, albeit to varying degrees. Supervisors and senior managers, on the other hand, are generally male, especially in the agricultural sectors. Tasks are assigned gender-specifically, which means it is mostly women who perform low-pay, low-prestige work. As the supply chain deepens, the proportion of women workers grows.
- The presence of women is strongest where employment is predominantly informal, unprotected and unregulated. Informality increases with supply chain length. Formal and informal types of employment are not worlds apart; they form a continuum.
- Working conditions often pose a threat to workers' health, sometimes to their lives, not only but especially where work is widely unregulated and informal.
- Wages are systematically and consistently low, sometimes below the absolute poverty line of USD1 per day, often below the statutory minimum wage and usually far from sufficient to provide a secure livelihood. The lack of living wages and the persistence of unequal wages for equal work are crucial factors of gender discrimination.
- Excessive overtime is wide-spread and closely linked to the problem of indecent wages. Due to the persisting double burden of reproductive work and wage labour for most women, the issue of working hours has a strong gender dimension.
- Freedom of association, collective representation and collective bargaining are largely absent from these sectors. Where unions are active, women are underepresented as unions often have a male-dominated structure.
- Sexual harassment, disparaging treatment and discriminatory recruiting practices are part of many women's everyday working experience. Women are stereotyped as 'supplementary' earners and cheap 'willing' labour.
- Corporate Social Responsibility (CSR) initiatives have not yet been able to tackle fundamental problems of gender discrimination.

Existing impact analysis show gender equality has been under-represented among the impacts of CSR instruments. Many workers, male and female, also remain ignorant of the rights granted to them by the codes of labour practice. The less secure but more frequent forms of work like temporary, seasonal, contract and migrant work generally persist and it is here that employment conditions are found to be poorest and codes' impacts are least felt. Therefore, any CSR instrument will remain weak as long as it does not build upon an understanding of the complex forms of discrimination at work.[17]

- Non-compliance with existing laws is a problem in most countries and that a focus on enforcement of existing legislation continues to be important. For example, according to a report from the United Kingdom's national human rights institution, 83 per cent of employers surveyed believed that they could violate equality laws with impunity. Soft regulation also plays a major role, particularly in the form of market pressures and expectations, though here again gender equality has received less attention than other human rights issues.
- States might not be meeting their human rights obligations under international law if they fail to consider gender equality when they enter into trade and investment agreements.
- A company, if 'gender sensitive' and is not 'gender responsive', will not empower women or correct embedded discrimination. Many countries still have gender-biased laws on their statute books; here companies may need to develop processes and policies that respect the spirit of gender equality, while not contravening local or national laws.[18]

Position in India

Status of women freedom depends on economic conditions even more than political. If a woman is not economically free and self-earning, she will have to depend on her husband or someone else, and dependents are never free. These were the ideas of Pandit Jawaharlal Nehru, the first Prime Minister of India, who vividly highlighted the importance of economic independence of women. 'When women move forward, the families moves, the village moves'. These words of Pandit Jawaharlal Nehru are often repeated because it is accepted facts that only when the women are in the mainstream of progress can any economic and social development be meaningful.[19]

Over the last few decades, while women have come forward to establish their own enterprises, their numbers remain few and far between. The entrepreneurial world is still male dominated. In developed countries women tend to perform secretarial or low-level managerial jobs in the corporate sectors – indeed, less than five per cent of senior management portions are held by women in the USA. In developing countries such as India even in the small-scale sector, less than seven per cent of the enterprises have been set-up by women. But probably what is noteworthy is that women have plunged into the field of entrepreneurship and have been found effective in emerging social, economical role. Women had been a manager since long, from the time the concept of living in a family emerged. She had been an entrepreneur within the four walls where she was innovative in terms of budgeting with the limited income resources, using the waste material for making some useful products. With the changing role that women accepted ever since mid-eighties, the role of entrepreneurship amongst women has gained a considerable importance.[20] Women entrepreneurship in India was earlier limited to the three Ks: Kitchen, Kids and Knitting; then came the three Ps: Powder, *Pappad* and Pickles; at present there are four Es: Electricity, Electronics, Energy and Engineering. 'Women in business' is considered a recent phenomenon in India. The fact that almost half the population of this large country comprises females while businesses owned and operated by them constitute less than five per cent is a reflection on social, cultural as well as economic distractions in the decades of development. Indeed, women's participation in economic activity and production of goods and services is far greater than formal statistics might reveal, since much of it takes place in the informal sector as also in the households.[21]

The Constitution of India guarantees equality, liberty and dignity to the women of India. The Fundamental Rights, The Directive Principles of State Policy and Fundamental Duties, etc. virtually assure equal status to women and provide special protection. After independence, a gamut of laws have been passed and some have been altered so as to award equal share to women in property as well as to eradicate some of the injustices meted out to women. However, there are many shortcomings and ambiguities in the enforcement of laws. Some of the labour laws are never enforced and some enforced in a mutilated form. In spite of the Equal Remuneration Act 1976, there is discrimination in promotion, training and transfer on the basis of sex. By and large undoubtedly more than six decades of efforts since Independence by the government and spell of fights and struggle under the immense pressure of women lib activists in the country, have indeed brought certain changes in social, psychological, economic and political spheres of life. Consequently, it becomes an imperative need to look into problems and issues and their implications upon women particularly in matters of business and entrepreneurship.

The chief constraints faced by the Indian women in terms of assessing their rights of economic development, is mostly the existing social and moral conditions coupled with the legal insecurities. Some of them are: lack of confidence, market-oriented risks, lack of managerial skill, lack of freedom and autonomy, lack of education and awareness and motivational factors.[22] The greatest deterrent to women entrepreneurs is that they are women. A kind of patriarchal, male dominant social order is the construing block to them in their way towards business success. Male members think it a big risk financing the ventures run by women. The financial institutions are skeptical about the entrepreneurial abilities of women. The bankers consider women loonies as higher risk than men loonies. The bankers put unrealistic and unreasonable securities to give loan to women entrepreneurs. According to a report by the United Nations Industrial Development Organization (UNIDO), 'despite evidence that women's loan repayment rates are higher than men's, women still face more difficulties in obtaining credit,' often due to discriminatory attitudes of banks and informal lending groups (UNIDO, 1995b). Entrepreneurs usually require financial assistance of some kind to launch their ventures – be it a formal bank loan or money from a savings account. Women in developing nations have little access to funds, due to the fact that they are concentrated in poor rural communities with few opportunities to borrow money.[23]

Women's family obligations also bar them from becoming successful entrepreneurs in both developed and developing nations. 'Having primary responsibility for children, home and older dependent family members, few women can devote all their time and energies to their business. The financial institutions discourage women entrepreneurs on the belief that they can at any time leave their business and become housewives again. The interest of the family members is a determinant factor in the realization of women folk business aspirations. Though the risk tolerance ability of the women folk in day-to-day life is high compared to male members, while in business it is found opposite to that.[24]

One of the greatest hindrances has been by way of sexual harassment. Sexual harassment at workplaces existed in India since a very long period, but the evolution of the right against sexual harassment is a new phenomenon. A woman may seek remedy under the Law of torts; National Commission for Women Act, 1990 or the Protection of Human Rights Act, 1993. The Supreme Court of India has also recognized sexual harassment at workplace as a legally distinct type of prohibited activity. The Supreme Court, in the absence of enacted law to provide for the effective enforcement of the basic human right to gender equality and guarantee against sexual harassment and abuse, has laid down the guidelines against sexual harassment at workplace in the landmark case of *Vishaka* v. *State of Rajasthan*.[25] What can be assessed and understood is that commonly the issue of sexual harassment at workplace revolves around the women who are employed under a male employer or boss, and as a result of which she is often discriminated and harassed owing to her gender. It is discriminatory when the woman has reasonable grounds to believe that her objection to the behaviour of the employer or next boss would disadvantage her in connection with her employment. But when we are emphasizing on women's role in business as an important parameter to determine the index of economic development, both the legislature and judiciary are silent. Perhaps, this is also a less-spoken and less-revealed arena of gender inequality. In a country like India, where cottage, small-scale industries, micro-financing institutions are all reflective of active female participation, its expected success is missing due to the menace of sexual harassment of these enterprising women. In fact, there have been various instances where such women have been harassed by their associates owing to their gender; the local authorities and, at times, even by their subordinates and the nature of such harassment is undoubtedly within the meaning of sexual harassment. While it is often said that sexual harassment can be prevented in women-run organizations; but what if the entrepreneur herself is a victim of such a wrong. However, the much awaited Protection of Women Against Sexual Harassment at Workplace Bill, 2010 finally received the assent of the President on 22 April 2013 thereby giving the Sexual Harassment of Women at Workplace (Prevention, Prohibition and Redressal) Act, 2013. But unfortunately, this piece of legislation suffers from a number of defects and it only limits itself to female employees and misses on the rights of women entrepreneurs. Hence, the law and the judiciary have miserably failed to recognize the rights of this invaluable human resource. It is often said that India is a safe game for entrepreneurs but not for women.

Another menace is that of domestic violence. According to a 2000 study in India, a woman loses an average of at least five paid work days for each incident of intimate partner violence. Though the Protection of Women from Domestic Violence Act has been enacted, but how it has actually affected the women's role in economic development is far from assessment.

In addition, gender-based discrimination, systematically and consistently low wages, underepresentation in unions, lack of 'gender responsive' attitude in companies, majority of the female workforce being in the unorganized sector, non-recognition of skill – all add up to the woes of women's active participation in business.

So far as the UN Global Compact Women Empowerment Principles are concerned, till date, of the 466 signatories only four Indian companies have come forward to ratify the seven principles which aim at gender sensitive approach to the business and human rights perspective. Perhaps, it is reflective of the nation's apathy towards women in business vis-à-vis human rights. Although the government has taken a positive step in the form of SEBI guidelines, but that is too small a step in a country where women mostly belong to the informal sector.

Suggestions

Human rights due diligence requires a systematic approach to the problem of gender discrimination in global production networks and supply chains. The business and human rights agenda of the United Nations and the Guiding Principles on Business and Human Rights should be an integral part of global efforts to bridge existing governance gaps and safeguard protection and respect for human rights in the context of economic activities. The entities and mechanisms of the United Nations system already contribute towards that end, but the sheer scale and complexity of the issue requires a coordinated strategic effort by the United Nations system as a whole. In order to achieve system-wide coordination and coherence with regard to business and human rights, the business and human rights agenda and particularly the Guiding Principles, should be embedded throughout the United Nations system at the strategic policy level. At the same time, it would be worthwhile to note that in the Indian context it is equally important to build on the principles of women corporate leadership and entrepreneurship. The other suggestions include:

- For CSR instruments to be able to strengthen gender equality, clear norms and criteria must be laid down. The two main labour standards aimed at securing gender equality are those referring to a fair remuneration for both women and men (equal pay for work of equal value) and to non-discrimination in the workplace.

- Addressing the whole supply chain and tackling informal employment should be a priority. So far, legislation and CSR initiatives have primarily affected the formal, regulated spheres of the economy, not the whole supply chain. To take stronger account of informality, more research and analysis of experiences from which to deduce strategies need to be done. Another matter for further discussion and field experiments is the question of how precisely brands' and retailers' responsibilities for the whole supply chain is to be conceived. In view of the hierarchical structure of production chains, delegating large parts of companies' responsibility for social standards to suppliers does not seem advisable.[26]
- Integrating a gender perspective into measures such as government procurement requirements, export guarantees and tax incentives would mirror efforts that have been suggested in order to promote other human rights issues in these areas.
- Concrete steps to check sexual harassment of women employees as well as employers.
- Checking instances of domestic violence.
- Financial assistance to women entrepreneurs.
- Increasing gender sensitivity and identifying structural discrimination in trade unions.
- Formulating guidelines to respect and protect the rights of women in the unorganized sector.
- Enactment of a legislation with emphasis on incentives to women run organizations.

Conclusion

Even as much has been accomplished through the assimilation of principles and actions on corporate responsibility, diversity and inclusion, the full participation of women all through the private sector – from the CEO's office to the factory floor to the supply chain – remains disappointed. Present research suggesting that gender diversity helps business perform better signals that self interest and common interest can come together. UN Women, the UN Global Compact, other leading UN agencies, the World Bank and the World Economic Forum, highlight these findings. Governments also recognize that women's inclusion drives development and admit that achieving the Millennium Development Goals and national economic and development plans necessitates rapidly moving towards gender equality. So far as India is concerned, the promise of equality of opportunity in economic sphere still remains a misnomer. The government-sponsored development activities have been advantageous to only a small section of women. The large majority of them are still impervious by change and development activities have benefited only a small section of women, i.e. the urban middle class women. The present CSR activities of the corporate in India also lack a gender responsive approach. Voluntary corporate instruments have so far been insufficient to solve these problems and that the issue of gender discrimination is closely entangled with other major human rights issues, is a much recognized fact. Hence, whether from the aspect of women leadership in business to women concern in business activities – there has been a laid-back outlook. Consequently, the present challenge is to craft a vivacious business milieu involving a wide spectrum of actors, collaborators, contributors and innovators to open opportunities for women and men; and enable the active and interactive participation of governments, international financial institutions, the private sector, investors, non-governmental organizations, academia and professional organizations to work together.

Notes

1. *Women, Business and the Law: Removing Barriers to Economic Inclusion*, Washington: World Bank and the International Finance Corporation, 2011, p. 2.
2. Ibid., p. 3.
3. Jean Davison and Richard Strickland, *Leveling the Playing Field: Promoting Women's Economic Capabilities and Human Rights*, Washington: International Center for Research on Women and the Centre for Development and Population Activities, 2000, p. 7.
4. Ibid.
5. Supra note 1, p. 5.
6. Submission to the UN Working Group on Human Rights and Transnational Corporations and Other Business by the Gender, Business and Human Rights Reference Group. View full report at www.ohchr.org/.../TransCorporations/Submissions/.../GenderBusinessAndHumanRightsReferenceGroup.pdf, last visited on 31 October 2012.
7. Supra note 1, p. 6.

8. Kathryn Dovey, 'Putting Gender on the Business and Human Rights Agenda', Scoping Paper, June 2009, p. 6, http://www.realizingrights.org/pdf/Gender_and_Business_and_HR_Scoping_Paper_Draft_for_circulation_June_2009.pdf, last visited on 31 October 2012.
9. http://www.unglobalcompact.org/issues/human_rights/equality_means_ business.html, last visited on 1 November 2012.
10. Ibid.
11. Supra note 1, p. 1.
12. Matthias Doepke, Michèle Tertilt and Alessandra Voena, 'The Economics and Politics of Women's Rights', *NBER Working Papers 17672*, National Bureau of Economic Research, Inc., 2011, p. 1.
13. http://www.unglobalcompact.org/docs/issues_doc/human_rights/Women's_Empowerment_Principles.pdf, last visited on 30 October 2012.
14. Ibid.
15. Ibid.
16. Ibid.
17. 'Gender and Corporate Responsibility in Global Production Networks', Wrap-up of Workshop Results, Berlin, 29 March 2011, pp. 3–4. View full article on www.humanrights-business.org, last visited on 31 October 2012.
18. http://www.humanrightsbusiness.org/files/inef_gender_summary_workshop.pdf, last visited on 31 October 2012.
19. S. Tarakeswara Rao, G. Tulasi Rao and M.P. Suri Ganesh, 'Women Entrepreneurship in India: A Case Study in Andhra Pradesh', *The Journal of Commerce*, 3 (3), 2010, pp. 43–45.
20. Ibid., p. 45.
21. Ibid., p. 46.
22. Mu. Subrahmanian, 'Women Entrepreneurs: The Emerging Economic Force', *THAVAN IJREB*, 1 (1), October-December 2011, p. 12.
23. Nagendra Kumar Jha, 'Development of Women Entrepreneurship – Challenges and Opportunities: A Case Study of Bihar', Ninth AIMS International Conference on Management, 2012, pp. 219–20.
24. Ibid.
25. AIR 1997 SC 3011.
26. Supra note 8.

16

Impact of SHGs on Personal and Social Development of Women

A Study of Indira Kranthi Patham in Prakasam District of Andhra Pradesh

A. KALPANA

A Self-Help Group (SHG) is a village-based financial intermediary usually composed of 10–20 local women members, making small regular savings contributions over a few months until there is enough capital in the group to begin lending. Funds may then be lent back to the members or to others in the village for any purpose. In India, many SHGs are 'linked' to banks for the delivery of *microcredit*. Self-Help Group may be registered or unregistered. It typically comprises a group of micro *entrepreneurs* having homogenous social and economic backgrounds; all voluntarily coming together to save regular small sums of money, mutually agreeing to contribute to a common fund and to meet their emergency needs on the basis of mutual help. They pool their resources to become financially stable, taking loans from the money collected by that group and by making everybody in that group self-employed. The group members use collective wisdom and peer pressure to ensure proper end-use of credit and timely repayment. This system eliminates the need for *collateral* and is closely related to that of solidarity lending, widely used by microfinance institutions.

Microfinance institutions consist of refinance institution, bank, Non-Government Organizations (NGOs) and Self-Help Groups (SHGs) which provide micro credit to the poor in rural, semi-urban and urban areas, encourage thrift habit to enable them to raise their income levels and thereby, improving their standard of living. Micro credit concept is a linkage programme executed by the SHGs and bank. T. Ramesh has explained that microfinance means improving very poor families with very small loans to help them engage in productive activities or grow their tiny businesses. Overtime, microfinance has come to include a broader range of services credit, savings, insurance and so on. Thirty years back, experiments started but microfinance became prominent in the 1980s. It was started in Bangladesh, Brazil and many Asian countries for the upliftment of the poor.

Objective and Methodology of the Study

In recent years, SHGs are popularizing day by day. Women are improving their social and economic condition through these SHGs. The main objective of this study is to review the work of Indira Kranthi Patham (IKP) and assess the impact of SHGs on the social and economic status of the members. The study is based on secondary data and primary data (through fieldwork).

Indira Kranthi Patham

The main objective of Indira Kranthi Patham is to enable all the rural poor families in 22 rural districts of Andhra Pradesh (AP) to improve their livelihoods and quality of life. All the households below the poverty line, starting from the poorest of the target groups, are covered by Indira Kranthi Patham.

Institutional and Human Capacity Building

The institution and human capacity building facilitates the formation and strengthening of self-managed institutions of the poor and help in building social and human capital. There are 1,01,82,181 SHG members in 8,50,671 SHGs organized into 35,525 Village Organizations (VOs) and 1,099 Mandal Samakhyas (MSs) in Andhra Pradesh. The SHGs in Andhra Pradesh constitute 25 per cent of all SHGs in the country. In addition to above MSs, there are 126 Mandal Vikalangula Sangams, 17 Chenchu Mandal Samakhyas, 15 Fishermen Mandal Samakhyas and 20 Yanadi Mandal Samakhyas in the State. District Federations called Zilla Smakhyas (ZS) have come into existence in all the 22 districts. As many as 33,147 (935) Village Organizations and 1,086 (99%) Mandal Samakhyas are registered under the Andhra Pradesh Mutually Aided Co-operative Societies Act 1995, to provide a legal entity and status to the federations.

Table 1

SHG Bank Linkages

Parameters	*2001–2002*	*2002–2003*	*2003–2004*	*2004–2005*	*2005–2006*	*2006–2007*	*2007–2008*	*2008–2009*
Coverage of Groups	88,575	1,65,429	2,31,336	2,61,254	2,88,711	3,66,489	4,31,515	4,37,003
Amount of Loan (₹ in Crores)	197.70	454.10	752.90	1,017.70	2,001.40	3,063.87	5,882.79	72,03.53
No. of Branches	3,263	454.10	752.90	3,853	3,853	3950	4,000	4,150
Per Group Finance (₹)	22,322	3,701	32,549	38,954	69,322	83,601	136329	1,64,839
Groups per Branch	27	45	60	68	75	93	108	105

Source: Society for Elimination of Rural Poverty 2009.

During the year 2009–10, SERP has facilitated ₹ 277.74 crores of bank loans to 20,009 SHGs up to June 2009.

Progress of SHG Bank Linkages

The SHG-Bank Linkages is a great success story in Andhra Pradesh. As many as 25 Commercial Banks, 16 Regional Urban Banks and more than 4,000 branches are participating in the programme. Bank-lending has dramatically increased from ₹ 197.70 crores in 2001–2002 to ₹ 5,882.79 crores in 2007–2008. AP leads the country in SHG-bank linkage programme with 50 per cent of all the bank loans given to SHGs in India and recovery of SHG loans is above 98 per cent. The year-wise progress up to March 2008–2009 is given in Table 1.

Financial Access and Pavala Vaddi Incentive

To encourage the women's groups further and also to achieve 100 per cent repayment, the State Government has introduced the PAVALA VADDI scheme, wherein the government is reimbursing to the SHG member the interest paid by the SHGs over and above 3 per cent per annum. This has led to significant improvement in loan repayment. Under this initiative, 4,75,164 SHGs were given ₹ 52.67 crores in 2004–2006; 2.90,825 SHGs were given ₹ 50.02 crores during 2006–2007 up to March 2007 and 5,54,359 SHGs were given ₹ 112.30 crores during 2007–2008 up to March 2008. During the year 2008–2009, ₹ 195.31 crores as interest subsidy was given to 7,14,930 groups. In the financial year 2009–2010, an amount of ₹ 38.96 crores was given to 1,76,384 groups. Thus, an amount of ₹ 450.26 crores was given to 20,35,278 SHGs (repeated finance) as Pavala Vaddi incentive from the inception of the Scheme.

Dairy Intervention

Dairy activity is a major livelihood opportunity for the urban poor in Andhra Pradesh. Milk procurement activity was taken up on a pilot basis in Mahabub Nagar and Nizamabad districts during 2006–07 and it has helped the milk procurement. Those also triggered intervention in milk productivity in the villages. Based on the success evidenced in the pilots, the same model was replicated in 18 more districts in the State during the year 2008–09. Bulk Milk Chilling Units (BMCUs) with a capacity of 2,000 to 5,000 litres to collect and chill milk to the desired temperature of 4^0 C, were established in 158 Mandals in the State. In collaboration with the APDDCF Ltd., the SHGs and their federations contributed 2.57 lakh litres of milk per day during the peak season and 1.808 lakh litres per day during the lean season. The total quantity and value of the milk procured and supplied by the SHG managed BMCUs during the year 2008–2009 is 51541 MTs and ₹

7,473.47 lakh. About 640 acres of perennial fodder varieties (APBN) are grown by community members for supply of green fodder to the milk animals in 361 villages of 16 districts.

Collective Marketing

The marketing strategy of the project is to enable the small, marginal farmers and Non-Timber Forest Products (NTFP) collectors to obtain the best price for their forest produce and agricultural commodities. It also aims to minimize the cost of inputs to the rural poor farmers and offer remunerative prices for their produce. The marketing intervention of IKP has registered a significant increase in this financial year with pick-up in paddy procurement activity. The VOs have successfully implemented village level collective marketing of neem, red gram, green gram, chillies, paddy, maize, cashew and NTFP besides agricultural inputs. Details of the marketing intervention of last five years and current year are furnished in the following table:

Table 2

An Overview of Collective Marketing

Item	*2004-'05*	*2005-'06*	*2006-'07*	*2007-'08*	*2008-'09*	*2009-'10*
No. of MMS involved	502	710	533	1036	845	408
No. of VOs involved	1,154	2,010	783	2,071	2,071	1662
No. of families covered	1,18,497	2,57,280	1,01,790	3,01,172	2,16,792	2,30,436
No. of commodities handled	57	81	81	79	65	29
Volume (in lakh quintals)	1.80	24.94	18.25	47.30	59.30	62.92
Turnover (₹ in crores)	16.0	141.90	126.38	320.15	492.16	582.02

Source: Society for Elimination of Rural Poverty 2009.

Various marketing initiatives were undertaken by Society for Elimination of Rural Poverty (SERP) in 2008–2009, among them paddy procurement is predominant in many districts. In the current financial year, up to June 2009, the VOs have procured a total of 62.92 lakh quintals of agricultural output and NTFP commodities worth ₹ 582.02 crores.

In the lean agricultural season, many of the rural poor have barely one square meal a day. The Food Security Credit is a direct intervention to tackle the hunger gap in rural areas. Village Organizations (VOs) estimate the balance requirement of SHG members, in respect of rice and other essential commodities to negotiate and buy better quality of commodities in bulk from the open market and sell to their members at a price lower than the retail outlets. Under this initiative, 23,63,735 families in 2,06,241 SHGs in 15,989 VOs were provided food security by March 2009.

Disability

Recognizing that people with disabilities are among the poorest and most vulnerable of the poor, IKP has adopted a participatory development approach to support them by building their capacities to improve life skills and self esteem. IKP has extended the support to enhance their livelihoods by creating accessibility to government benefits and entitlements. Provisions of assessment, treatment and rehabilitation services are made through community managed interventions. Intensive activities are carried out in 128 Mandals. However, activities are also undertaken in the other programmed Mandals. As many as 2,13,197 persons with disabilities (PWDs) were organized into 23,069 exclusive SHGs and 126 Mandal Vikalangula Sangams in the State; 72,685 PWDs were given an assistance of ₹ 55.40 crores through Cost, Insurance and Freight (CIF), bank loans and revolving fund for enhancing their livelihood. Further, 6,777 surgical corrections were carried out and 64,187 PWDs were issued assistive devices at no cost to them both in the programme and non-programmed Mandals.

Education

Support is being continued for the community-governed pre-primary schools in Adilabad, Visakhapatnam, Vizianagaram, East Godavari and Warangal districts. There are 275 pre-primary schools with an enrollment of about 5,000 children in 3–5 years of age group. The SHG women in the three Mandals of V.R. Puram, Chintoor and Kunavaram in Khammam district actively participated in the programme of Child Right Protection and Quality Improvement in schools. English language programme is being continued in 50 schools of Kothaguda and Gudur Mandals of Warangal district.

In 2009–10, support was continued to the talented among the rural poor who were admitted into corporate junior colleges in 2009–10 or graduated into second year intermediate course. The proposal for continuation of scheme of providing technical education to the talented poor candidates in 2009–10 is under active consideration.

Pensions

Village organizations today are the nodal points of fund dispersal. This has resulted in more efficient way of disbursing pensions and has also plugged leakages in pension distribution system. The government is distributing ₹ 200 on the first of every month to old age persons, weavers, widows and ₹ 500 to disabled persons. ₹ 476.34 crores was distributed to 66.97 lakh pensioners up to June 2009.

Women Empowerment and SHGs

Empowerment is a comprehensive process and something that can be given to the people. The process of empowerment is both individual and collective, since it is through involvement in groups that people must often begin to develop the awareness and the ability to organize to take action and bring about change. For the socio-economic empowerment of women various self-help groups have been formed in the country. They are the major forms of micro-finance in India and are playing a predominant role in the socio-economic development.

The SHGs are playing an important role in socio-economic change of women. The researcher personally came across many SHGs which are trying to improve the social conditions of women in villages. The increasing membership of villagers in SHGs and changes taking place among the members motivated the researcher to take up this study. Self-help groups of women in Andhra Pradesh are focusing on economic activities like saving, collective marketing and promotion of individual enterprises and are in the process of moving into the mainstream of society. In the process, leadership qualities blossom, discipline prevails and true democracy begins to function. This also helps to add value to the work they do, to their families and their communities. A heartening fact is that 50 per cent of such self-help groups in the country have been formed in Andhra Pradesh alone. Ever since the inception, self-help groups are making great strides in the country and Andhra Pradesh stands foremost in ranking with 3,73,044 SHGs 1999–2000 and the number of SHGs increased to 4,36,579 in 2002–2003 and non-governmental organizations are doing yeomen service in motivating the women to form self-help groups. Here researcher has examined the socio-economic backgrounds of the respondents and their association with SHGs.

Age, Literacy and Education of Respondents

The age of the respondents is a crucial factor while gathering data about the impact of SHGs because the person who shares the information should be one who can narrate the actual development in the village. The data in Table 3 shows that about 56.34 per cent of respondents are educated and 43.66 per cent are illiterate. About 28 per cent are educated up to primary level. Only 5.63 per cent respondents received education up to Intermediate or above. The inference is that as most of the samples are educated, they participate in self-help group activities actively and with higher level of awareness.

Age-wise, the lowest number of respondents are between 25–35 years and 45–55 years. There are a sizeable number of respondents (18, 25.30%) below 25 years. It shows that most of the SHGs members are young and middle aged. This may also be the reason for the groups being very active.

Table 3

Age, Literacy and Educational Level of Respondents

Age (in years)	*Education*					
	Illiterate	*Primary*	*Secondary*	*Higher Education*	*Total*	*%*
Below 25	4	5	7	2	18	25.30
25–35	4	3	6	2	15	21.13
35–45	10	11	2	–	23	32.39
45–55	13	1	1	–	15	21.13
Total	31	20	16	4	71	
%	43.66	28.17	22.53	05.63		100.00

Caste-Wise Composition of Respondents

The Table 4 shows the caste-wise composition of the respondents. 7.04 per cent of the respondents belong to Scheduled Tribes, 42.25 per cent of the respondents belong to Schedule Castes, 30.98 per cent of the respondents belong to Other Backward Classes and the remaining 19.71 per cent of the respondents are of general castes. Thus 49 per cent of the respondents belong to Schedule Castes and Schedule Tribes.

Table 4

Caste Composition of Respondents

Caste Category	*No. Total*	*%*
ST	5	07.04
SC	30	42.25
OBC	22	30.98
Higher Caste	14	19.71
Total	71	100.00

Occupation and Income of Respondents

Data in the table shows the occupation and income level of the respondents. It is found that most of the respondents, i.e. 69.01 per cent are agrarian labour earning mostly less than ₹ 40,000 p.a. There are just two farmers with less than the same amount of income. The respondents doing private jobs and in business also earn less than the same amount. Only one of the two, doing a government job, earns more than that amount.

Table 5

Main Occupation and Income of Respondents

Income (in ₹)	*Occupation*						
	Agri. Labour	*Farmer*	*Private job*	*Government job*	*Business*	*Total*	*%*
Less than 20,000	10	1	2	–	2	15	21.13
20,000–40,000	29	1	10	1	4	45	63.38
40,000–60,000	10	–	–	–	–	10	14.08
Above 60,000	–	–	–	1	–	1	01.41
Total	49	2	12	2	6	71	
%	69.01	02.82	16.90	02.82	08.45		100.00

Competence after Entering into SHGs

The competence acquired by the respondents after becoming members of SHGs was also gathered from them. Information was gathered on competence involving skills such as (1) ability to sign, (2) ability to talk to others, (3) going out alone and (4) ability to talk to leaders. Table 6 summarizes the results.

Table 6

Competence of Respondents

Competence	*No. Total*	%
All skills (No improvement)	25	35.21
Three skills	39	54.93
Four skills	7	09.8
Total	71	100.00

Type of Habits

It is quite natural that when women became member of SHGs, they may acquire new habits and hobbies. Most of the respondents (56.34%) like to watch TV. Just 9 respondents (12.68%) read news papers or books. Substantial number (10, 14.04%) makes handicrafts. Twelve respondents (16.90%) engage themselves in other habits.

Table 7

Types of Habits

Habits	*No. Total*	%
Reading books, news paper	9	12.68
Watching TV	40	56.34
Handicrafts	10	14.04
Others	12	16.90
Total	71	100.00

Improvement of Qualifications After Joining SHGs

Data in Table 8 the table shows that members of SHGs members have improved their qualification after joining it due to motivation. About 26.76 per cent of the respondents have improved their qualifications after becoming members of SHGs and 73.24 per cent respondents have not acquired any new or higher qualifications.

Table 8

Improved Qualification of Respondents

Improved Qualifications	*No. Total*	%
Yes	19	26.76
No	52	73.24
Total	71	100.00

Self Confidence to go to Various Places

The respondents were asked whether they could visit different places outside home like markets, banks, etc. to find out whether they have acquired any self-management skills. Happily, an overwhelming number (65, 91.55%) can go on various errands to all the places mentioned in the schedule. Only six members reported that they visited only banks and not others. That means, all the respondents can manage on their own.

Table 9

Self Confidence of Respondents

Name of Places	*No. Total*	*%*
All places#	65	91.55
Banks	6	08.45
Total	71	100.00

\# Places include nearby town and such other places.

Taking Help of Other Members when Taking Decision

From the sample, it was found that SHGs members are taking help of other members when taking decisions. Data in Table 10 shows that about 84.51 per cent of the respondents have been taking decisions with the help of others. 15.49 per cent respondents do not take any help as they take decisions independently.

Table 10

Taking Help by Respondents

Take Help	*No. Total*	*%*
Yes	60	84.51
No	11	15.49
Total	71	100.00

Acquiring Self-respect due to Membership in SHGs

The Table 11 shows the self-respect dimension of the SHGs members. About 97.18 per cent of the respondents claim to have acquired self-respect after becoming members of SHGs. This is a welcome feature as membership in SHGs enhances the self-confidence which would, in turn, instill in the members problem-solving skills.

Table 11
Self Respect of Respondents

Self Respect in Society	*No. Total*	*%*
Yes	69	97.18
No	2	2.82
Total	71	100

Suggestions

- It is suggested that the SHGs should gear up for new challenges such as use of science and technology in the urban areas and human resources development.
- Most of the members of the SHGs are self-employed. Therefore, both the government and non-government agencies should encourage them to build their own resources so that, in the long run, they can stand on their own feet.
- The SHG members should become politically more active by organizing workshops on sensitization, mobilization and leadership matters so that, on the one hand, the grassroots democracy is strengthened and on the other, the women empowerment is achieved.
- The academicians and the media, both print and electronic, should highlight success stories to inspire other members and groups.

Conclusion

It can be inferred from the study that the SHGs have, by and large, played a positive and welcome impact on the rural women. While this may be contested with an argument that other processes like education, urbanization, marketization, etc. have also been affecting the rural populace, including women, it should be admitted that the SHGs have successfully instilled a 'group' or 'collective' sense which has consequently led to enhancement of self-confidence and acquisition of abilities to analyse issues and problems and the skills to communicate and represent on various matters to the attention of the groups as well as external agencies such as banks, revenue, panchayat and other officials.

It is understood from the results of the study that a majority of SHG members are educated which creates a higher level of awareness and problem-solving skills. Most of the SHGs function among the marginalized groups such as Scheduled Castes, Scheduled Tribes and

Other Backward Classes are indicative of the fact that the women among these sections are willing to change. But the economic levels of the SHG members are still to improve considering their present status. An overwhelming number of the respondents hail from poor and very poor families.

Membership in SHGs have enabled them to acquire competences like putting signature, ability to talk to others, venturing to go out alone or being in a position to represent to leaders. A few of the members are also interested in improving their knowledge by the reading of books or newspapers and learning handicrafts besides engaging in entertainment like many others. A significant number of them have improved their educational qualifications. Almost all of them feel confident of going to nearby towns, markets or banks and at the same time, consult family members or co-members before making any important decisions on matters such as loans, education of children. Nearly all the members assert that joining the SHGs has boosted their self-respect in society.

References

Gupta, M.L. and Namita Gupta. 2006. 'Economic Empowerment of Women through SHGs', *Kurukshetra*, 54, February, pp. 23–26.

Indira Kranthi Patham. *Society for Elimination of Rural Poverty*, Community Managed Sustainable Agriculture, Hyderabad.

Krishnamurthy, H.R. 2007. *Women Empowerment Programme: Economic Development of India*, Bangalore: Sapna Book House, pp. 269–70.

Mahajan, V.S. 1993. *Women's Contribution to India's Economic and Social Development*, New Delhi: Deep and Deep Publications.

Nadarajan, S. and R.P. Ponmurugan. 2006. 'Self Help Group: Bank Linkage Programme', *Yojana*, 50, December, pp. 37–38.

Pillai, B. Vijachandran and V. Hari Kumar. 2006. 'Self Help Groups in Kerala', *Kurukshetra*, 54 (9), July, pp. 30–32.

Ramesh, T. 2008. 'Microfinance: A Drive to Combat Poverty', *The Management Accountant*, 11, November, pp. 822–26.

Sharma, Abijit. 2007. 'Micro Finance: Hope for the Poor', *Yojana*, 50, December, pp. 31–36.

Suguna, B. 2006. *Empowerment of Rural Women through Self Help Groups*, New Delhi: Discovery Publishing House.

Women and Child Development Department Report 2008. Bangalore.

Part IV

Women Empowerment

17

Empowerment and Emancipation of Women

SADHNA GUPTA

> A woman feels as keenly, thinks as clearly, as a man. She in her sphere does work as useful as man does in his. She has as much right to her freedom – to develop her personality to the full – as a man. When she marries, she does not become the husband's servant but his equal partner. If his work is more important in life of community, her's is more important in the life of the family. Neither can do without the other. Neither is above the other or under the other. They are equals.
>
> — Lord Denning (The Due Process of Law)

Empowerment is used to ensuring social transformation and economic development of a society. It includes political participation and also influencing the political decision (Saxena, 1994). Participation as empowerment is related to redistribution of power in society (Mohanti, 1995). Participation denotes sharing or taking part in development process. It can empower the marginalized section of society to participation and improve their social status. According to the UN Summit 1994, empowerment is the process which strengthens the competence of people in general and of the oppressed section of society. The betterment of the deprived section of society can be expected only by enabling them to participate in socio-economic and political affair of society.

Empowerment is the effective answer to oppression, exploitation, injustice and other maladies which are done on women. It is about skill formation. The focus on empowerment has given a new emphasis to the building of economic and social capability among women. It is seen as a way of addressing the problem of right that remains un-enforced (Beteille, 1999). In discussion of women's empowerment, emphasis is often placed on women's decision-making roles, their economic self-reliance and protection against all forms of discrimination. The evidence of empowerment can be seen in terms of indicators that measures women's control, both extrinsic and intrinsic. These include women's participation in household decision-making process, freedom of movement and working outside their houses (Sachdeva, 1997: 29).

Education is the process of developing and reflecting individual skill and ability which enhance social mobility by allowing for social selection based on the merit of individual. Education brings self reliance, personal development, social development, productive capacity, social integration and political understanding (AIU, 1999: 37). It is a productive investment, which brings conscientization that helps individuals to perceive, interpret, criticize and transform their environment. It is one of the channels to empower the people. Education helps to empower them by equipping information and means of function effectively, especially in global world. It widens their capacity and efficiency for better opportunity in life and brings lot of job opportunities, employment particularly for cash and in non-traditional occupation, empowers them by providing financial independence, which helps in social mobility. Not only can employment be a source of economic independence, but it can help to give women a sense of self-worth. It can expose them to the world outside their houses and kin members. Employment can not bring empowerment until decision-making power is given to women in household activities. Poor women are being provided credit facility on easy terms for purchasing bullocks, goat and poultry; they are also being given craft training for generating self employment by government agencies which is considered as a step towards empowerment. Empowerment of rural women should be the priority area of non-formal, adult and continuing education programmes (Trivedi, 1991). The idea of empowerment is a theory of social change, in particular a change from a hierarchical to an egalitarian society.

Women empowerment can be seen through Pachayati Raj Institution (PRI) at grass roots level (Mehta, 2002). The present Pachayati Raj is based on the recommendation of Ashok Mehta Committee, which had asked for transformation of the Panchayat from an implementing agency to a political institution, in which political parties were to be allowed to enter into fray. The 73rd Constitutional Amendment Act legalized a political party's entry into Panchayat and election to Panchayati Raj are contested on party line after this Act was passed in 1992. Article 243D (3) of the Indian Constitution provides that not less than 1/3rd of the total seats to be filled by direct election in every Panchayat to be reserved for women and such seats to be allotted by rotation to different constituencies in a Panchayat. The objective of constituting Pachayati Raj is mainly decentralization of power, development of village and participation of people in the nation-building process. The present Pachayati Raj is not an implementing body to the development programmes but it is a decision-making body and rules over the governance of the village (Malik, 2002).

The membership to (PRI) is reserved vis-à-vis the member of the weaker section of society, i.e. SC, ST and women (Agnimitra, 1996: 441). Article 243T (4) of Constitution provides reservation of offices of Chairperson in Municipalities for SC, ST, women in such manner as the legislature of a State may by law provide. The reservation of one-third seats to weaker section is the landmark decision towards empowerment of women, as it helps to develop their competence so that they may be able to influence and affect the development and decision-making process independently at the grassroots level. It has provided political space for marginalized groups and women for subsequent exposure to decentralized governance, planning development and capacity building to some extent through imparting training. It has been found that one of the significant achievements of the provisions of the 73rd Amendments Acts concerning reservation of seats and political offices in favours of women is that it has improved their awareness and perception level and has created an urge in them to assert their rightful share in the decision-making process at the local level. This political empowerment certainly improves women's economic and social status and helps in social mobility.

Constitutional Provisions

The framers of the Indian Constitution were aware of the social problems of emancipation of the female sex. They also knew that gender equality was crucial for national development. It was evident that in order to eliminate inequality and to provide opportunities for the exercise of human rights and claims, it was necessary to promote them with special care towards educational and economic interests of the women and to protect them from any social injustice and exploitation (Anand, 2003). The Constitution of India did well by declaring in its Preamble the desire to secure justice that is – social, economic and political, and to secure equality of status and opportunity and did its best to ensure translation of these objectives into reality by incorporating provisions ensuring equality of status and of opportunity in the fields of education, public employment and participation in political life. It directs that women shall not only have equal right and privileges with men but also that the state shall make provisions – both general and special for welfare of women. Apart from ensuring *equality before law* and *equal protection of the laws* in wider sense of the term, the Constitution took great pains to specifically prohibit the state from discriminating against women on the ground of sex, in such areas as education and public employment and to direct the state to take special care to promote women's welfare, particularly the protection of their health as mother's and their dignity as individuals.

Special provisions have been made for women under the Indian Constitution. Article 15 (3) permits the State to make special protective laws for women and children. For this reason, establishing educational institutions by the State, exclusively for girls or reservation of seats for women in colleges is not violative of Article 15. Provisions for special maternity relief under Article 42 can be made in favour of women. Article 51A (e) imposes a Fundamental Duty on every citizen to renounce the practices derogatory to the dignity of women.

Legislative Enactments

In course of interpretation of the Constitution and various enactments, the Supreme Court has consistently upheld the protective laws in favour of women. Parliament too has a fair share of protective legislation. Parliamentary legislation according protection to and ameliorating the lot for women has been tackled by passing the Dowry Prohibition Act, 1961, and finding it to be ineffective, the toothless amendment had been made in 1984 and 1986. The legislation has tackled the problem of dowry death, cruelty to women on account of dowry and of battered wives by amending the Indian Penal Code, Criminal Procedure Code and the Indian Evidence Act. In 1983, Section 498-A of the Indian Penal Code defined a new cognizable offence, namely, 'cruelty by husband or relatives of husband'. This law takes particular cognizance of harassment, where it occurs with a view to coercing the wife, or any person related to her, to meet any unlawful demand regarding any property or valuable security, or occurs on account of failure by her, or any person related to her, to meet such a demand. Another amendment was also made under the Indian Penal

Code naming the crime as 'dowry death' under Section 304-B. The section states that if the death of a woman is caused by burns or bodily injury, or occurs under abnormal circumstances, within seven years of her marriage and if it shows that prior to death she was subject to cruelty by her husband or his relatives, in connection with demands for dowry, such a death would be called 'dowry death' and the husband or relative would be deemed to have caused her death. By inserting a new Section 113-B in the Indian Evidence Act, the lawmakers stipulated that in cases that are registered by the police as those of 'dowry death', the court shall presume that the accused is guilty unless he can prove otherwise.

The problem of rape has been solved by drastically amending the penal laws. Section 228A was incorporated in the IPC w.e.f. 25.12.1983 whereby the disclosure of the identity of a victim of rape was made punishable. Amendments to criminal law made in 1983, provides for a punishment of seven years in ordinary cases of rape and 10 years rigorous imprisonment in cases of custodial rape. The maximum punishment can extend to life imprisonment. Burden of proof has also been shifted to the accused under the Evidence Act and new Sections 376-A; 376-B; 376-C and 376-D are inserted relating to the various categories of custodial rape. A new Section 114A lays down that once a raped woman stated that she did not consent, there was the presumption that she did not consent and it is for the alleged rapist to prove that she consented. Section 327 has been incorporated in the Criminal Procedure Code (CrPC) which provides for in-camera proceedings for rape and sexual offences and prohibits publication of such proceedings without previous permission of the court. *Section 46* of the said Act was amended in 2005, which provides safeguards for women in terms of bar on arrest after sunset and before sunrise, except in exceptional circumstances.

To tackle the problem of Sati, the Parliament passed the Commission of Sati (Prevention) Act, 1987. This enactment came to be passed after the Roop Kanwar case in Rajasthan, when a young widow was burnt alive as a *Sati*. The South Indian states have passed the Devadasi System (Prohibition and Dedication) Act to tackle with the ancient problem of prostitution. The Immoral Traffic (Prevention) Act of 1956 as amended and renamed in 1986 makes sexual exploitation of male or female, a cognizable offence. The Child Marriage Restraint Act, 1976 raises the age for marriage of a girl to 18 years from 15 years and that of boy to 21 years and makes the offence under the Act cognizable. The Factories Act of 1948 (amended upto 1976) provides for establishment of crèches where women are employed (including casual and contract labourers). The Act further provides that women will not be employed to work beyond 9 hours between 6 am and 7 pm. The Medical Termination of Pregnancy Act of 1971 legalizes abortion by qualified professional on humanitarian or medical grounds. Another landmark enactment is the Pre-natal Diagnostic (Prevention) Act, 1994 which prohibits the use of pre-natal techniques for the purposes of sex determination. The Maternity Benefit Act, 1961 prohibits employment of women in any establishment for a period before and after child birth, and provides for payment of maternity benefits to them. Various studies revealed that only a very small percentage of women workers avail of this benefit. The Equal Remuneration Act, 1976 as amended in 1987, a landmark enactment was introduced, which provides for payment of equal wages to both men and women workers for the same work, or work of similar nature. It also prohibits discrimination in matter of promotion, training, transfer, etc.

With the passing of The Hindu Succession Act, 1956 it provided for the first time that daughters would have an equal right of inheritance in the father's self-acquired property. But it did not apply to ancestral property which was governed by the concept of Mitakshara copercenary property. The Hindu Copercenary did not include a female member of the family. The legislature has now passed a further amendment to Section 6 of the Hindu Succession Act on 9 September 2005, whereby daughters have an equal right in copercenary property, as that of a son. The Hindu Adoption and Maintenance Act, 1956 has brought some changes that relates to the status of women. The original law gave father the unquestionable power to adopt irrespective of the wishes of the wife. But the Act now makes the wife's consent essential. Under the original law there was no provision for a daughter's adoption, but now a daughter can be adopted. The Act also provides that a wife can live separately from her husband and still claim maintenance if the husband is guilty of cruelty, bigamy, desertion, etc. Regarding the Hindu Minority and Guardianship Act, 1956 mother is the natural guardian of her illegitimate children. She can appoint a guardian at will. Even mother's re-marriage does not deprive her of guardianship and a widowed mother can appoint a guardian at will. Women can claim maintenance under the Hindu Marriage Act, 1955. Under Section 24, a spouse is liable to be maintained during pendency of the proceedings before the court if he/she does not have sufficient independent source of income. Section 125 of the Criminal Procedure Code, 1973 provide maintenance to neglected wives, discarded divorced wives, abandoned children belonging to any religion, community or nationality.

Previously various tax benefits were introduced in favour of women. But now it is at par with men. Also, some state enjoy 1 per cent or 2 per cent rebate on stamp duty and property tax. Other provisions have been made in statues to protect and safeguard the interest of women in various spheres so as to provide them economic independence and equality in various walks of life. These include; The Employees State Insurance Act 1948; The Plantation Labour Act 1951; The Family Courts Act 1984; The Special Marriage Act 1954; The Contract Labour (Regulation and Abolition) Act 1970.

The Indian Penal Code and the Criminal Procedure Code did not adequately protect the women against domestic violence. But The Domestic Violence Act, 2005 (Act No. 43 of 2005) seeks to protect the rights of women. It is an act to provide for more effective protection of the rights of the women guaranteed under the Constitution who are the victims of violence of any kind occurring within the families and for matter, connected therewith or incidental thereto. The most salient features of the act are:

- Recognition of the fact that men and women live in relationships that might not always be legal;
- Recognition of the right of women to live in their marital homes;
- Provisions of positive entitlements – maintenance, protection from future violence, the right to custody over children as opposed to mere penalization of the husband.

On 8 April 2008, the Vidhan Sabha of Himachal Pradesh passed three Bills [Himachal Pradesh Panchyati Raj (Amended) Bill, 2008; Himachal Pradesh Nagar Palika (Amended) Act and Himachal Pradesh Municipal Corporation (Amended) Act.)] for reserving 50 per cent seats for women in panchayats, nagar panchayats and nagar parishads. After the Governor clears the Bill, Himachal would become the third State after Rajasthan and Madhya Pradesh to give 50 per cent reservation to women in panchayats and local bodies, showing the empowerment of women.

Conclusion

Despite the constitutional guarantee of equality of sexes and constitutional mandate of social justice, rampant discrimination and exploitation of women continues. The incidence of bride burning, women battering, molestation and rape, and brazen ill-treatment of women are on the increase in this country where women are worshipped as Goddess of wealth (Laxmi); learning (Saraswati); purity or purifier (Ganges); power (Durga). Women constitute almost half of the population of world. In India, they are referred as better half of men; still women had worst deal at the hands of society till date and are exploited in all possible manners. More than sixty seven years after independence, violence against women in public and private sphere is strongly persisting thereby violating women's human rights. Their discrimination and exploitation in father's house and in-law's abode and at work place are still the orders of the day. There has been number of commissions and committees on women's problem. Reports have piled, numerous suggestions have been made and many solutions have been offered. As a sequel to this long-drawn battle for real equality for women and prevention of their exploitation and discrimination, at long last, National Commission for Women has been stipulated which was established under the National Commission for Women Act, 1990. The Department of Women and Child Development in the Ministry of Human Resource Development has prepared a 'National Policy for the Empowerment of Women' in the year 2001. The goal of this policy is to bring about the advancement, development and empowerment of women.

Women Reservation Bill has been introduced in the Parliament. It was tabled in the Rajya Sabha on 6 May 2008, as the Constitution (108 Amendment) Bill 2008. This Bill will provide 33 per cent reservation for women in Parliament and in the State Assemblies. This step would go a long way in empowerment of women.

Though we stand at the 21st century still we are unable to boast of a society where there is total gender equality. Fight for justice by females or cry for gender equality is not a fight against men. It is fight against those traditions which have chained the women by laying down different norms for men and different norms for women. It is men who must have to realize and accept the fact that women are equal partners in life having an equal identity. Indian society is still largely male-dominated and most women do not have real freedom. A cultural struggle is needed to sweep away the feudal and medieval mentality from which such a situation stems. The Indian Constitution, in Articles 14, 15 and 16, provides for equality between men and women. But in practice there is often denial of equality for women in large parts of India, particularly in the rural areas, due to the disgusting survival of remnants of feudalism and medievalism.

References

Agnimitra, Neera. 1996. 'Women in Panchayats: Empowerment or Illusion', *Gandhi Marg*, January-March.

Agnes, F. 1992. 'Protecting Women against Violence: Review of a Decade of Legislation, 1980–89', *Economic and Political Weekly*, April.

Anand, A.S. 2003. *Justice for Women*, Delhi: Universal Law Publishing Co. Pvt. Ltd.

Association of Indian University. 1999. *Education and Women's Empowerment*, New Delhi.

Beteille, Andre. 1999. 'Empowerment', *Economic and Political Weekly*, 6–13 March.

Mohanti, Manoranjan. 1995. 'On the Concept of Empowerment', *Economic and Political Weekly*, XXX (24).

Malik, Shamser Singh. 2002. *The New Panchayati Raj*, Jaipur: Aalekh Publishers.

Mehta, G.S. 2002. *Participation of Women in the Panchayati Raj System*, New Delhi: Kanishka Publishers and Distributors.

Mittal, J.K. 1991. 'Equality for Women under the Indian Constitution: A Study of Judicial Interpretation', *Central India Law Quarterly*, 4 (II).

Nagala, B.K. 1994. *Violence in India: A Sociological Analysis*, paper presented in the 23rd Conference of Society of Criminology, New Delhi.

Pal, Mahi. 2004. 'Panchayati Raj and Rural Governance', *Economic and Political Weekly*, 10 January.

Saxena, Kiran. 1994. 'Empowerment of Women: The Indian Context', *The Indian Journal of Political Science*, 55 (4).

Sachdeva, Nirmal. 1997. 'Women Empowerment: Myth or Reality', *Third Concept*, March, 29–31.

Sen, Gita and Srilatha Batliwala. 1997. 'Empowering Women for Reproductive Rights', in Harriet Presser and Gita Sen (eds), *Women's Empowerment and Demographic Processes*, New York: Oxford University Press.

Trivedi, Abha. 1991. 'Law and Their Side: The Changing Legal Status of Indian Women', *Central India Law Quarterly*, 4 (IV), October-December.

18

Economic Empowerment of Slum Women

A Study of Slum Area in Jaipur City

AMBEY KUMAR SRIVASTAVA

Promotion of gender equity and women empowerment is the third goal among the eight Millennium Development Goals. It means that women's empowerment is a prominent indicator of human development throughout the world. Gender dimension in economic development should not be ignored at any cost because women constitute about half of world population. But an increasing number of studies indicate that gender inequalities are extracting high economic costs and leading to social inequities and environmental degradation around the world (Stevens, 2010). Here, we take a look at some of the results of report *Women in Labour Markets,* 2010 released by International Labour Office, Geneva:

- About 48.4 per cent of the productive potential of the female population remains unutilized compared to 22.3 per cent for men.
- Rate of female labour force participation has increased from 50.2 per cent to 51.7 per cent during 1980 and 2008, while the male participation rate decreased slightly from 82 per cent to 77.7 per cent. Hence, the gender gap in labour force participation rates has reduced from 32 percentage points (in 1980) to 26 percentage points (in 2008).
- More than six in ten women remain economically inactive in three regions: South Asia, the Middle East and North Africa.
- Globally the female unemployment rate in 2009 was 7 per cent compared to the male rate of 6.3 per cent.

- The share of women in wage and salaried work grew during the last ten years from 42.8 per cent in 1999 to 47.3 per cent in 2009 whereas the share of vulnerable employment decreased from 55.9 per cent to 51.2 per cent.
- The high incidences of time-related underemployment for some women tend to lend support to the premise that many women take up part-time work as the only solution to balancing work with family responsibilities (ILO, 2010).

After this brief scenario of women participation in labour at global level, when we compare India, the picture is gloomier. The country is ranked at 134th position in Human Development Index (HDI) 2011 report. Regarding gender inequality index the position is 129. The female labour force participation rate is 32.8 per cent compared to 81.1 per cent in males (HDI, 2011). Women empowerment in male dominant Indian society is a very crucial issue because despite being one of the fastest growing economies in the world, the gender disparities are deep seated and persistent in the country. India's growth rate could jump by 4.2 per cent if women were given more opportunities (Inderfurth and Khambatta, 2012) and gender discrimination is not institutionalized.

Within the country as well, the status of women differs from state to state. Extreme disparities continue to prevail with respect to various indicators of women's status at state level and the states which are economically least developed are the ones where status of women is low (ibid.). Female work participation rate (WPR) is positively associated with sex ratio and negatively associated with mean age at marriage (Kumar, 2011). Both these indicators exhibit low performance when we talk about Rajasthan, which is listed among the Empowered Group Action[1] states. The issue of women empowerment is also crucial for Rajasthan, because some of the malpractices like female foeticide, infanticide, son preference, *nata system*[2], child marriages and dowry are still prevalent in the state. The state has poor human development indicators as shown in Table 1.

Table 1

Human Development Indicators of Rajasthan

Human Development Indicators	*Rank*
Human Development Index (Rank out of 23) (Year 2007–08)	17
Gender Related Development Index (Rank out of 35) (Year 2006)	31
Gender Empowerment Measure (Rank out of 35) (Year 2006)	24

Source: Rajasthan Economic and Human Development Indicators, UNDP.

In Census 2011, among 35 states, Rajasthan in terms of sex ratio comes at number 21 and in case of child sex ratio the position is 29 (Census of India 2011). The sex ratio of the state is 926, whereas at national level it is 940. The child sex ratio of the state is 883 in comparison to 914 at national level. Overall sex ratio has improved by 5 points but the child sex ratio has declined by 26 points in census 2011. Among the major states, the highest mean age at effective marriage is 22.6 years for Kerala and the lowest is 20.1 years for Rajasthan (Women and Men in India, 2012). According to Women and Child Department reports, nearly 30 per cent of girls were married off at the age of 13 and 50 per cent were mothers by the time they were 15. Women literacy rate (52.66%) in Rajasthan is also lower than male literacy rate (80.51%) by 27.85 points (Census of India, 2011). The female work participation rate was apparently lower than male and worse in urban areas than rural areas. Further analysis shows that gender difference in work participation is wider in urban areas (see Table 2).

Table 2

Selected Indicators on Status of Women

Indicators	*Rural*	*Urban*	*Total*
*Sex ratio (2001)	921	930	890
*Sex ratio (2011)	926	932	911
*Child Sex ratio (0–6 years) (2001)	914	887	909
*Child Sex ratio (0–6 years) (2011)	886	869	883
*Literacy rate (male) (2011)	77.49	89.16	80.51
*Literacy rate (female) (2011)	46.25	71.53	52.66
**Workforce Participation Rate of males (2001)	50.74	47.42	49.95
**Workforce Participation Rate of females (2001)	40.63	9.55	33.49
**Workforce Participation Rate of total (2001)	45.87	29.59	42.06

Source: * Census of India 2011 and
** Population Census 2001; Office of the Registrar General, India.

The current paper looks into the issue of women empowerment in terms of participation in household economy and decision-making in urban poor segment of society. The urban poor constitute 26.8 per cent (Report of the Working Group, 2011) of the total urban population of the country. India is getting urbanized at rapid pace, but the growth of slums is also faster. The 2–3–4–5 phenomenon has often been used to describe the character of Indian demography. This implies that in the last decade India grew at an average annual growth rate of two per cent, urban India grew at three per cent, mega cities at four per cent, and the slum population rose by five to six per cent (Chatterjee, 2002).

Both men and women are exposed to different vulnerabilities of a slum like poor housing, absence of urban basic infrastructure services, insanitation, overcrowding, poverty and unhygienic environment but the woes and challenges faced by women get compounded because of gender inequities, low literacy level, low accessibility to health care services in slums. Married women migrating along with their partners for the sake of livelihood are aware of the availability of domestic jobs in the city, relative higher wages (Joshi, 2003) and other attractions of city life. She often comes to the city with very limited resources and job skills. However, many women end up in urban slums where they can be close to commercial areas and work opportunities (COHORE, 2008), but their work is badly remunerated and hardly noticed at all, sometimes even stigmatized (Thorbek, 1995). Women not only perform paid work but also engage in unpaid household work (Joshi, 2003). Globally, nearly one-fourth of women remain in the category of unpaid contributing family workers, meaning they receive no direct pay for their efforts (ILO, 2010). Still her economic participation is not so manifested and decision-making is not encouraged because of gender discrimination. In the current paper, an attempt has been made to look into this issue in more detail on the basis of study in some slums of Jaipur city.

An Overview of Slums in Rajasthan

In 2001, Rajasthan had slum population of 12.94 lakh in 26 towns, constituting 16.9% of population of cities reporting slums and 9.8% of all urban population (Census of India, 2001). Literacy rate of slum population in 2001 was 65.6%. The literacy of female (51.9%) was lower than the male (77.8%). The sex ratio among the slum population in 2001 was higher at 902 compared to non-slum sex ratio of 886 (Rajasthan and MDGs, 2007). Female work participation as marginal worker in slum areas of Rajasthan was 29.81% whereas in non-slum areas it was 21.30% (Census of India, 2001).

Methodology

The study was carried out in Jaipur city in the year 2005–06. Jaipur city has the highest slum population in the state. As per Census 2001, the slum population was 350,535, which was 15.07 per cent of total population (2,324,913) of the city and 29 per cent of slum population of the state. Jaipur city has got worldwide recognition for its scientific town planning. But the growth of slums in and around walled city and fringe areas indicates unplanned expansion of city to absorb the migrant population. Jaipur is rapidly urbanizing and growing as the centre for education and employment opportunities. The city offers jobs in commerce, services and the informal sector and shows a high economic growth compared to several other Indian cities. The main economic drivers in the city are trading, administration and tourism activities and local handicraft industries. In Jaipur, there are number of factories of carpet, gem stones, block printing, dyeing, jewellery, glass work, textiles, etc. These industries need cheap and intensive human labour, which is provided by the inmigrants.

In Jaipur city, there are 211 slums[3] called as *katchi basti* in local parlance. A representative sample of 128 women respondents was randomly selected from eight slums, namely, *Bhojpura*, *Jawahar Nagar Tila –2*, *Biharion ka Tila*, *Fauji Nagar*, *Kathputli Nagar*, *Reech Bandar walon ki basti*, *Jhalana Mahal* and *Tamil Colony* (see Table 3).

Table 3

Study Slums

Study Slums	*Characteristic Feature*
Jhalana Mahal Kunda	Located in foothills of Jhalana, before legally banned Jhalana was mining area
Tamil Basti	Rehabilitation of some families by Jaipur Development Authority
Bhojpura Kacchi Basti	Agricultural land of village named as Bhojpura
Jawahar Nagar Tila–2	Located on sand dunes of Jhalana forest, along National Highway no.8,
Fauji Nagar	Located along Amanishah ka nallah and credit of formation goes to an army man
Biharion ka Tila	Located on undulating sand dunes
Kathputli Nagar	Located on private land in main city, famous for puppet work by Bhat community
Reech Bandar Walon ki Basti	Along National Highway 8

The data was collected through structured household level questionnaire and qualitative discussion was held with respondents. The collected data is analysed using excel software. In the current chapter, only issues which are related to economy and women empowerment are analysed and discussed.

Results and Findings

Socio-Economic Profile of Respondent Women

Out of 128 women respondents interviewed, 79.69 per cent were Hindu and 20.31 per cent were Muslim. Table 4 shows the caste composition of respondents, in which majority (59.38%) belongs to Scheduled Caste, followed by castes of general category (21.88%). Women respondents of Scheduled castes were mainly from *Bhat, Bairwa, Harijan, Khateek, Muslims, Dhobi, Keer, Kalbeliya, Dholi* and *Nayak*. Scheduled Tribes women were from *Meena* and *Bhil* tribes. Respondent women of general category were mainly *Rajput, Brahmim* and *Muslim*. Women respondents of Other Backward Castes (OBC) were largely from *Darjee, Nai, Jat, Yadav, Muslim* and *Mali* castes.

Table 4

Distribution of Respondent Women by Caste Category

Category	*Number (%)*
Scheduled Caste	76 (59.38)
Scheduled Tribe	6 (4.69)
General	28 (21.88)
Other Backward Castes	18 (14.05)
Total	128 (100)

Age

Table 5 is about the age distribution of respondent women in study slums. Majority women respondents were in the age group of 20–49 years, except 7.81 per cent women respondents, who were above 50 years of age.

Table 5

Distribution of Respondent Women by Age

Age Group	*Number (N=128)*
20–24	24 (18.75)
25–29	14 (10.94)
30–34	23 (17.97)
35–39	24 (18.75)
40–44	17 (13.28)
45–49	16 (12.50)
Above 50	10 (7.81)
Total	128 (100.0)

Marital Status

Table 6 shows that about 90 per cent women were married where as 10 were widows. Three women respondents were unmarried.

Table 6

Distribution of Respondent Women by Marital Status

Marital Status	*Number (N=128)*
Married	115 (89.84)
Widow	10 (7.81)
Unmarried	3 (2.34)
Total	128 (100.0)

Educational Status

Distribution of respondents by their education is shown in Table 7. More than half (53.13%) respondents were illiterate, followed by 28.13 per cent, who were just literate. Only one respondent was educated up to senior secondary. The literacy rate comes down as we climb up from primary (8.59%) to middle (5.47%) and then secondary (3.91%).

Table 7

Distribution of Respondent Women by Educational Status

Education	*Number (N=128)*
Illiterate	68 (53.13)
Literate	36 (28.13)
Primary	11 (8.59)
Middle	7 (5.47)
Secondary	5 (3.91)
Sr. Sec	1 (0.78)
Total	128 (100.0)

Occupation

The distribution of respondent women by occupation in Table 8 shows that about 32 per cent women were skilled labourers, followed by 16.41 per cent unskilled labourers. Women were also employed as private (6.25%) and government (3.91%) servants, whereas 8.59 per cent were pursuing their own business.

Table 8

Distribution of Respondent Women by Occupation

Occupation	*Number (N=128)*
Unskilled Labour	21 (16.41)
Skilled labour	41 (32.03)
Private service	8 (6.25)
Government service	5 (3.91)
Business	11 (8.59)
Not in any occupation	42 (32.81)
Total	128 (100.0)

Slum Women as an Earner

Slums prove a house of opportunities for migrant women. They earn through vending, job work at home, as maidservant, as a factory women, or as a mason, breaking all the barriers of illiteracy, skill incompetency and social inhibitions. Among the women respondents, only 67.19 per cent were engaged in some sort of earning besides performing the role of housewife as well.

Some women at *Kathputli Nagar, Jawahar Nagar Tila–2* and *Jhalana Mahal Kunda* slums were fruit and vegetables vendors. Women occasionally put stall on road side and near temples on particular festivals like *Raksha Bandhan, Ganesh Chathurthi, Karwa Chauth, Diwali, Janmastmi, Holi*, etc. for vending festival's specific items. Some women were found running petty shops in their houses and some women were pursuing work of *Moti* (cheap quality beads) fitting in *Duppatta, salwar* (female dress), table cover, etc. Their daughters were also giving a helping hand to them. Women were found giving help to husband in occupations like *Bindai* (drilling of gem stone) work at *Jawahar Nagar Tila–2* slum; tailoring, washing and iron cloths at *Fauji Nagar* slum and *Jhalana Mahal Kunda* slum; puppet making at *Kathputli Nagar* slum. Some women, especially those who belong to Rajasthan, were going for labour in construction work with their husband. Migrant women of Bihar, West Bengal, southern states were mainly engaged as maidservant.

Castes like *Kalbeliya* (snake charmers), *Bhat* (Puppeteers, also known as *Kathputli wale*), *Madari* (monkey showmen), *Jadugar* (Magician) and *Dholi* (drum beaters) are performing castes. Women of *Bhat* community work with male counterpart in puppet making. Some Muslim women too were earning by contributing in puppet making like filling body parts of puppet with cotton and stitching work. Puppeteers were also skilled in musical instruments and various traditional dances like *kacchi ghori*, puppet show, *panihari* dance, fire dance, *bhangara dhol*, etc. Women and young girls too support male members of family in performing these dances and musical shows in marriages and parties. They also get work offers from government departments like Health Department to organize information, education and communication shows for public awareness on issues like HIV/AIDS, health, etc. They are the patrons of traditional folk media.

Some educated women and young girls were engaged in teaching profession. At *Jhalana Mahal Kunda katchi basti*, a Rajput woman was teaching in a school run by NGO. Some women respondents of Scheduled Castes at *Kathputli Nagar* slum were government employees on contractual basis at Jaipur Municipal Corporation. Women were also found running *Aanganwari* centres in slums.

Although not quantified, but the reasons mentioned by women to pursue earning activities were like 'want to support husband', inflation, 'husband don't give money', 'husband wastes his earnings on alcohol', 'traditional profession', 'want to save money', 'husband passed away', etc. In Indian society, the role of married woman is naturally perceived as a 'housewife' and 'homemaker', whereas that of a husband is perceived as a 'breadwinner'. But the participation of slum women in different economic activities has presented altogether a different picture in which she is ready to work, willing to help her family and want to become a pillar of household economy. Involvement of slum women in household economy has also given rise to some important issues, as shared below:

- *Disguised income:* The role of women in household income was found extensive. Not only married women, but also the girls of adolescent age were providing support in household economy. Ironically, the contribution of a woman has not been measured as segregated income but as a helping hand, especially in traditional castes like *Bhat, Dholi, Dhobi*, etc. in which male and female of family works together by dividing the tasks among them.
- *Competitive behaviour:* Competitive behaviour of slum women becomes evident when they complaint that how women of other states like Bihar, West Bengal, etc. have snatched the labour of Rajasthan women. They said that women of other states get ready to work on lower wages. Local business men and people used to take advantage of this issue. They get preference over *Rajasthani* women in getting employment on lower wages. Among professional castes as well, like *Bhat*, the women perceived that if they quit their traditional job the other caste people can encroach upon

their profession. Women used to share problems related to health, conflicts with husband and other local issues of slum but not about their earnings.

- *Work preferences:* Slum women have their own job preferences. Like *Rajasthani* women of some castes (who are usually involved in labour work) prefer to go with their husbands for labour work. Muslim women and women of upper Hindu castes prefer to work at home. Women of professional castes like to pursue the traditional occupations. *Rajput* women at *Jhalana Mahal Kunda*, *Bhojpura* and *Biharion ka tila* said that they were not habituated to do labour work and feel proud to continue with traditional occupation. They perceive that other caste people couldn't excel in their occupation. Migrant women of South Indian states at *Tamil basti*, *Bihari* women at *Bhojpura basti* and *Jawahar Nagar Tila–2* prefer to work as maid servant.
- *Social and cultural issues:* In Rajasthan, *purdah* (face covered with veil) system is prevalent and it is not appreciated if married women stepped out for job, mainly in rural society. This culture was found prevailing in slums as well. There were many migrant women, especially in *Rajput*, *Brahmin* and *Muslim* castes, who hesitated to work outside so they were earning through job work at home like tailoring, embroidery, making quilts, etc. It also allows them to look after household work.
- *Entrepreneurship:* Slum women don't lose any opportunity coming at their doorstep. Their involvement in spectrum of jobs reflects the entrepreneur nature, self-confidence and desire to become self-reliant.
- *Division of labour:* There is no role division found in household chores like cooking food, care of offsprings, collecting water every day for domestic purpose, etc. But in economic activities like in Washerman caste, Puppeteers, *Kalbeliya,*[4] etc. husband and wife divide the work between themselves on the basis of nature of work. Like in puppet making the hard work of cutting and sharpening wood is done by males whereas stitching cloth, filling cotton, decorating puppet, etc. is done by women. Selling of puppet is mainly the job of males.

Participation in Decision-Making

After removing the 10 widow women respondents, Table 9 shows the analysis of remaining 118 women in decision-making. About 45 per cent respondents said that husbands consult them in all decisions followed by 35.60 per cent who shared that they were seldom consulted. The women were consulted mainly in matters related to marriage, education of children, shifting of house from slum and going to village, but not about changing the profession, business issues, going out with friends for leisure and remittance of money at home. Issues like borrowing money or lending money are seldom discussed. Among professional castes it is not customary to discuss the issues like selling of puppet, fixing shows, or business contracts with wife. All those women, who were pursuing any job outside home, had consent of their husband. Also, majority women shared that if they want to go out with neighbouring women for any purpose, then they have to take permission of their husband or have to inform him. About the children as well, the women don't have full freedom. Children too need to take permission from father, especially when they reach adolescent age. Responsibility of adolescent girl, like her health-related issues, is the responsibility of mother but if she wants to pursue education or any job then she needs to take permission of her father, told by respondent women.

Female participation in decision-making about 'number of children a couple should have' is very important issue. But most of the husbands don't consult sex related issues, including the use of male contraceptives. Female always consult husband while using any contraceptive. Issues like health check-ups during pregnancy, delivery, consultation with doctor are generally always discussed between husband and wife in families where husband and wife were literate. In illiterate families, such decisions are taken when other neighbouring woman said or any health worker does counselling.

Table 9

Involvement of Women in Decision-Making

Frequency of Involvement	*Response (N=118)*
Always	53 (44.91)
Seldom	42 (35.60)
Never	23 (19.49)
Total	118 (100.0)

Freedom to use earnings is an important issue to analyse the economic empowerment of women, after all she is making handsome contribution in household income. But very few number of women said that husband consult them before spending money. On the other hand, most of the women asked their husband to make any major expenditure. Table 10 shows that only 18.75 per cent women were able to use their earnings as they want but 48.44 per cent women said that they had to consult husband before spending money. In most of the cases, husband was aware about the income of wife but woman was not.

Some women said that they spend their earnings in purchasing essential household items for use in kitchen, small items of routine use, cosmetics, vegetable for daily cooking, fruits, cloths for self and children and other minor things of their use without seeking prior permission of husband. But in purchasing costly items, they either need to seek prior permission of husband or take him along while purchasing. Some of the wives of drunkard husbands were highly annoyed with their husbands. They said that if husband can waste his earnings on alcohol then why should they consult him in using the earnings? Such women spend their earning without seeking prior permission of husband. Women give priority to family and children while spending their earnings.

Table 10

Women Using their Income

Options	*Response (N=128)*
Yes	24 (18.75)
No	62 (48.44)
Not in any occupation	42 (32.81)
Total	128 (100.0)

Factors Affecting Female Participation in Decision-Making

- *Mutual understanding:* Relationship of husband and wife was a factor, which affects the participation of woman in decision-making and using their earnings. Women had the opinion that in slum, husband and wife are not living with parents, so they feel it necessary to develop a mutual understanding. Majority women didn't perceive any harm in seeking permission of husband because by doing so they were able to avoid any tension in relationship.
- *Nuclear family:* Living in nuclear family system was mentioned as a major reason to involve women in household level decisions because there is nobody around with whom husband can discuss the problem. This is also one of the reasons that women are ready

to bear all hardships of slum life but don't want to return to the village. Quantitatively also 56.25 per cent women thought that it is better to live in slum than to go back to village. Most of the women respondents preferred to live in nuclear family.

- *Urban culture:* Women have the opinion that city life has broadened the thinking of their husbands because they interact with people of different backgrounds and see the differences in rural and urban lifestyle. Respondents also accepted the impact of urban society on slum women, as they too interact with the outside world more frequently and easily than at village. It has built their capacity to argue with the husband.
- *Space shortage:* Space shortage in house is a barrier in discussing the issues privately between husband and wife. Sometime husband and wife don't get time and space to consult issues, especially related to reproductive health and sex.
- *Habit of alcohol:* Women were very much worried with the habit of alcoholism of their husbands. Women of alcoholic husbands were found to be a little bit aggressive. They were of the opinion that if their husband can waste his earning on alcohol then why can't they spend it on their own and children?
- *Domestic violence:* Many women admitted that husbands resorted to violence towards them when drunk. Cases of domestic violence after intoxication with alcohol were reported in all the slums. A woman at *Bhojpura* slum complained about her abortions due to violence of the husband. In such cases, women don't give importance to consult with husbands.
- *Attachment with social institutions:* Slum women mentioned about their association with institutions like Self Help Groups (SHGs) and Non Governmental Organizations. Mahila Mandals were formed in *Kathputli Nagar, Jawahar Nagar Tila–2, Bhojpura* and *Jhalana Mahal Kunda katchi basti* slums. NGOs were also functioning at *Bhojpura, Jhalana Mahal Kunda, Jawahar Nagar* and *Kathputli Nagar* slum. Women associated with SHGs were able to save money and borrowed at the time of need. Women associated with such institutions felt more informed and empowered.
- *Education:* Families where both the spouses were literate discuss the issues with each other. They felt that now the time is changing and in cities, unlike in villages, husband and wife emphasize more on education. Still, the views about education differed starkly in

people of different cadstes and occupations. Higher education of female was not favoured by many slum dwellers. They had the opinion that marriage ultimately decides the fate of a girl.

- *Gender complex:* Some women shared that a husband feels inferior in consulting his wife. If they insist on it, it can cause a row between husband and wife. So to prevent collision they avoid arguing with husband.

Conclusion

Mobility of women from rural to urban areas has improved the economic freedom of women but when it comes to issue of spending own earning and involving them in decision-making, women are not so empowered. Her contribution in household economy is commendable because management of the home and care of the children are generally considered exclusively women's responsibility. Measuring the participation of women in economy of slums is a challenge but very important and should be deeply explored. It will help in recognizing her participation in household economy more strongly and improving her social status. Also, it will reduce the gender gap in labour force participation in urban areas. Better understanding about her role in household economy will also help in institutionalizing the entrepreneur skill of slum women and her economic empowerment.

Notes

1. The EAG states are those with high fertility rates and weak socio-demographic indicators. The EAG was created in the Ministry of Health and Family Welfare (MoHFW) especially to ensure population stabilization and intersectoral convergence. (Source: http://www.frontlineonnet.com/fl2210/stories/20050520001508600.htm)
2. The *nata* is a practice of establishing a second alliance, when a male partner dies in marriage or deserts a woman or when a couple separate due to conflict.
3. Figure of slum is taken from the website of Jaipur Municipal Corporation on 2 January 2013, http://oswal.selfip.com/jaipurweb/UI/Static/staticpage.aspx?pageid=9
4. Kalbelia is one of the dance forms of Rajasthan, performed by a Kalbeliya tribe woman.

References

Census of India 2001 and 2011.

Chatterjee, G. 2002. *Consensus versus Confrontation: Local Authorities and State Agencies Form Partnerships with Urban Poor Communities in Mumbai*, Nairobi: UN-HABITAT.

COHORE. 2008. *Women, Slums and Urbanisation: Examining the Causes and Consequences*, Geneva, Switzerland: Centre on Housing Rights and Evictions, p. 11.

Human Development Index 2011. *Sustainability and Equity: A Better Future for All*, United Nations Development Programme, p. 126 and 141.

ILO. 2010. *Women in Labour Markets: Measuring Progress and Identifying Challenges*, Geneva: International Labour Office, pp. 3–4.

Inderfurth, K.F. and P. Khambatta. 2012. 'India's Economy: The Other Half', *India Policy Studies*, 2 (2), Centre for Strategic and International Studies (CSIS), Wadhwani Chair in US, p. 1.

Joshi, S. 2003. 'Marriage, Migration and Labour Market: A Case Study of a Slum Area in Delhi', *Indian Journal of Regional Science*, 37 (1), pp. 6–13.

Kumar, N.P. 2011. 'Status of Women and Economic Development: A Decadal Analysis Based on Indian States', *Socio-economic Voices*, September-October, indiastats.com, pp. 5–7.

Rajasthan and MDGs: Status and Progress at Half Way Mark, a Citizen's Report. 2007. Jaipur: Institute of Development Studies, pp. 25–28.

Report of the Working Group on Urban Poverty, Slums and Service Delivery System. 2011. Steering Committee on Urbanization Planning Commission, New Delhi, p. 2.

Stevens, C. 2010. 'Are Women the Key to Sustainable Development?: Sustainable Development Insights', The Frederick S. Pardee Center for the Study of the Longer-Range Future, Boston University, 003, April, p. 1.

Thorbek, S. 1995. 'Women's Participation in Slum Organisations: Does it Make a Difference?', Feminist Research Centre in Aalborg, Department of Development and Planning, Aalborg University, p. 2.

Women and Men in India. 2012. 14th Issue, National Statistical Organisation, Ministry of Statistics and Programme Implementation, Government of India, p. xxi.

19

Tribal Women's Education and Empowerment

Realizing an NGO's Importance in Odisha

SAROJ KUMAR DHAL

Tribals are at the bottom of social and political ladder in India. Development projects have not only bypassed them, but have often harmed them by taking away their lands and other resources on which their livelihood was based. Unless the processes which result in their proletararianization are identified and corrective action taken to prevent it, chances are that new programmes will continue to ignore their interests as in the past. Articulation of such processes will not only lead to appropriate solutions but it also helps in sensitizing field officers who in the past often held a negative stereotype about tribals.

From the viewpoint of policy, it is important to understand that tribal communities are vulnerable not only because they are poor, assertless and illiterate compared to the general population; often their distinct vulnerability arises from their inability to negotiate and cope with the consequences of their forced integration with the mainstream economy, society, cultural and political system, from which they were historically protected as the result of their relative isolation. Post-independence, the requirements of planned development brought with them the spectre of dams, mines, industries and roads on tribal lands. With these came the concomitant processes of displacement, both literal and metaphorical – as tribal institutions and practices were forced into uneasy existence with or gave way to market or formal state institutions (most significantly, in the legal sphere), tribal people found themselves at a profound disadvantage with respect to the influx of better-equipped outsiders into tribal areas. The repercussions for the already fragile socio-economic livelihood base of the tribals were devastating – ranging from loss of livelihoods, land alienation on a vast scale, to hereditary bondage. As tribal people in India perilously, sometimes hopelessly, grapple with these tragic consequences, the small clutch of bureaucratic programmes have done little to assist the precipitous pauperization, exploitation and disintegration of tribal communities. Tribal people respond occasionally with anger and assertion, but often also in anomie and despair. However that too is branded as a typical 'law and order' problem, ignoring its socio-economic dimensions (Gupta, S.K., V.P. Sharma and N.K. Sharda, 1998).

Role of Tribal Women

In tribal society, the women play a key role not only by involving themselves in household activities rather they also play major roles in social and agricultural spheres by giving equal company to the men, collection of minor forest produce and other economic activities in the family. In spite of their enormous contribution for the society, they have remained as underprivileged and ever-neglected in the society. The problem in tribal areas is rather more acute than it is in other areas, where women face many kinds of oppression from a whole range of denials, beginning from schooling at the early stages, due payment for work done, property ownership, limited access to social and political life, violence at home and outside, and socio-psychological conditioning from childhood that they must play second fiddle. Tribal women are playing a very significant role in the economic development of tribal area as they are contributing in various economic activities, which are related with different sectors and education is one of them. The tribal female literacy rate is very low but with the effect of modernization and urbanization and due to the efforts of various voluntary organizations, missionaries and social workers, education is being spread over tribal areas through constant motivation. Tribal women are now obtaining education and the educated tribal women are also providing education to other students and their family members. The educated tribal women also encourage female education among them for the upliftment of their society. Those tribal women who are uneducated also send their children to school and even colleges for higher education. Thus, they also cooperate in the development of education among tribal society. This makes their contribution significant. (Mohapatra, B. and Vimla Ramchandran, 2001). But the continuing gap between literacy levels of STs and the general population is shown in Table 1.

Table 1

Literacy Rates of STs and Total Population (in%) in India

Category	*1971*	*1981*	*1991*	*2001*
Total Population	29.45	36.23	52.21	65.38
STs	11.30	16.35	29.60	Not Available
Gap	18.15	19.88	22.61	Not Available

(Census of India).

Table 2

Female Literacy Rates of STs and Total Population (in%) in India

Category	*1971*	*1981*	*1991*	*2001*
Total Population	18.69	29.85	39.29	54.16
STs	4.85	8.04	18.19	Not Available
Gap	13.84	21.81	21.10	Not Available

(Census of India).

Thus, the gap in literacy levels, both for tribal men and women, is increasing despite the fact that the largest proportion of centrally sponsored programmes for tribal development are related to the single sector of education. This sector tends to dominate budgetary allocations in state governments too. In states like Madhya Pradesh, tribal education is administered directly by the tribal welfare department and separate from the education department on the premise that the educational needs of tribal communities are at variance from the needs of the rest of the population. The strategy of special tribal hostels and residential schools makes immense sense, because tribals reside traditionally in extremely small and dispersed settlements in difficult and remote areas. Therefore, the logistics of serving each of these settlements with day schools are unmanageable. The solution has been found in locating residential tribal schools and hostels even in the deep forest interiors, although quality and basic amenities remain a problem. The amounts paid as scholarship and stipends to tribal students have enabled resource-strapped tribal families to invest in education and there is even evidence that part of the money is diverted by some families for non-educational purposes. A recent evaluation carried out by the Ministry on the scheme reveals that the performance of certain states in providing matching grant, maintenance of services and management of hostels is not encouraging and the pace of construction of hostels has also been very slow and the basic amenities provided therein are of substandard. A review of the scheme of Ashram Schools revealed that some of the schools are very badly maintained and deprived of even basic facilities. Also, no separate sections exist in the hostels for primary school children, which is a pre-requisite. Tribal hostels and residential schools in remote interiors are notoriously poorly managed, plagued by badly maintained buildings and leakages and delays in payments to students and purchases. Teachers, if they teach at all, are often poorly motivated and sometimes display prejudices against tribal children. The greatest failing has been in the context of education in tribal schools. The sensitive rhetoric of stated tribal policy of 'integration' and enabling tribal communities to 'develop according to their own genius' is entirely forgotten, as mainstream school curricula are imposed wholesale on tribal schools. The problem is not merely the medium of instruction; again, contrary to stated national policy of enabling children at the primary level to study in their mother-tongue, there are almost no tribal schools in which teaching is in tribal languages. Even more serious is the cultural bias of school curricula, which tends to be urban, upper-caste Hindu in content. Studies have also established patriarchal and communal trends. Even the dedicated Ramakrishna Mission schools in remote regions of Bastar and Arunachal Pradesh, which have been actively promoted by the Indian state, provide high-quality education but of a kind that is exclusively and unapologetically Sanskritized Hindu in terms of its cultural moorings, values and idioms. The Christian missionary schools in tribal regions country-wide have been equally aimed at assimilation, although into a different cultural ethos (Mukherjee, K.K., 1994). However, despite all these limitations, education is a growing and powerfully felt need of tribal communities. The most visible evolution in tribal aspirations even in remote tribal hinterlands and among so-called primitive tribes, has been for education. The attraction is partly for eligibility for employment, particularly in government. However, the major impetus is to acquire skills to negotiate the complex, exploitative external world. The challenge remains of meeting these aspirations without alienating tribal communities from the roots that sustain them.

Although, literacy is very crude indicator of educational development, even after 68 years of independence, tribal women are the most disadvantaged lot. Thus, even a large percentage of tribal women are illiterate but both the literate and illiterate tribal women are contributing in the development of education as by sending their children to schools and colleges, by obtaining education of different levels and by providing education to other members of the society. So, their contribution became significant.

Problems

To impart education to the tribals and to make successful the different programmes for the development of education, which are, running out by government, there are so many impediments, which stand on the way such as:

- First and foremost, the factor of extreme poverty operates as a check on educational development in tribes. Due to this they prefer to send their children to earn some wages rather than send them to school. Therefore, there is positive correlation between poverty and illiteracy.
- In tribal family, girls give every kind of help to their mothers in the work at home. During the agriculture season they work in the field with their parents. Even tribal women have interest in educating their girls but other members of the family do not want to educate them because they think that if girls will be educated they will be idle and fashionable only while they have to work hard in father-in-law's house.
- The tribal students have to walk long distance without any conveyance facility and this discourages them to go to school.
- The major impediment is the language barrier. So, the communication gap between teacher and the taught alienates the tribal child from the school.
- The tribal students are not attracted to the curriculum, as it is not their life oriented. Therefore, they have no interest in getting formal education.
- After getting education, today only a part of the educated tribes get good employment and the rest are unemployed or under-employed. Therefore, the unavailability of employment restricts other tribal persons to educate other members of their society. No guarantee of service after education generates lack of interest for education among tribal.
- Lack of awareness, skills, vocational training, motivation towards education and new techniques limits the achievements of tribal women.

Hence, there is the need to change the way of thinking of tribal to motivate them towards education and it can be done by following these suggestions:

- When every educated tribal person make his sincere efforts to motivate the people of his society towards taking education as it is a necessary condition for the development of their society.
- Capable persons should be recruited from both the urban as well as tribal areas, they should be posted in tribal areas and it should be made compulsory for such persons to live in non-tribal areas for a certain period to provide their service regularly. Priority should be given to young persons and salary of such persons should be very attractive so that they can't refuse it.
- Those tribal persons who participate in the development of their area, in the economic upliftment of women of their society and in encouraging female education in them should be honoured.
- Special attention should be given and measures have to be taken to increase women literacy among tribal.

NGO's Intervention

NGOs have become active agents of the civil society. They have acquired both grassroots level reach through community participation and expertise in their activities. They have been fairly successful in providing a flexible, efficient, local delivery system and effective programme implementation mechanisms in addition to mobilizing citizens for developmental efforts. NGOs contributed to the strengthening of the civil society by bringing about a diversity of structures and a deepening of political participation. NGOs are one set of institutions within civil society. They are, therefore, part of the public domain of governance by civil society. This implies that NGOs need to be seen as public institutions, of civil society, engaged in the process of strengthening civil society in its relationship vis-à-vis the State and the ruling elites. As Gangrade and Sooryamoorthy (1995) have discussed about the factors that have promoted the rise of voluntary action in India. This can be summed up as Hindu Tradition, Missionaries role, Gandhi's role and perception.

History of the NGO, Agragamee (Means Forward Movement)

The situation of the tribal community struggling with starvation, hunger, diseases and malnutrition forced a group of young men in the year 1981, to initiate some voluntary action in *Kashipur* Block of the old *Koraput* district, which falls under the district of *Rayagada* at present. The problem of money lending, bondage, payment of low wages, landlessness, low literacy rate, non-functioning of primary schools over and above lack of political will and local leadership were the main factors attributed to such a socio-economic scenario of the tribal of the region. Food scarcity was considered to be an additional factor for the underdevelopment of the this tribal area. Low land which is considered to be the prime land of this area belonged to the non-tribal land lords, who have their origin mostly from coastal Odisha, who settled here and took advantage of the backwardness, simplicity and the above mentioned socio-economic situation of the various communities like *Soura, Kohl, Ho, Santhal, Munda, Juang* and *Mankadia Kandha* apart from *Kondhs* and *Parajas*. The living standard of large number of scheduled caste population was also no better than the tribes but some of them have been used by the local land lords and *sahukaras* to establish their authority over the poorest section. *Agragamee* took its first experiment in a tribal area like *Kashipur* being fascinated by the overwhelming response and initiatives of the tribal to development. The team was supported by a group of tribal youths who joined them in the second year of its action. The organization was in search of a strategy after introducing itself to the tribal community and was looking for alternatives for the awakening of the tribal to come up in order to bring about a change in their socio-economic condition. With the above mentioned objectives in mind *Agragamee* has taken an attempt to create alternative leadership being closely associated with the tribal situation and problems of the area. The efforts of *Agragamee* since 1981 till date have been replicated in various tribal districts of Odisha.

Education: Experiments and Innovations by Agragamee

Agragamee's (means forward movement) intervention for tribal development combines educational input along with economic development activities for a holistic development of the community. Apart from this, *Agragamee* has made systematic effort for enabling primary age group children access education in terms of literacy, numeracy and other basic skills. This has been necessitated since the majority of the tribal children cannot avail the benefits of the existing system of education provided by the government due to a combination of reasons, including poverty, non-functioning of the existing government mechanism, and the necessity to work. The education taken up attempts to overcome these reasons for inaccessibility by adjusting schedule, timings, educational content and approach to suit the needs and priorities of the tribal people with special focus on the tribal child. Further, institutional support has also been built up for this process so that teaching-learning materials of relevance can be developed. To facilitate all this, the

Ministry of Human Resource Development has funded this organization for programmes of non-formal education, as well as for a district resource unit for adult and non-formal education. The focus of the programmes taken up by *Agragamee* is as under:

- Tribal children
- Drop outs
- Girls
- Inaccessible areas

Training and Community Capacity Building

Organizing communities, building up their capability and self-reliance has been the major thrust of the organization since its inception. It has been *Agragamee*'s conviction and now experience that the development programmes can be effectively implemented if the community is fully involved in the planning, implementation, management and follow-up levels of any development work. In these years, these activities range from formation of grain banks to providing backup supports to the block level people's organizations. *Agragamee* helps the communities and people's organizations to build up their capacities by imparting adequate training and exposing them to other areas to improve their knowledge and skill.

Training of Multi-purpose Community Trainers and Organizers

Based on the experience of *Agragamee,* training programmes for community organizers have been conducted by various units of *Agragamee*. Ten tribal youths have undergone this orientation programme for developing their understanding of the social conflicts and their reasons of economic backwardness, which has culminated in the form of poverty and oppression of masses. The training period is for three months; partly in-house on leadership and communication skill development. Their placement in various field centres to conduct village meetings with a team has enlightened the vision and widened their knowledge with a package of thought-provoking inputs.

Infrastructure Development for People's Organizations

Agragamee's work has a major focus in the formation and strengthening of grassroots people's organizations. A number of organizations have emerged with the back-up support of *Agragamee*. Now-a-days *Agragamee* has taken up the task of providing some of them with basic minimum infrastructure to facilitate learning processes. Training centres in *Padhan Sahi, Satkosia village* of *Thakurmunda* block under the patronage of the local organizations and Development Education and Environment Project (DEEP) at village *Halia Sahi* of *Kashipur* block for the *Mandibisi Mahila Mandal* have been supported. These two organizations have been struggling for the people's rights in their locality for the last five years.

Formation of Communication Group

Local tribal youths, instructors of Non-Formal Education (NFE) centres and animators have been trained at different project areas and have formed local communication teams by upgrading the existing skills in the locality based on the problems at the village level. It is observed that the tribal youths have picked up the skill well and it is seen that the message through the above media by the local teams is clearly reaching out to the people. A number of communication groups have been formed in different project areas of *Agragamee.*

Training and Exposure

Agragamee has good number of professional and non-professional staff members with various backgrounds and educational qualifications. There are a number of tribal youths and women who are just literate and illiterates. The organization has provided the scope for the growth of individual members through training, orientation, exposure and interaction at various levels within its limitations. The quarterly workshop cum training programmes for staff members of different projects have not only become a forum for sharing experiences and ideas but also an excellent opportunity for dissemination of information related to the issues concerning the tribals, marketing of forest products, the policies of the government of tribal development and so on. In some workshops a number of renowned resource persons are invited to share ideas and knowledge with the staff and animators.

Agro Service Centre

Agro service centre has basically three functions:

- Provide training to NGO functionaries, technical staff, government officials or National Relief Network (NRN), especially on watershed development.
- Provide inputs (technical and material) to farmers.
- Organize workshops and training camps for various stakeholders dealing with NRN.

Table 3

Training and Activities in Different Tribal Areas

S. No.	*District/Block*	*Federation*	*Membership*	*Activity*
1.	Rayagada/ Kashipur	Ama Sangathan; Registered: 1996; Turnover: ₹ 700,000 p.a	25 groups; 1,000 women	–Processing and Marketing of agriculture and Minor forest produce, –Organized action for education, minimum wages, accountable delivery and against alcohol
2.	Kandhamal/ Phiringia	Phiringia Anchalika Mahila Mahasangh; Registered: 1998 Turnover: ₹ 50,000 p.a	25 groups; 500 tribal women	–Processing leaf plates, consumer store, organized action for education, PDS, BPL identification; minimum wages, accountable delivery and against alcohol
3.	Koratput/ Dasamantpur	Dasamantpur Mahila maha Sangh; Registered- Turnover: 50,000 p.a	80 groups; 200 tribal women	Processing leaf plates, Organized action for education, PDS, BPL identification, minimum wages, accountable delivery and against alcohol
4.	Nabarangpur/ Tentulikhuti	Indravati Mahila Maha Sangh: Registered: 2001 Turnover: ₹ 1,50,000	40 groups; 500 tribal women	Processing and Marketing of agriculture and Minor forest produce, –Leasing in of cashew plantations; –Organized action for education, minimum wages, accountable delivery and against alcohol

Agro service centre (ASC) has been recognized by CAPART (Council for Advancement of People's Action and Rural Technology), an autonomous development agency under the Ministry of Rural Areas and Employment, Government of India, New Delhi, as one of the national level support voluntary organizations (SVO) since 1997.

Area of Operation

Initially ASC was operating in *Kashipur* block of *Rayagada* district and other resource degraded areas of the state of Odisha. Presently, the area of operation of ASC has gone beyond the state and the centre and now it is imparting training and providing field level support services to the Project Implementing Agencies (PIAs) supported by CAPART, New Delhi, under its watershed conservation and development programme.

Capacity Building Training

This programme organized grassroots level people's organizations to help them carry on their networking and take up issues of democratic rights and justice. The outcome of the training programme:

- The trained community members have started asserting their legitimate rights and privileges.
- Existing leadership skills of the trainee activists have been improved.
- People's participation in local governance has improved and Gram Sabhas are calling Panchayati Raj Institutions (PRI) representatives as well as local government functionaries to account.
- People have become aware of their right to information and of role and functions of PRIs.

Objectives

- To generate proposals on drought proofing intervention.
- To introduce to NGOs to the significance, principles and objectives of the drought proofing programme.
- To provide orientation to the inexperienced NGOs regarding the procedural technicalities.
- To facilitate entry of NGOs with proven track record in social mobilization and empowerment into CAPART mainstream.
- To educate users on community management of natural resources and their role in the same.
- To orient the community on proper utilization of natural resources for sustainable development.
- To empower people about their rights on common property resources.

Conclusion

Hence, the NGO *Agragamee* has been playing a vital role in the tribal region of Odisha for more than two decades in spite of occasional setbacks and strains. Its main task has been to prepare an appropriate base, which will make its clientele aware and empowered and equip tribal women through education, for further take off that await them in the process of empowerment and development. Really it is a commendable task done by *Agragamee* for the Tribals of Odisha what may be expected from any NGO. Last but not the least, we can not avoid the participation of those tribal women in the process of development and empowerment through education.

References

Annual Reports: Agragamee, 1993–99 and 2002–03, Agragamee Publications, Kashipur (Rayagada), Orissa.

Baviskar, B.S. 2001. 'NGOs and Civil Society in India', *Sociological Bulletin*, 50, March, pp. 1–5.

Dantwala, M.L., Harsh Sethi and Pravin Visaria (eds). 1998. *Social Change through Voluntary Action*, New Delhi: Sage Publications.

Gangrade, K.D. and R. Sooryamurthy. 1995. 'NGOs: Retrospect and Prospect', in R.B. Jain (ed.), *NGOs in Development Perspective*, Delhi: Vivek Prakashan.

Gupta, S.K., V.P. Sharma and N.K. Sharda (eds). 1998. *Tribal Development: Appraisal and Alternatives*, New Delhi: Indus Publishing Company.

Mathur, H.M. 1997. 'Participatory Development: Some Areas of Concern', *Sociological Bulletin*, 46 (1), pp. 52–95.

Mehrotra, Nilika. 2004. 'Situating Tribal Women', *The Eastern Anthropologist*, 57 (1), January-March.

Patnaik, S.M. 1999. *NGOs and Tribal Development in Orissa*, Research Study Sponsored by Ministry of Tribal Affairs, Government of India, New Delhi.

Mohapatra, B. and Vimla Ramchandran. 2001. *Agragamee: Stock-Taking Exercise*, A Report on Agragamee, Kashipur (Rayagada), Orissa.

Mukherjee, K.K. 1944 'Societal Changes and Voluntary Organizations', *Gandhi Marg*, 15, pp. 389–414.

20

Meira Paibi Movement in Manipur

A Socio-Historical Analysis

KHANGEMBAM INDIRA

Social movement has been defined as an organized effort by a group of people either to bring or resist changes in the society. Women's movement is one of such social movements, which endeavours to bring changes in the institutional arrangements, values, customs and beliefs in the society that have subjugated women for so long. Women's movements have emerged in almost all regions of the world though they remained isolated and sporadic. In the nineteenth century, women in many regions of the world have mobilized collectively in pursuit of a wide variety of goals, women began to organise against inequalities based on sex and to demand legal reforms, aimed at removing patriarchal controls over women in the family and in society at large (Molyneux, 1993).

The struggle for women's rights in India has a long history. The emergence of the women's movement dates back to the beginning of the nineteenth century and connects it with the social reform movements of this period. Linking the reform of women's status with the modernization agenda, the reformers who were mostly men such as Rajaram Mohan Roy, Iswarchand Vidyasagar and Swami Dayananda opposed practices like child marriage and spoke up for the remarriage of widows and the education of women..Women's right and equality was seen as an integral part of the struggle for national independence. Women leaders of the freedom movement, including Sarojini Naidu and Margaret Cousins, gave greater importance to the issues concerning women's rights. The post-independence period witnessed women belonging to various denominations raising their voice against the adverse impact of patriarchal, demeaning and discriminating personal laws (Desai, 1985). With the passage of time, they extended their struggles to the legal front and conducted many battles to effectively implement these laws (ibid.). The contemporary women's movement in India gives emphasis on violence against women. Women's groups in different cities and regions of India joined in anti-violence campaigns, especially against dowry deaths, rape, and sati (Fuchs and Linkenbach, 2003). They were also active in the anti caste movements and tribal and peasant struggles in different parts of India. Several struggles are still carried out by women in different parts of the country on various issues affecting their livelihood.

Role of Women in Manipuri Society

The high social and economic status of Meitei women (a majority group) in Manipuri society was frequently remarked upon by British colonial officers. Despite the dominance of Hinduism in the plains of Manipur, Meitei women suffered none of the humiliating oppression of their sisters elsewhere in the subcontinent (Parratt and Parratt, 2001). Above all, the women controlled the food supplies and the markets and were, therefore, a dominant economic force. Still, their social status is much lower than that enjoyed by men. To quote Devaki Jain, 'yet the Manipuri women are subjected to traditional hierarchies, in which men are the stereotyped heads of households, often marrying more than once, beating women after drunkenness and so on' (Jain, 1980). According to Kalpana Sharma, despite the leadership they have shown in many protests, in their homes they continue to function in a highly patriarchal structure. The women of Manipur despite running the main market and are visible in public spaces have no right to inherit property, women's literacy levels are substantially lower than those of men and very few of them hold public office and a very few of them are in the legislation (Sharma, 2009).

In this backdrop, it would be pertinent to examine the importance of women's movements in Manipur. These movements have played a significant role in shaping up the Manipuri society. This paper takes up the task of examining the evolution of women's movement in Manipur by focusing on a popular movement called *Meira Paibi* and traces the nature and extent of changes affected by this movement over the years. The paper also throws some light on the role it played to bring peace in the conflict ridden Manipuri society and discusses the limitations of such kind of movement from the societal perspective.

Meira Paibis: A Profile

Meira Paibi is the largest grassroots human rights movement in Manipur. It is formed by the Meitei women of Manipur valley and is acting as the guardian for the civil society. The term *meira* is occasionally used to connote initiative, progress, achievement and leading a light towards brightness. In literal terms, *meira paibis* means women bearing flaming torches or women torch bearers. The *meira,* made up of bamboo, fueled with kerosene and a piece of cloth, at the first glance may appear to be just another source of light in the dark. But if one looks deeper, it has a significant meaning. To quote Bhabananda, 'holding the lit up *meira*, the *Meira Paibis* feel confident to face any untoward incidents. It gives them a sense of strength and inspiration. It gives them the courage needed to face and protect themselves and others in the face of adversaries. It is a reminder of the sacred oath that they took, to fight injustice' (Takhellambam, 2002). Above all the *meira* is the mascot of solidarity inside their own *meira paibi* group as well as among other meira paibi groups all over the state. At present, almost all the localities have *meira paibi* organizations and most of the organizations have an office called *meira shang.*[1]

The established objective of the *Meira Paibis* is to defend and save the Manipuri society from unrest. It is the watchdog of civil rights violations at the community level, and initiates campaigns against these violations. The Manipuri women condemn any forms of rights violation and launch agitations against undemocratic repressive acts.

Origin of the Meira Paibi

The prevailing situation of human rights violations have compelled the women of Manipur to organize themselves to defend their human rights as the government failed to perform the duty of guarding the society from these violations perpetrated by the army and paramilitary forces. According to Parratt and Parratt (2001), the *Meira Paibi* movement began in 1979 after a period of continuous abuse of power, including several cases of rape and indiscriminate arrest and violence, by the Indian army forces occupying Manipur. Initially, it was a voluntary grassroots vigilante women's movement organized in each locality of the Manipur valley aiming at protecting citizens' basic rights. But circumstances made it compulsory for each Meitei woman to represent her respective family in the movement.

In order to understand the relevance of *meira paibis* movement it is important to trace the history of women's movement in Manipur since the British period and after. It can be seen that even during the British period the women had showed as being capable of organizing themselves to register their protest when occasion demanded.

Nupi Lan (Women's War)

Historically, Manipuri women have fought two wars against the British. The first *Nupi Lan* or 'Women's War' in 1904 was against the British orders of punitive punishment to male members to rebuild the new state bungalow of the government which was burnt down by some unidentified miscreants. The women had effectively revolted against the British Colonial policies for imposing forced labour upon the male population and forced Major Maxwell, the political agent to withdraw its order and this set in motion a tradition of women's political protest which continues till date.

The second *Nupi Lan* Movement of 1939 was based on genuine fears and apprehensions arising out of uncontrolled export of rice from Manipur. These fears were further aggravated by the heavy rains and floods of 1939. Thus, fuelled by the impact of price rise and scarcity of food grains, the womenfolk in the state, who were more vocal and volatile as compared to their male counterparts, led a movement against the unscrupulous traders who exported local foodgrains to meet the war time demands (Yambem, 1976). It was they who initiated the agitation and sustained it. While a movement for constitutional reforms in Manipur had been initiated in 1938, it was the *Nupi Lan* which focused on the inadequacies in both the economic and administrative policies of the Manipur State. While the original demands of the women were confined to the banning of rice export, their later demands also included changes in the Durbar and administrative set-up. So, the agitation, which started with a demand for banning export of rice from Manipur, took the form of anti-monarchial and anti-imperialist uprising. The boycott of the market for more than one and a half years certainly convinced the state authorities that the women of Manipur could take up any form of agitation once they were convinced of their purpose (ibid.).

The *Nupi Lan* movements were against imperial hegemony, exploitation and malpractices of the British administration. It would, perhaps, not be very far from the truth to conclude that the *Nupi Lan,* which started as a rice agitation directed against the economic policies of the Maharaja and the Marwari monopolists, later on changed its character to become a movement for constitutional and administrative reforms in Manipur.

The uniqueness of the movement, however, lies in the fact that it was the women of Manipur who were in the vanguard of change. Due to this movement many reforms were introduced and changes were made in the administration of Manipur. A chief court was established and many Acts such as Manipur Constitution Act and Manipur State Election Act were passed. Subsequently, in 1948, Manipur Assembly was established.

In the post-independence period, women played active roles in public spheres and displayed high political consciousness. In 1954 and 1959, women took active part in agitations demanding establishment of responsible government in Manipur. In 1960, women formed 'Women Assembly Demand Committee' to press the central government to grant responsible government in Manipur. Women's participation in 'Statehood Demand Movement' was also very significant in late 1960s.

Night Patrollers or Nisha Bandi Movement

The *Meira Paibi* Movement of today has its predecessor in another movement popularly known as the *nisha bandhi* movement, a movement which specifically focused on tackling the social menace like alcoholism, domestic violence and others. Women in Manipur mobilized themselves into what is popularly known as the night patrollers in 1975. It was a movement against the sale and consumption of intoxicants especially liquor. Under this movement, groups of 30 to 50 women patrolled the streets after dusk and were on the alert for inebriated men returning home after an evening at the wine shop (Jain, 1980). The All Manipur Women Social Reformation and Development Society announced a Manipur bandh on 4 April 1980 and intensified the campaign against intoxication. The movement had spread to almost all parts of the state. The main objective of the night patrolling by women is to prohibit manufacturing, selling and drinking of alcohol. To quote Jain: 'the overall objective of the night patrollers was to introduce temperance in the drinking habit so as to ensure that alcoholism did not erode family life, children's health and the potential for productive participation by the consumer of alcohol' (ibid.). In the year 1991–92, their efforts finally paid off. The then Government of Manipur led by Manipur Peoples Party of R.K. Ranbirsana passed the order prohibiting the sale and manufacturing of liquor in the state. Later, Manipur was declared a dry state, and the status is still continuing. Surprisingly, there is no conclusive evidence of a decline in liquor consumption in Manipur. After the government of Manipur declared the state as a dry state the *Nisha Bandi* Movement has transformed itself into the *Meira Paibi* Movement. The nature and content of the movement changed when it shifted focus from social to more political issues such as human rights violations, demand for repeal of repressive acts, etc.

The Meira Paibi Movement

The transformation in the focus and role of the women movement in Manipur calls for an understanding of the political unrest and the sense of frustration among the masses around 1960s and it also coincided with the birth of the first generation insurgent outfits in the valley. The period of mid-1960s also marked the beginning of contestation between the state and non-state actors on political issues. The trouble became widespread and took a violent turn in the 1980s when the army was asked to curb the increasingly threatening insurgent movement in the state. The then government headed by R.K. Dorendro declared Manipur as a disturbed area and imposed the Armed forces (Special Powers) Act in 1980. Following this, the central government sent battalions of Army personnel to the state and they are posted everywhere in the hills and the valleys. The central forces brought their own problems with the coercive measures they adopted against the locals.

In the state of Manipur, peace has become a distant dream with many of the younger generation not even able to afford a nostalgic remembrance of what a peaceful society was like. People, especially villagers, are caught in the crossfire between security forces and underground groups (UGs). In fact, countless insurgent groups are literally holding the entire population, besides the administration, demanding money from the public and resorting to violence. Living in a violent society, the people of Manipur are most hungry for peace.

Today, the *Meira Paibis* are protesting against the 1958 Armed Forces Special Powers Act (AFSPA) which they have branded as the 'black law'. It had initially been enforced in the Manipur hills to contain the Naga insurgency movement. The Act was extended throughout Manipur state in 1980, following intensification of activities by the insurgents in the valley as well. The Act gives the security personnel the right to pick up or even kill anyone on mere suspicion alone. The state government is on record saying that the security forces have been abusing the provisions of the Act, arresting, torturing and even crafting fake encounters.

The *Meira Paibi* Movement became more dominant when women organized themselves as human rights defenders against state terrorism. Women condemned human rights violations by the state and launched actions against undemocratic repressive acts. This movement, in effect, can be regarded as the logical outcome of the rise of insurgency and counter insurgency policy in the state. To counter the menace arising out of this conflict, the women started spending nights outside the comforts of their homes, patrolling the streets and guarding their locality against any surprise search operations of the armed forces. The *Meira Paibi* Movement is particularly aimed at defending the human rights of the people such as the sexual harassment, killing of innocent citizens, tortures and atrocities perpetrated by the army and paramilitary forces of the Indian security force. Majority of the women who were involved in the movement against the consumption of alcohol and drugs are now participants of the *Meira Paibi* Movement. On 29 December every year, Manipuri *Nupi Samaj* (Manipuri women association) celebrates the anniversary of the formation of the *Meira Paibi* Movement which shows that if they come together they can fight the menace in the society.

The *Meira Paibis* intervene and rush to face challenges from the armed forces whenever they violate human rights in the name of military combing operation. The security forces always indulge in human rights violations especially in the night and the *Meira Paibis* are more active during this time. They keep vigil on any arbitrary arrest, extrajudicial killings, torture, etc. They have been demanding peaceful negotiation between the Government and the insurgents. They organize and conduct protest rallies, road blockades, sit in protests, boycott, hunger strikes and public meetings from time to time for the cause of defending human rights. At times, they also organise street corner meetings and poster campaigns in different parts of the State. In addition to it, they also support individual fighters such as Irom Sharmila, a peace activist who has been fighting while on a fast for the last 12 years in pursuance with the demand for withdrawal of AFSPA.

Whenever there is injustice, killing and encounters, especially to Meitei youth either by the security forces or the different insurgent groups, the *Meira Paibis* always protest against such act. Thus, in contemporary Manipur one can see different forms of protest against the state, state agencies, and the form of protest ranges from simple rally to mass protest. Even self-immolation occurs though such cases are rare. The three prominent incidents which occurred in the last few years are highlighted here. The agitation against the removal of the AFSPA following the alleged rape and killing of Th. Manorama on 15 July 2004 in the custody of the Assam Rifles, lasted for more than two months. One month later, on 15 August, as part of the same protest, another young man, Pebam Chittaranjan, a student activist immolated himself on the main street of Bishnupur Bazar, about 30 km from Imphal.

In February 2009, Manipuri women staged a sit-in demonstration for many days on the roads of Imphal in protest against the killing of Thingnam Kishan Singh, a subdivisional officer and two others. In this case, Kishan Singh was killed by the rebel groups of NSCN (IM), an insurgent group involved in extorting government funds.

The third important incident was on 23 July 2009 morning, a pregnant woman and a young man were killed, and five others injured in a shooting incident in the crowded Khwairamband Keithel of Imphal. The incident provoked massive public outcry against the killings. There was outrage and protest by the Apunba Lup of Manipur consisting of more than 30 organizations, in which *Meira Paibis* is a prominent one, which led to demonstrations on the streets and all the educational institutes, including school and colleges, were closed down for more than three months in demand of justice to the victims. These incidents show that the *Meira Paibis* take a leading role and protest with determination for days or months while expressing their solidarity with the victim's family if they feel injustices have been meted out to the victims or their family.

The demand for withdrawal of the AFSPA is met with resistance from the state and army engaged in counter insurgency, while the civil society groups, including the *Meira Paibis*, question the extra-judicial powers given to them. On the other hand, there exist a number of doubts on the functioning of the movement. Has the movement's excessive preoccupation with the repeal of AFSPA resulted in the neglect of other gender issues by the movement? Are some women members misusing or maligning the ethos of the movement? Does the movement need to be more inclusive?

Setback in the Movement

The contribution of Manipuri women in the socio-economic and cultural life of the state is evidently significant. They are highly mobile as they do all the buying and selling of goods in the market. Besides doing the household work, agricultural-related activities and producing handloom and handicrafts products, many of them are also actively involved in selling the products and come collectively to support the issues concerning the society. Hence, many scholars have highlighted that women in Manipur enjoy a comparatively higher status than their counterparts in other parts of India. In reality, women are subjected to traditional hierarchies, the women do suffer very much from rights abuses because of their gender, and they are not accorded adequate protection. The society follows patriarchal system, men can have more than one wife, preference of male child is still there and women lack any role in the decision-making process even in their family.

Like in many parts of India, in Manipur also, gender-based division of labour is very much prevalent. Normally women are loaded with multiple responsibilities of carrying out household activities as well as engaging in activities outside home. Usually men do not have to worry about any domestic chores since they consider it as the domain of women. Women also suffer from domestic violence and do not have right to inherit property. Their literacy rates are substantially lower than those of men and very few of them hold public office. The representation of women in Legislative Assembly is substantially low with only three out of 60 members in the Manipur Legislative Assembly being women.

Interestingly, the *Meira Paibis* movement has failed to address any of the gender issues mentioned above. It is, perhaps, for the reason that since they have been brought up in a patriarchal set-up, decision-making is considered to be the right and domain of men. In fact, it is ingrained in them to such an extent that women have accepted the dominance of men without questioning. In spite of various rights guaranteed to the women by the Constitution of India, it will not be wrong to say that the culture and tradition has got dominance over the modern rules. However, the movement needs to give special attention to create a general consciousness among the women about women's rights and need to strive consistently for improvement of the status of women.

Findings of the North East Network study, 2004, suggest that a lot of women and women's groups have not been able to fight this violence and articulate their rights because most of them are unaware of these rights. 'Even though the solidarity amongst these women's groups is fairly strong, the *Meira Paibis* are little concerned with women's rights by themselves and believe that they must get general civil rights implemented first,' says L. Anna Pinto, a member of the Imphal-based NGO, Centre for Organisation, Research and Education (Pinto, 2000). Hence, the *Meira Paibis* have not addressed the question of marginalization of women. Also they do not address the issues of gender discriminations and all kinds of inequalities persisting in the society.

Besides manpower, any movement needs money/funding also. The inherent weakness of the movement lies in mobilizing the money as it relies solely on voluntary contribution of the members and through fund raising events. Such contribution is insufficient in the long run as women protests for months for a particular cause. As a result of this, their earning gets affected as many of them depend upon the market for their living. Moreover, their health also deteriorates due to irregularities in their eating habit. As women spend more time outside home and fail to keep an eye on their children, there is increasing numbers of school dropouts, youth joining insurgent groups and increase in the number of alcohol and drug addicts.

Another limitation of the movement is that many consider the movement to be too community specific and it becomes alive only when it affects the Meitei community. For instance, the incidents such as sit-in protest and *dharnas* for months happened mostly when the affected person was a Meitei. There were many incidents of killing of people belonging to other communities by the Army or insurgent groups but such incidents did not receive greater attention and the leaders of the movement just condemned such incidents and long mass protests that can be recalled has hardly happened. There has been some changes in the situation in recent years as the *Meira Paibis* have started addressing issues that affect a woman's dignity such as molestation or rape, whether the victims belong to Meitei or not. So, the support of other communities is on the increase in the recent years and this policy is commendable. However, there still needs a lot of work to be done and the movement needs to broaden its horizon and become more inclusive in its character so as to get mass support from other communities.

There is also an increasing report of many of the women members of the *Meira Paibi* Movement having nexus with the underground outfits.[2] Such reports give a maligned image of the movement and, hence, seriously question the credibility of the movement. To the public, these women were giving the impression of belonging to *Meira Paibi* Movement while actually they were working for the insurgent group, the sole reason being the easy way of earning money. It can be argued that not only such incidents but it is a common belief that children especially son of many women involved in *Meira Paibi* Movement have joined insurgent groups. Such incidents brought bad name to the organization and they lost their integrity. In addition to it, most of the women who are educated and working in public sector shy away to join the movement as they claim that they do not have sufficient time.

Meira paibis are pre-occupied with Armed Forces Special Powers Act (AFSPA) and have taken to the streets many a times to demonstrate against the imposition of AFSPA. Skeptics have often pointed out that they are a facade for a stronger force and only representing the magnified maternal instinct of the society. It is even argued that the movement acts as a mouthpiece for insurgent groups in the state. The army officers carry the opinion that though the *Meira Paibis* protest against the actions of security personnel, they create a slipway for insurgents to get through arrest or detention.

These charges were denied by a representative of the movement. To quote Ramani, a leader of the movement: 'We have nothing to do with the underground (militant) organizations. Our struggle is to protect the people caught in the crossfire between militants and security forces. We are neither protecting militants nor fighting the security forces. Our only concern is the safety of our children. Our fight is to protect human rights which are being misused under the AFSPA' (*The Telegraph,* 2004). The army, on the other hand, started organizing Military Civic Action Programme (MCAP) for the *Meira Paibis.* Under this programme, new sheds were constructed, sewing machines and yarns were distributed and excursion trips exclusively for the members were arranged. The *meira paibis* feel that the Military Civic Action Programme, which lures the *meira paibis* to the programme, is one among the many reasons for the weakening of the *Meira Paibi* Movement in the State.

Conclusion

This region has witnessed a strong women's movement during the colonial period and this has given rise to local groups that have successfully changed policies of the past and spoken for the rights and roles of women in strife torn areas. During British rule Manipuri women fought against humiliation to their honour and identity, forced labour, social injustice, illegitimate taxation, economic exploitation, political subjection and brutal repressions.

Post-independence, in mid-1970s there was *Nisha Bandhi* Movement in Manipur, a movement which focused on alcoholism, drug abuse and domestic violence and this movement gradually transformed into *Meira Paibi* Movement. The *Meira Paibi* Movement is gender, regional and community specific and they are identified as a group of Meitei women from the valley of Manipur. Of late, the movement seems to be losing its strength but its organizational skill is very much evident during crises. There is a need to keep supervision to women who in the name of *Meira Paibi* are spoiling the image of the organization/movement. It, however, needs to be stated that it was because of the courage and grit of *Meira Paibis* that the Manipuri society could overcome various issues and challenges that plagued the society.

Even though there is very little tangible means to bring peace in the society, unity among women and solidarity in their woes can certainly mitigate the situation to a certain extent. Through its perpetual service for the people of Manipur, they have gained a distinct legitimacy – the legitimacy not based on the legal sanction of the state but on the moral and social approval from the people of the state. Since the movement has sustained for more than three decades, they have occupied a prominent place in the Manipuri society. Women, with this social and moral command over the larger populace, can play a pivotal role in facilitating peace in the state. In order to sustain the movement in the long run, the role of the educated woman will become critical. Moreover, participation from other community members is also required to give the movement an inclusive character.

Notes

1. *Meira Shang* is a shed constructed by the *Meira Phabi* organizations for guarding the locality during the night.
2. Two women were arrested by a team of Imphal West commandos on 10 April 2012 in Imphal as revealed by a local newspaper, *Sangai Express*. According to the police, these women who were also leaders of *meira paibis*, were working for an insurgent group, PLA.

References

Delhi Solidarity Group. 2009. *Independent Citizens' Fact Finding Mission to Manipur, Imphal*, Report on Democracy 'Encountered': Rights Violations in Manipur.

Desai, A.R. 1985. 'Women's Movement in India: An Assessment', *Economic and Political Weekly*, 20, 8 June, pp. 992–95.

Fuchs, Martin and Antje Linkenbach. 2003. 'Women's Movement', in Veena Das (ed.), *The Oxford India Companion to Sociology and Social Anthropology*, Vol. II, New Delhi: Oxford University Press, pp. 1546–52.

Jain, Devaki. 1980. *Women Quest for Power: Five Indian Case Studies*, Ghaziabad: Vikas Publishing House.

Molyneux, Maxine. 1993. 'Women's Movement', in William Outhwaite and Tom Bottomore (eds), *The Blackwell Dictionary of Twentieth Century Social Thought*, Oxford: Blackwell Publishers.

North East Network. 2004. *Violence against Women in North East India: An Enquiry*, New Delhi: National Commission for Women.

Parratt, John. 2005. *Wounded Land: Politics and Identity in Modern Manipur*, New Delhi: Mittal Publications.

Parratt, Saroj N. and John Parratt. 2001. 'The Second 'Women's War' and the Emergence of Democratic Government in Manipur', *Modern Asian Studies*, 35 (4), pp. 905–19.

Pinto, L. Anna. 2000. *Women's Rights in the Context of Insurgency: A Report from Northeast India*, 6 August, http://www.cceia.org

Rehman, Teresa. 2009. 'Murder in Plain Sight', *Tehelka Magazine*, 6 (31), 8 August.

Sharma, Kalpana. 2009. 'Disturbed in Manipur', *The Hindu*, 22 March.

Singh, N. Joykumar. 1992. *Social Movements in Manipur*, New Delhi: Mittal Publications.

Takhellambam, Bhabananda. 2002. *Women's Movements and Nationalism in Manipur*, Second Civil Society Dialogue on Peace: A Report, Kolkota: Mahanirban Calcutta Research Group.

Thokchom, Khelen. 2004. 'She Stoops to Conquer', *The Telegraph*, 25 July.

Yambem, Sanamani. 1976. 'Nupi Lan: Manipur Women's Agitation 1939', *Economic and Political Weekly*, XI, pp. 325–31.

Index